Loving Zelda

Sue Anne Kirkham

Carpenter's Son Publishing

Loving Zelda: A Stepdaughter's Caregiving Journal

Published by Clovercroft Publishing, Franklin, Tennessee. Published in association with Larry Carpenter of Christian Book Services, LLC. www.christianbookservices.com

Edited by Robert Irvin

Cover Design by Debbie Manning Sheppard

Interior Layout Design by Suzanne Lawing

Printed in the United States of America

978-1-946889-51-5

Disclaimer
This is a memoir-style work. It is based on the observations and impressions recorded in my journal during the time period covered in this book. While all the experiences relayed actually occurred, some names and identifying details have been changed to protect the privacy of the people, businesses, and institutions involved.

Contents

ACKNOWLEDGMENTS

Many thanks to the following: my stepsister, Joan Leffler, for her understanding and support; the Rockwall Christian Writers Group for the invaluable technical education, encouragement, and modeling of high standards; Chris D'Alleva for her generous investment of time and expertise; and Dr. Pamela Hearn, whose early demonstration of belief in me helped keep the dream alive.

DEDICATION

To Jack, who was the calm center of my whirlwind self.
To Terri, who always believed I could do it.
And to Patti, who wouldn't allow me to give up.

"No one is useless in this world who lightens the burdens of another."

CHARLES DICKENS

Chapter One

A Dose of Reality

August 1958. I am nine years old, teetering on the lip of the high dive board ten feet above the sickly green water of the high school swimming pool.

The sting of chlorine scorches my nostrils as I picture the last fourth-grader who was unwilling to take this final step in summer swim class. The embarrassed tears. The fists clenched to his chest in a plea for mercy. The surrounding gasps of horror as the instructor stole up behind him and dropped his rigid body off the end of the board.

I look down. It seems more like twenty feet than ten. I inhale, but can't push the air back out again. Couldn't a person die on impact under these circumstances?

Except . . . I am not there. I am home in bed, feigning a stomach-ache. Confined to my room by my irritated, perfectionist mother who can't understand why I shy away from scary things, things I might not be good enough at.

It directs my future, this pattern of walking away from challenges. Fear of failure. Lack of guidance. Defective character. Who knows why, but I become lazy about engaging in life. The upside to this sorry state of affairs? All that unspent potential mushrooms over the decades—creates a hunger for a taste of success, for a worthy endeavor to pour itself into.

~~~

January 2005. Look out, World. Swooping in to help my aging father and stepmother remain in their townhouse could be my shot at Worthy Endeavor of a Lifetime. My excitement bubbles into giddiness. I'll stop pushing papers and start making a difference. I will single-handedly shore up their quality of life, rerouting it from mudslide to terra firma—and perhaps justify my own existence in the process.

> Bursting into 2412 Afton Circle that first Monday morning, I startle the dogs—calf-high, mixed-breed, curly-headed brunettes, Chloé and Fergie.

Bursting into 2412 Afton Circle that first Monday morning, I startle the dogs—calf-high, mixed-breed, curly-headed brunettes, Chloé and Fergie. Dad squirms in his easy chair as the vacuum whines and my dust cloth flutters nearby. Retreats to his office as I dismantle Christmas decorations, clean bathrooms, collect household litter.

Necessity drives me to attack the cobwebs and clutter. This accumulation results partly from stepmom Zelda's philosophy that there are more important things than housekeeping. But it's mostly a product of her increased inability to focus, organize her thoughts, and coordinate intention with action.

These first weeks, Zelda hugs me often. Tells me tearfully how glad she is to have me here. Dad is less expressive, but I sense in him resignation and relief.

I also begin to grasp the extent of their decline.

Journal Entry: 1-4-05: *Z still does a little reading but fatigues quickly. And in general interactions, she's okay until she encounters* *the unfamiliar. But we used to talk for hours on topics of substance. About the quirks of human and animal behavior. About nutrition and social issues and childhood disappointments. Now, there is a distance in her gaze, a locking-off of herself within herself. Sentences no longer knit together quite right, and dropped conversational stitches make for choppy, shallow discourse.*

~~~

Doctor's appointments. They anchor the week and all else orbits around them. The urologist, the general practitioner, the oral surgeon, the podiatrist. Such easy access is both a blessing and a curse. This first month, I attempt to map out all the doctor-patient relationships.

I also catch myself wanting to will Dad and Zelda out of the stereotypical scenario they've stepped into, with its underlit rooms, worn furnishings, and 78-degree thermostat settings. As rank optimism gives way to whatever this is, I learn to clean as surreptitiously as possible and to expect the unexpected from this pair. Their days, once filled with productive activity, are now devoted largely to self-maintenance; simple tasks like nail trimming or laundry folding require assistance. Then there is mealtime.

1-5-05: *For lunch, Dad brings home a Subway sandwich. Just one Subway sandwich. So I pull my own turkey on whole wheat out of the fridge and warm up leftovers for Zelda. She exerts a noble effort to get through her toast and meatballs but constantly interrupts herself—getting up to wash her hands, go to the bathroom, search for eyedrops. Dad says, tense with defeatism, "I can't remember the last time she sat through an entire meal."*

But how Zelda loves the all-you-can-eat buffet: the effortless plate-filling, the colorful array, the limitless bounty, the no-extra-charges. Here she can concentrate on getting fork to mouth and putting away a good calorie load to carry her through skimpy breakfasts and early bedtimes. Trips to the local outlet are a midday reward for all of us, until a thread of tension weaves its way in.

1-6-05: *Settled into our booth at Old Country Buffet, there are moments when everything seems so normal. But I have to push back against the urge to rescue Z as I watch her make her way through the serving lines only to lose track of where we are seated. As I debate with myself, white-knuckled, Dad dives into his plate of baked ham and au gratins, and Z snakes her way back to the table without calamity.*

~~~

As the month chugs along, sorting, cleaning, and tidying give order to my days and keep melancholy from shrouding my thinking. Sadness seeps in when I break away from busywork and focus on the erosion in Dad and Zelda's relationship. He does his own thing. Completely gives over Zelda's care to me. No more little taps on her elbow, their private signal that she is starting to stoop and needs to correct her posture. No more sideways hugs, his tall lankiness dwarfing her in an embracing, ballet-like curving of his torso. It's as if he has washed his hands of trying to relate to this stranger who now shares his life.

1-7-05: *Z had a particularly bad day today, not recalling that I knew mutual friends in Michigan or that I was living with her and Dad in '78 and was best buddy to Sally, the Wonder Dog. A small ache creeps into my heart whenever I see her go blank, then withdraw into denial as we hit on details that have slipped through the widening cracks in her memory.*

It must be, for her, like clutching at so much steam in the air and knowing that you can't do a darned thing to get the elusive stuff to form up for you, to become graspable.

The first danger signals flickered eighteen months ago when Zelda got so overwhelmed trying to put together a family dinner that she had to lie down and turn the preparations over to me. An hour later she reemerged, dazed and exhausted, baffled by what had happened. I told myself it was fatigue. After all, they'd just made the long car trip back from wintering in Florida. Or low blood sugar. Glucose levels can plummet when you lose your senses of smell and taste. The appe-

The first danger signals flickered eighteen months ago when Zelda got so overwhelmed trying to put together a family dinner that she had to lie down and turn the preparations over to me.

tite dwindles. You forget to eat.

Within weeks of that episode, she forgot having made a breakfast date with her best friend. Distressed over this "first," she confided to me later, "I guess this is the way it's going to be," then teared up and collapsed on my shoulder. I blustered in dissent even as my diaphragm cramped in apprehension.

The changes in my father also burden the heart. I watch him clench his jaw and slide into a state of anger with little provocation, this good-natured man I have idolized from earliest memory. This man who treated me to a dime-store chocolate Coke and explained away my fears after a tactless dentist sentenced me to oral surgery at the age of ten. Who sat at the foot of my bed, patting my knee and speaking consolation, when John King snubbed me at a seventh-grade dance.

I'm not sure I know this man. He is different. He is hurting. And he won't let me close enough to return the kindnesses.

~~~

The kitchen soon becomes an island of refuge—a place I can navigate with certainty, where I have control over outcomes. I can enter this haven, assess what needs to be done, tackle it, and measure my success in tangible results. No guessing about whether I've been effective or helpful or have made matters worse. There I feel grounded, secure, competent. There I can produce nutritious offerings to meet a genuine need and take joy in Dad's and Zelda's pleasure at receiving them— despite the fact that the temperature dial on this decrepit oven spins like the Wheel of Fortune without any of the happy surprises.

Ribeye soup—a rich, beefy broth combined with crushed tomatoes, pinto beans, cubed zucchini, onion, celery. Grilled ham and Swiss on rye. Navy bean soup and tart-sweet raspberry muffins. Papa's favorite shrimp egg foo yung with fried rice. Zelda's favorite egg salad sandwiches. And everybody's favorite chocolate-chocolate chunk cookies with pecans.

As gray wintry skies cast a pall and the cold numbs noses and toes, crock pot beef stew with cheddar wheat biscuits. Pigs in a blanket. Banana pecan muffins and blueberry brunch cake. Another batch of chocolate-chocolate chunk cookies. Food. The universal elixir.

Walks with the dogs are another source of regeneration. I laugh out loud at Fergie's gleeful romps through banked snow, an explosion of black fluff springing rhythmically above the mounds of white. But tiny Chloé demurs. Back she turns toward the warm shelter of home, or else I carry her the distance, tucked into my down-filled jacket like a baby kangaroo. And these two are delirious at my daily arrival—a problem for late-sleepers.

1-10-05: *At the trumpet call of the Dueling Yelpers, Z awakens and staggers into the living room wearing a rumpled turquoise T-shirt and baggy gray sweatpants. Competing for our attention, all four chiming clocks bong the hour in a discordant rumble of rhythms as the hen tea kettle warbles away unattended on the stove. Z turns to me with an amused smile and says, with crystal clarity, "Suz, you have to write about this."*

~~~

Irony surrounds us. There is the role reversal, Dad's and Zelda's loss of a sense of usefulness stoking my discovery of one. And the demonstrated paradox of amassing decades worth of memorabilia, too precious to part with, yet all but lost anyway in a jumble of intermixed collections that fill every available space.

Dad's defense is to avert his focus. He writes essays, makes lunch dates, does crossword puzzles, takes classes. Zelda zeroes in on the physical and the treatable, and doctoring becomes a minor obsession.

Dad's defense is to avert his focus. He writes essays, makes lunch dates, does crossword puzzles, takes classes.

She makes new appointments, forgetting that she was just seen, and discusses bodily functions without inhibition.

1-11-05: *Today Z is fretting over infrequent bowel movements—she who takes in about six ounces of solid food a day and ignores the stockpile of doctor-recommended stool softeners marching toward their expiration dates in the dark recesses of the bathroom vanity.*

The tightrope dwindles down to a thread. How much do I try to dissuade, and how much do I take on Dad's "if another appointment makes her feel better" attitude? I silently fret that Zelda's beloved Dr. A will stop taking her seriously if she keeps popping in for no legitimate reason.

Back to the sanctuary of conquerable challenges: dog walks, cleaning, cabinet reconditioning, and scrubbing this accursed kitchen floor with its ten-by-ten off-white ceramic tiles—about as practical as a white silk apron in a spaghetti sauce factory. I take Zelda to the YMCA to scout out indoor walking options. She's bound to profit from moving more and sleeping less. To the library, where meandering through the familiar stacks brings her contentment. To the community center to pick up brochures on art classes, straining hopefully toward the stimulation of old hobbies.

I also reorganize the linen closet, Zelda's most vexing bugbear. Every section of every shelf gets a label to help her locate what she's looking for and know where to stack laundered items. I start the process while she naps because she feels guilty seeing someone else take on a task that she herself loathes. Later, I convince her I'm having fun. And it is somehow more satisfying to tackle someone else's chaos rather than my own.

~~~

This month's biggest hurdle is medications. Zelda has a prescription that lessens her confusion and softens her mood swings, which, in turn, keeps depression at bay. But there is abundant evidence she is not taking the pills.

1-12-05: *As I putter about, I find trash-filled plastic grocery bags that never made it to the garbage can, a package of energy bars tucked in with the bath towels, and eggs in the freezer. "Don't tell her," Dad admonishes, so I secretly dispose of the frostbitten ovoids, knowing how Z would shudder at the waste and at the private conspiracy.*

Dad tells me that she was very confused last night after napping from 3:30 'til 5. She couldn't think of my name and had to be convinced it was actually evening and not morning. He talked her through it, but the strain on him carries over to today while a night's sleep has washed it from her awareness.

~~~

It is a frigid Minnesota winter, and I am frozen in place. Stuck to the pavement. Getting my father to accept that laissez-faire may not be the best approach to take with an increasingly childlike wife is obstacle number one in this drug war I am waging. Until I can convince him there's a problem—that Zelda can no longer stay on task long enough to oversee her own dosing schedule—there is no hope of improvement on that front. Meanwhile, she assures me, "Papa and I will manage it."

I count her pills every few days, and things don't add up—or subtract down—right. Not knowing what she gets and when leaves me batty with frustration. But numbers are the evidence I need to win my case with Dad.

Elated to have him on my side, I run up against resistance from his bride. She rejects a plastic pill-minder, confused by all the abutting little boxes with their Monday through Sunday snap-top lids. So I stand by helplessly as she talks about taking her meds, then fails to do it. Plummeting hope plops like a swallowed boulder into the pit of my stomach.

And so it is that I often find myself operating at the remorseful end of a very short fuse. I snort blue smoke at the clinic rep who misinforms Zelda that it's time for another appointment even though she has just seen the doctor the week before—and when I have just convinced her it's too soon for another visit. I erupt in anger in the Sam's Club

Elated to have him on my side, I run up against resistance from his bride. She rejects a plastic pill-minder, confused by all the abutting little boxes with their Monday through Sunday snap-top lids.

parking lot when a vehicle invades our crosswalk. Driving home alone at day's end, I screech foreign obscenities at other drivers who do the same dimwitted things they have always done.

As my moods teeter-totter, I nosedive into a mucky pool of self-recrimination. I remind myself that this is uncharted territory for all of us. That Zelda gets more upset with the unseen gremlins that turn her thought processes into a kaleidoscope than she does with me. But it's scant comfort. If my reactions disturb her at all, then I am at cross-purposes with my reason for being here.

I'm thinking it would be a keen idea to remind myself "Jesus Wants Me for a Sunbeam" by sticking a perky yellow Post-It note to my dashboard. That is until I picture going from lost composure to mild hysterics with every blown opportunity to measure up. Rejected, the perky yellow note plan gets refiled in a corner of my brain. If only I could stow my raw nerves somewhere as easily.

~~~

Minor events can yield major pleasure. People who face daunting obstacles discover this little truth. So do the parents of challenged children for whom a single step or the first delayed utterance of "mama" becomes grounds for celebration. So, sometimes, do imperfect daughters who lug their own overstuffed emotional baggage to the doorstep of every relationship they approach. One minute, I feel weighted down by the prospect of sifting through the endless stashes tucked away in every corner of this place; the next, uplifted by the small allotments of grace that nudge a day along.

1-13-05: *On this glimmering, twelve-degrees-below-zero morning, golden rays flood the dining nook and spill over into the kitchen, and my spirit swells with cheerful confidence. All burdens lighten as Z and I bag bushels of now-oversized clothes for delivery to the Salvation Army.*

With Zelda weighing only ninety pounds, there is no reasonable hope that her old wardrobe will ever again hang from her wisp of a frame. So seeing this sparrow of a lady plunge enthusiastically into her lunch is always cause to rejoice. We present ourselves at the combined Taco Bell/Long John Silver's counter—bean burritos and Diet Pepsi for me, fish and chips with coleslaw for her. She eats half, covers the leftovers with a paper napkin, rides home with them in her lap, then sets the cardboard serving boat on top of a margarine tub in the refrigerator. I later sneak back and re-pot them.

I can also count on Chloé and Fergie for infusions of joy. They tow me along as they investigate the townhouse grounds where we meet charming animal friends who are leashed to some rather nice human beings. But some days, exploring is out of the question.

1-14-05: *With a minus-twenty-degrees windchill, the dogs are having no part of a trek outdoors. As she and I round the first corner and step headlong into the biting gusts, even robust Fergie shoots me an accusatory look and hightails it back toward the front door. With our walk curtailed, I lift her up and over three-foot snow drifts to tend to necessities.*

Chloé snorts at the very notion of stepping foot outside, so I carry her across the threshold to the small, snow-covered patch of yard beyond the front door and huddle over her as she scribbles a hasty citrine signature.

On one of those magnificent days when the winds calm and the sun shimmers in a cloudless sky—Nature's apology for the bitter temperatures—Fergie snoops out a tennis ball belonging to a neighbor's dog and proceeds to lift her leg on it. Apparently, she feels no obligation to act like a girl. Or to practice the Golden Rule.

Back home, she trots her little lump of kibble into the living room, tosses it into the air, and then pounces on it over and over again as if it were a toy. This rite of frivolity ends in a gleeful series of munches. Her delight is contagious, and I release a healthy chortle. Pet therapy in action.

And Chloé. Endearing, demanding, vocal little faux Cockapoo, Chloé. Between her hearing loss and supplemental attention from me, she is less high-maintenance—and less high-volume—than in her puppyhood. She can't go nuts over an outside noise she doesn't hear. And regular walks wear her out, so she sleeps more soundly.

Her mealtime manners are still lacking. But she does an admirable job of keeping the table-side whimpers dialed down until the strain of self-control overpowers her, at which point pained, strangulated, high-pitched throat-whines escape. She is past the point of no return. She must have a bite of whatever it is. Bedroom confinement is the only recourse.

~~~

Bumping along on the undercurrent of My Own Life, as Dad likes to call it, distractions develop at home. My mother-in-law, Corine, who lives with my husband Jack and me, is diagnosed with hyperparathyroidism, suffers side effects from her blood pressure medications, and endures headaches and facial pain from a cranial nerve infection. Inside Jack's eyes, blood from ruptured vessels swirls, disrupting his vision—years of blood sugar fluctuations making a militant declaration.

Then, just when we need it most, my former employer gets stinky about promised healthcare benefits. Fallible creature that I am, resentment now keeps me awake at night. That and a pesky little syndrome called menopause.

1-17-05: *Accursed insomnia. It's 4:45 a.m. Do I assume defeat and*

get up or risk two more stress-tousled sleepless hours in bed? Hormones.
Can't live with 'em, can't live without 'em.

~~~

As Dad copes privately, Zelda and I do the girl thing—we lean on each other. She still has a very good sense of direction. I still do not. Whenever I get turned around trying to get us somewhere, she navigates us through it. And her eagerness to do whatever it takes to improve her health amazes.

When I won a complete Hoist exercise apparatus from a local radio station a few years ago, I had it set up in Dad and Zelda's lower level, hoping to inspire my exercise-averse ("I'd rather read") father. He gave it a few tries, but the novelty wore off quickly. Now it just sits, a smirking reminder of all he can't do. He uses it for a coat rack.

Zelda's enthusiasm almost makes up for Dad's indifference. She needs to be shown the exercise technique in careful, repetitive detail, and for me to count out the reps for her. But she is so willing.

Adopting a novel medication regimen is a different story. Revised agendas rattle the dementia-invaded brain, and so she must resist any plan for pill delivery that doesn't have the reassuring feel of familiarity to it. More frustration. Hers is real and hard, like a granite stumbling block. Mine is subjective and malleable, like Play-Doh. I should be able to flatten it with logic. Instead, I allow little vexations to trip me up, like when Dad and Zelda fail to tell me they'll be out for breakfast when I show up for duty. Should I initiate a search? I am twelve again, trying to garner enough household respect to be kept in the loop.

Dad's cell phone lays impotent on his desk. He's been paying

Verizon $30 a month for two years, but he has yet to place or receive a call on the thing. I guess he's waiting for the right emergency situation. Meanwhile, I pray that situation doesn't arise away from home.

I do encourage them to do things as a couple—half altruism, half selfishness. Now I am parent, prodding them to follow through on a plan to see a matinee of *The Incredibles*. Coaxing them into an early lunch of grilled Gruyère sandwiches and tomato basil soup. Easing Zelda out the door as she waffles and finds excuses to dodge back into the house. While they are gone, I purge the refrigerator of fuzzy gray bloblets and the freezer of unrecognizable frozen packets. Tear into areas that cry out for deep cleaning.

I also push back against the wave of panic that revisits during quiet times alone and sometimes at night before sleep pushes in to rescue me. Zelda can no longer hold onto a thought long enough to get from the kitchen sink to the kitchen wastebasket. Dad has to sit hunched over the side of the bed after a nap, concentrating to get control of his labored breathing. And his knees, which have been creaky for years, get less reliable week by week. What do I do with these raw facts?

~~~

On grumpy days, when I'm somnambulating through my walk-on role in their lives, I almost start to believe in karma. Negative karma.

> On grumpy days, when I'm somnambulating through my walk-on role in their lives, I almost start to believe in karma. Negative karma.

Of course, the true trouble-magnet is my own shroud of gloom.

1-23-05: *It's a Monday through and through. As blowback for my earlier grouchiness, my last act of the day is to clog up the garbage disposal. Jack stops to help on his way home from work. This unfortunate episode climaxes with my sopping up ground cabbage splatter and his reassembling the reamed-out drain.*

At home I settle into my snare of a

recliner, where 16-pound JJ plants himself in the space between my ankles like a feline ball and chain. Two hours later I feel the downward tug of sluggishness and an uneasy conscience. My own house needs cleaning, my own files need organizing, but the evening drip, drip, drips away. I'd make a resolution, but I'm too darned whacked.

Guilt shows up on Fridays, too. As I heave a sigh of relief that the weekend is here, I'm visited by a premonition of what Saturday will hold for Dad and Zelda without me there. Quiver. Droop.

Then Providence moves in with comic relief.

1-27-05: *Dad answers a call from my telephone provider—I had given their townhouse number as my daytime contact—and the service tech says, "Hi, this is Pete from Qwest." My father, knowing the lead-in to a sales pitch when he hears one, says, "It is?" and slams the receiver back on its cradle. Fortunately, Pete calls back, and Jack and I now have a repaired phone line at our place. Pete is my hero for the day.*

~~~

General knowledge games play into my scheme for keeping everybody's neurons firing. As we work through the color-coded categories, Zelda is modest even when she comes up with a right answer, Dad a bit cocky even when he does not. Immediate experience does nothing to reshape self-images so firmly gelled.

One frosty day in late January, Zelda treats me to the Panda Oriental Buffet. We eat mounds of crisp, steamed green beans, veggie fried rice, chicken wings, mushrooms with peppers. And for a finale, the best deep-fried shrimp I have ever consumed.

When she and I return to the townhouse to walk the dogs and quiz through some trivia questions over tea, it's as if I have my dearest friend back—even though occasional memory glitches derail the conversation. "How do you know Barb McC?" she asks about a long-term family friend. I quell the twitch of apprehension in my gut, nonchalantly retrace the history, and we wend our way back to the reality of that shared friendship.

To help her stay on track, I affix big honkin' labels to wallpaper-covered boxes on the shelf in the front closet: GLOVES. HATS. SCARVES. Install drawer dividers with illustrations of scissors and tape and paperclips. These not achieving glaring success, I learn to schedule weekly re-sortings instead of bemoaning the failure of the system. Or at least to cut the moaning sessions short.

As the days flip by, fresh concerns crop up to offset any sense of complacency. The flux of microcosmic life, in other words. But in my organizing, I rediscover cherished old photos, and Zelda lets go of certain outdated clippings. Progress. My father declares a 100 percent improvement in the household and calls my presence a bargain. Jubilation. My mother-in-law finds a caring doctor who talks her through concerns about Prednisone. Relief. I learn to talk myself past my own bouts of visual wriggles, like oil on water—a quirky physical response to sleep deprivation and tension. Mercy granted.

And—hallelujah!—Dad works out a plan to smooth out the wrinkles in Zelda's erratic medication schedule. This one uses a one-column weekly pill-minder, with each compartment relabeled as a daily dose: number one, thyroid; number two, antidepressant; number three, morning memory pill; and so on. Numbers six and seven are for evening doses. Dad and Zelda refill the box together at the end of each day to ensure nothing gets missed.

1-30-05: *Before she lies down for an afternoon nap, Z informs me that Chloé and Papa are now helping with her pill-taking. Later Dad confirms that Z is agreeable. When I suggest that she may even be relieved to let go of that task, he rewards me with an eye-crinkling chuckle.*

And so another day headed for the shoals instead ends up drifting serenely into the sunset.

~~~

You grapple with yourself in this caregiving calling. At least I do. I guess it's the baby boomer version of wanting to have it all, do it all. The superwoman complex becomes an oozing layer in the club sandwich of attending to your own household's needs, worrying about your children's problems, and staving off the tidal pull toward the ultimate exit that aging parents force us to face.

It becomes preferable to spar with the inevitable rather than hop on a treadmill and burn off the anxiety. Easier to be angry at randomly encountered strangers who refuse to honor your circumstances, or fail to treat fading loved ones with respect, than to pull on your grown-up knickers and admit that they have their own issues. Easier to forget that you are not the center of any real-life universe but your own. And it is definitely easier to hoard hard-earned tension than to invite acceptance and serenity into your heart and mind.

> You grapple with yourself in this caregiving calling. At least I do.

This is where God hides in the details.

1-31-05: *As I succumb to the allure of The Food Network, that diabolical Barcalounger once again sucks me into its immobilizing depths, sapping away valuable evening hours. My metabolism clunks into low gear. My self-disgust ripens.*

At 10:30 p.m., I shuffle off to bed and sink into the same old weary-woman's prayer: "Lord, please grant me the stamina and the discipline to do all that I have set out for myself." And sleep comes—luxurious, untroubled sleep.

Chapter Two

Treading Water

When her first marriage began to flounder back in the '60s, Zelda built a teaching certificate onto her B.A. in home economics and soon became her family's sole support. With a husband in commission sales and four daughters to raise, she had always been careful with her dollars. As a single parent with college-bound teenagers, she forged thriftiness into a well-crafted tool.

Even putting her children first and dangling from a frayed shoestring of a budget, she always dressed nicely and was meticulous about her personal care. Forty years later, her powers of observation are based more on faded mental snapshots of previous experiences than on front and center reality. It's as if she can look right past something rife with obvious flaws and still describe it as she believes it to be. ("It looks wonderful, Suz," she says kindly of a spattered kitchen floor I have yet to mop.)

One month into this new venture, and I am still flailing at the unforeseen anxiety that creeps along my flesh at 2 a.m. like a million Velcro-footed centipedes. I pull at my own bootstraps, only to sink deeper into the quagmire of borrowing tomorrow's troubles. Roll out of bed and into whatever comfortable clothes are within reach. Not even a cursory swoosh of blush or swipe of mascara. Growing out a bad perm becomes my sole grooming effort.

Zelda and I make quite a pair. She sometimes mismatches socks or misbuttons her sweater. Sometimes grabs a frayed ragbag hat instead of the new hand-crocheted beauty her California daughter, Deb, sent for her birthday. But her mental energy is invested in more urgent concerns. She no longer accessorizes but instead wraps small bundles of costume jewelry in cotton hankies and tucks them away to be mailed to her daughters. She does this secretly as if fearful of interception or, worse yet, thievery. Her own collection of eye shadow and lipstick has gone untouched for months. Her mildly eccentric appearance is a product of a distracted mind; mine is sheer apathy.

On a day cold enough to form pea-size ice globules between Fergie's furry toes, Zelda and I start out in search of overdue haircuts. The trip does not begin well. First, my grand, galumphing Buick Roadmaster sputters to a stop in the mini-mall parking lot. Then I tangle with a shop manager who goes authoritarian on me about borrowing his business phone to report my car problems—a phone that does not ring the entire time we are in a salon that takes only walk-in clients.

I would love to say I'm handling all this with grace and poise, but I am not doing grace and poise very well lately. Instead, I bristle and seethe, then blush with shame for Zelda's sake. Changing the subject seems like a stellar idea.

2-1-05: *Waiting room chit-chat about hairstyles leads Z to disparage her own appearance against my objections. "Of course, you're young and beautiful," she responds, peering past me, out the sleet-streaked storefront window. There I sit, haggard and cosmetically naked in my frazzled ponytail and shapeless jeans, while the nice-looking, thirtysomething fellow next to me sneaks a sideways, incredulous peek. He is a portrait of gallantry even as his eyes widen in horrified bewilderment.*

A cringe grips my body, trapping a squawk of awkward laughter inside. "Beauty is definitely in the memory of the beholder," I'm thinking. Wish I had the nerve to say it out loud.

~~~~~

Zelda's dementia has a playful innocence to it. But somewhere in there lurks the sinister twin symptom of paranoia that surfaces according to no predictable cadence. In the past, she had always been agile at returning a swift volley against my father's cynical witticisms. While they were long-distance dating—Dad often visiting Royal Oak, Michigan, from his Minneapolis digs—he once sat across from her at a bridge table shared by two of her women friends. In a too-clever attempt at flippancy, with Zelda out of play and her hand exposed for him to draw from, he called out, "Hey, Dummy, why don't you get me a cup of coffee?" Ignoring the play on words, she quietly obliged, but laced the mug with a tablespoon of salt. As he choked back an urge to spew his first mouthful onto the living room carpet, she growled softly, "*Never* call me dummy."

Now, she dredges up decades-old comments, applies literal interpretations, and roils up anger and resentment as if they had been simmering on the back burner for years. Especially aggravating are Dad's appointments with a female counselor. Granted, a lot of spouses might view seeking outside help as a form of betrayal. But when you're no longer able to process explanations with a full measure of adult rationality, hurt and confusion can feed off each other like fermenting yeast giving volume to dough.

2-4-05: *I sort and file, then help Z through stretching exercises before she and I settle in to watch* Who Wants to Be a Millionaire *and* Jeopardy—*Dad off to a late counseling appointment. She fidgets and frets, complains that he uses these sessions to vent about her behind her back. She requires active assistance to mimic the limbering routine. I have less success guiding her through her suspicions about the counseling.*

And so the pot bubbles, and she recalls the time in 1972 when Dad joked that marrying an only child like her meant you wouldn't have to split your spouse's inheritance with siblings. A raw jest arising from his male sensibilities now strikes injury to Zelda's heightened sensitivities. Mars and Venus in their geriatric phase.

~~~~~

From the former chin-up confidence that allowed her to strike out alone in midlife as a self-sufficient career woman, Zelda has become a pixie waif. As she skips from one disconnected thought to another, she sometimes lands back on solid ground long enough to realize that she has removed the entire protective outer wrap from the box of powdered milk for absolutely no reason. "Why would I do that?" she laments days later, her brow contorted in anguish.

The original Zelda—the one who had been christened Mary Audrey but adopted the handle "Zelda" in her fifties because there were too many Marys in the world—had balanced self-determination and spunk with a fondness for whimsy. She loved devising costumes for Halloween, appreciated an occasional dose of Peter Sellers's lunacy, and searched for images in the clouds or in gnarled tree trunks. She also treasured art and music and literature. Today, mountains of records and tapes and DVDs, great stacks of Maxfield Parish illustration books, historical novels, and tomes on travel all sit—not simply untouched but unnoticed.

Unplugged from her passions as if to avoid sensory overload, she becomes a personality devoid of energy. Antiques and framed prints surround her, but she peers down a tunnel that leads to starkly practical destinations: a trip to the senior foot clinic, a jaunt to McDonald's with Papa, yet another nap. As I steer her toward talk of old interests, she is disengaged, like a jaded appraiser touring one more disappointing estate sale. The flame is extinguished, and a frosty breeze takes its place.

> Unplugged from her passions as if to avoid sensory overload, she becomes a personality devoid of energy.

2-7-05: *I steal a moment for a tea break and a sampling of Ogden Nash poems. Zelda urges me to take the six-volume collection home, as a look of revulsion crosses Dad's face. I decline. It is far too soon to begin* *bequeathals.*

To redirect, I lead her on a tour of household paintings and photo-graphs. We arrive at the monochrome oil of a wintry landscape that I gave them one Christmas after she had admired it on a store shelf, but then balked at the asking price. "I never much cared for this one," she says with calm detachment. "So gray and cold and depressing."

~~~~~

When meeting basic needs threatens to supplant aesthetic pursuits, you can lay down and roll over or you can chart another course. My days are still mellowed by turning out culinary delights: meatloaf with a cheesy hash browns casserole, fresh steamed green beans, and butterscotch peanut bars; ham hocks and navy beans with buttermilk biscuits and hot fudge pudding cake; crock pot jambalaya and custard flan; turkey breast sandwiches with tomatoes, sprouts, and avocado, and chocolate chip cookies. When Dad steps up with some creative ideas to help Zelda plug back in, we redouble our efforts in that arena. Outings are the lifeblood of this strategy, flexibility an essential ele-ment in pulling them off.

2-8-05: *I retrieve Z's boots from under the dining room table and her gloves from robe pockets, then talk her into a beauty school facial when a trip to the library is met with locked doors — CLOSED ON TUESDAYS. She deals well with students and staff, who patiently ease her through the credit card payment, a procedure she now finds puzzling. She later complains that the face lotion lingers like a coating of wax she can't wash off. Still, I smile inwardly: We actually pulled off a spontaneous minor escapade!*

Dad's treat of an art institute visit produces better results. But it's been awhile, and he isn't the adept navigator he once was. After a wrong turn or two and a few harrowing lane changes, we arrive unscathed, and Pa is off on his own as Zelda and I wander marble-lined hall-ways that echo with our footsteps. It's as if she remembers what she's supposed to like about this sort of thing but can't breathe the oxygen of enthusiasm into the venture. Still, mere exposure to fine art must benefit the spirit. At the very least, it's a change from the bland beige walls of home.

Fortunately, Zelda's intuitive connection to nature remains strong—God's lifeline for dimming senses. Sightseeing lures our imaginations back to unhurried Sunday excursions in the family car as we sink, full-body, into the downiness of those memories. Cruising by the townhouse Dad and Zelda once considered buying, a walk through a local Realtor's open house, a final stop at the Snail Lake pavilion to drink in the placid view across the lake's glassy surface. This last bit she savors the most.

It's as if she remembers what she's supposed to like about this sort of thing but can't breathe the oxygen of enthusiasm into the venture. Still, mere exposure to fine art must benefit the spirit.

~~~~~

When Zelda finds herself dithering, she sometimes jokes, "I should be on a leash." Here, I plunge into the mission of reassuring her of her tremendous worth to others throughout her lifetime—her students, her loyal friends, her family, her coworkers, the rescued pets. And me, the needy stepdaughter whose birth mother was two thousand miles away, both emotionally and geographically.

In the right mood, we can even share a hearty chuckle as we discover, a half-hour into an errand, that her boots "feel funny" . . . because she's put them on the wrong feet. She is less conscious, however, of the extent of her physical torpor.

2-10-05: *Z moves as if slogging through cold molasses. There is a cinematic trick where one person tracks in slow motion while the other whizzes around her at hyperspeed. This is Z and me. Today she tells me that I am wearing her out with my buzzing. Today, we are the ant and* *the bumblebee.*

It's easy to get wrapped up in my own agenda. To throw myself into recaulking the bathtub, clearing snow, cleaning up after Dad in the bathroom. Sneaking an over-soiled jacket into the wash without hurting anyone's feelings. And tidying, constant tidying. I welcome reminders to slow my roll and reorder my priorities.

2-14-05: *A touching exchange as Z kisses a seated Papa in thanks for his Valentine gift, then cradles his shoulders in her arm and leans her cheek against his forehead. His eyes well up as she murmurs tender words about having him there and their "helping each other." My Valentine gift is being here to witness this moment.*

~~~~~

For a long time, family wisdom held that Dad's limbs and joints weren't as reliable as they once were, but his mind was sharp. And Zelda was having difficulty with her memory but remained physically agile. He could oversee the household business, they reasoned, and she could be his legs. Both now sense a depletion of their respective strengths, and that awareness needs a place to hide—a cove of protection from the despairing thought of no longer having a productive role to play. Zelda naps; Dad writes acerbic essays on the threat of organized religion or the bigotry of moralistic right-wingers.

Last year, when my husband and I were helping clear out their winter place in Palm Harbor, Florida, for their final move back to the Minnesota townhouse, Jack commented on a clever arrangement of hardware for their living room drapes, to which Dad lightheartedly replied, "Yes, I wasn't always useless!" Since keeping up with ballooning handicaps has become a daily encumbrance, his lost abilities are no longer fodder for jokes.

In general, Dad does his stoic best, only occasionally speaking to me about Zelda's condition. Together, we three explore the idea of visiting the Mayo Clinic for a definitive assessment, for concrete recommendations with the weight of international renown behind them.

Meanwhile, not trusting her own judgment and unable to retain what she is told, Zelda continues to over-attend to physical issues she never used to find compelling. If her perpetually empty stomach gurgles, she wants to see a doctor to determine why.

Zelda's latest fixation is an elective referral to a periodontist about a tiny lump in her mouth that has not changed in appearance, size, or sensitivity since the dentist first noted it sixteen months ago. Thus, an appointment with the oral surgeon becomes both superfluous and necessary. But it does keep her involved in society. More traditional means of socializing don't always pan out.

2-18-05: *I so want to help Zelda stay engaged with the world, but her affliction has its own plans. Lunch out with my friend Barb S. is always a delight. But Z's attention floats somewhere above our table, and I can't seem to reel her back to earth. I itch to apologize to those who don't know the whole story of her ups and downs, then feel guilty for inclining in that direction.*

And then sometimes traditional means of socializing work just swell.

2-21-05: *Zelda greets me dressed in gray tailored sweatpants and a cross-buttoned, royal blue cardigan—heart-meltingly vulnerable like the underfed children in photos taken half a world away.*

After morning chores, naps, and dog walks, Pa, Z, and I bop over to Panda Buffet for a leisurely lunch and some light debate: Alfred Kinsey. Dedicated researcher or tool of Satan?

~~~~~

I am slowly learning that Zelda's condition is more advanced than I'd realized, but the situation is not as dire as my palpitating heart suggests when I'm awakened mid-dream by a quickened pulse and runaway thoughts. Yet as often as I scold my reflection in the mirror—*"It's not about you"*—I still spend too much energy tussling with my own angst. There is nothing like a glimpse of your parents' fragile mortality to send you careening back into the unresolved insecurities of adolescence. Grown-up me is no better, compulsively overanalyzing my moodiness, like the person who can't get relief from the misery of poison ivy because he won't stop clawing at it.

It's complicated. On days when Zelda shows improved stamina, I may be operating on less than four hours of sleep. May even be fighting the blues, anticipating another wasted evening of channel surfing at home. I'm allowing winter to lull me into stagnation—winter and insomnia and the inertia of a loosely structured day. I wanted this caregiving opportunity so much I could taste it, but the transition is no slice of strudel.

2-23-05: *I push through today as if wading in weed-infested water. Instead of putting every minute to constructive use, I flounder—fine intentions trampled by reality. The emotional wrestling match is draining. Disappointed in myself, I tie all lack of progress—mine or theirs—to my own deficiencies. In the end, I feel like a slug.*

I think I have just given myself a headache. What a perfect excuse to retreat to my bedroom.

More and more often, I eat a lean, mean lunch, then a sloppy fast-food dinner as my willpower erodes from the stresses of the day. The physical demands of the work are manageable, but emotional turmoil rumbles inside me. I watch Zelda fumble over things she once did with ease. I see Dad's pace slow to a crawl—his former zest for new challenges withered to nothing. It's insidious, the effect of these images.

And so, another point of clarity: While a "good day" does not necessarily indicate a trend, a "bad day" doesn't have to forebode a drop off the cliff, either.

2-25-05: *Z has no interest in leaving the house. She eats a few bites, talks, sleeps, eats a bit more, then sleeps again. Dr. A instructed Z to drink two Ensures a day, but she nurses one can for a week, not to be persuaded otherwise.*

I pound out a fifteen-minute weight-lifting workout and three fifteen-minute romps with Fergie, make corn bread to go with yellow pea soup, work on the half-bath remodeling project, sweep and mop the kitchen floor, and spot-clean the wallpaper. Valuable insights filter in when the hands are well occupied, Confucius say. Or maybe this is simply what it's like to relax and go with the flow.

A stop at the bank and another for Chinese carryout get me home by 5:45, where I manage fifteen minutes of Tae Bo before I flop into the abyss of lethargy that I like to call my recliner and pray for the resolve to hang on to tranquility.

~~~~~

If it's Monday, this must be serenity.

2-28-05: *After a solid night's sleep, I awaken to a bright, clear day. Z is thrilled when I produce in seconds the address of a Florida friend—the result of having cleaned out dining room drawers. You would think I had levitated the dogs.*

After our lunch of meatloaf sandwiches on sprouted wheat bread, Z hesitates about venturing out. She wants to go to Sam's Club with me, and then she doesn't. She becomes lodged midway between the two options. An excursion will be good for her, she says at last. It is an agonizing ordeal, deciding to walk away from the beckoning sanctuary of her warm, comfy bed. I see this. I feel this.

After our return, I take Fergie for a long walk and then coach Z through her weight machine workout while I do stair-climbing. As a reward, we share a pot of tea and a sliver of pumpkin pie—with thanks.

Chapter Three

Redefining Normal

You begin to fall into a routine of sorts even when things aren't all that routine—learn not to be shocked by the once unthinkable or bowled over by the bizarre. You also learn that if you don't take firm hold of the reins, circumstances can lead you where you don't want to go.

My husband tells me I've become bossy at home. This horrifies me. It's a bleeding over of the role I've fallen into with Zelda, and I question whether I am overbearing with her as well. More fodder for sleepless nights.

She is in need of some steering, but you can't take a course in knowing how far to crank the rudder without inciting resistance or damaging relationships. I read books and articles. I research websites. I apply the principle of abiding harmless delusions without judgment and faulty recollections without challenge. I pick my battles. But do I choose wisely? It's in the individual application that guidelines fail us.

Zelda's conversations are sometimes melancholy, and that seems like a good time to redirect. And when she's playful, that seems like a good time to hop on for the ride. Dementia has robbed her of the capacity for probing analysis, so talk of current events requires diplomacy. And tracking the present is much more difficult for her than plucking tufts of experience from history. Yet when she peers too intently into the past, she can get lost there as well.

3-2-05: *Z is distant today. Her eyes become saucer-like and glassy as they fix on some unknown point in space. I am eager to know what torments her mind at times like these. Sometimes she can articulate what it is and sometimes she cannot. It's almost better when she cannot, for then we just leap to a new subject far from the source of her distress.*

Randomness has become the new norm. Zelda may confidently dredge up nicknames from her college days. Fred was Spud. Mary was Stretch. Lois was Moonbeam. The next minute, she might ask where I went to school but never enjoy the spark of an "aha!" moment that my answer should ignite. Information bounces off the surface instead of sinking in and reestablishing its place.

For stimulation I contrive tactile activities, like a teacher making a lesson plan, and guide an afternoon of errands toward the art supply store. Sketch pads, pencils, and pastels—a grand strategy for getting Zelda drawing again. But fresh, inviting materials don't come with a potion to revive atrophied impulses. She follows my lead. Complies with the expectation. But after sketching a miniscule portrait of her beloved dog Sally in the bottom corner of the 11x14 sheet, she tires of the effort as if the thought of having to fill all that empty white space has worn her out. Looks like I'll be returning that stack of borrowed drawing books to the library.

~~~~~

This is, of course, new territory for all of us. And we don't always end up on the same page of the atlas. Dad drives Zelda to her regular appointments with Dr. A, who—Zelda assures me—is a geriatric specialist. This is good. It is time together and keeps him involved. But once there, he remains in the waiting room. Doesn't go into the inner sanctum to be a second set of ears. I sense that he is humoring her and doesn't expect

By the time they get home, details of the consultation are no more recoverable than the van's exhaust fumes.

anything helpful to take place. By the time they get home, details of the consultation are no more recoverable than the van's exhaust fumes.

3-5-05: *I pace the kitchen, washing and drying dishes as a pot of chicken thighs, rice, and mushrooms in wine sauce bubbles away on the stove. Next, a batch of lemon bars for dessert because Z loves them and it's one of the flavors she can still taste. I will be ready with pen and paper when they walk in the door to try and capture whatever she remembers about her doctor's visit.*

I need to find a way to connect with the doctor myself because the eating concern looms large and has potential for harm. Nutrition plays such an essential role in wellness. I indulge their tastes but try to sneak good stuff into the things I make for them: ground flax seed stirred into bar and cookie dough; olive oil substituted for butter; fruit incorporated into breads and muffins; a pot of vegetable beef soup, heavy on the vegetables.

Dad couldn't care less. He eats whatever appeals and is handy. Has no interest in talk of healthful options. But Zelda always has been on board with the idea of wholesome eating—that is, before she lost touch with the sensation of hunger and the concept of mealtime. Just getting sustenance into her system becomes the revised goal as I coach her to reseat herself and finish her scant half-serving of whatever. At times these situations become Cortisol-inducing standoffs. She sleeps it off. I store fat.

It's so easy to get entrapped in Cortisol's vicious cycle. The brain, the pituitary, the adrenals: all send out signals for stress hormone production. The pattern becomes self-perpetuating. Anxiety and depression cause lethargy and disrupt sleep patterns; lack of sleep leads to even higher blood levels of cortisol—the adipose-accumulating, muscle-robbing enemy of the female metabolism.

So food becomes an issue for me, too. I eat plenty of whole grains, fruits, and vegetables and stay active during the day, but I've gained eight pounds since Christmas. And there doesn't seem to be any logical connection between my own good or bad habits and how I feel on a given day.

3-8-05: *I glide effortlessly through the day in spite of getting less than four hours of sleep last night. No pasty-mouth sensation or weighted limbs, even after a pre-dinner, 30-minute Tae Bo workout at home. Thank you, Lord, for the opportunity to make a difference, for this beautiful sunny day, and for listening to my perpetual whining.*

~~~~~

I so wish Dad and Zelda could still appreciate their canine companions. The dogs seem contentedly readjusted to the slowed pace and the extra naps, loyally curling up at the feet of whomever, whenever. But I mourn the loss of shared delight over their antics and try to draw as much personal pleasure from Chloé and Fergie as I can.

Indeed, the pups are my tonic for a sagging mood. A reminder that life balances out in the long run if we can resist obsessing over the debit side of the ledger. No one here has suffered years of cancer treatments or dialysis; we still have our homes, food on the table, and family. All significant kindling for true gratitude. So it's not that things are so bad; it's just that they are sometimes so sad. That's when these two furry clowns can be more effective than a truckload of Prozac.

3-9-05: *Chloé stands lock-kneed on the top porch step, shivering in triple time. Turns a forlorn and pitiful face toward me as the leash extends taut between us. I release her back into the house where she straight-lines it for a pool of collected sunlight like a fish reintroduced to the lake from an angler's clutches.*

But intrepid Fergie tramps on, burrowing her nose into the snow like a miniature bulldozer. We scale to the top of an icy ridge on this cold, crisp, luminous day and are rewarded by a chorus of chirping birds and a stunning horizon capped by layers of multicolored clouds.

~~~~~

3-16-05: *During our double-dog walk, Chloé discovers a discarded French fry. I try to pry it from her mouth, but she clamps her jaws stubbornly as if around a miniature cigar, then totes her trophy back home where she can munch at her leisure.*

~~~~~

When my father remarried, I was blessed with four above-average stepsisters. They are scattered about North America now but had only recently left the nest when their mother made the move from Michigan to Minnesota with her new husband, M.H. Williams, PhD, also known as Bill—and soon to be dubbed by his bride with pet names suitable to various occasions: Papa, Milton Hugh, His Highness.

Visits from my stepsisters have been part of our shared history from the early years of Dad and Zelda's marriage. Now is no exception, and the appearance at the threshold of Rob, Joan, Deb, or Julie brings great cheer to the household. It also sets me off on a dizzying whirl of cleaning and prepping in a neurotic effort to assure them that everything here is proceeding flawlessly.

With the announcement that Julie will soon arrive, I plan vegetarian meals, redouble all cleaning efforts, and try not to nurse my disquiet over trouble spots. Her stay should be relaxed and pleasant and might even introduce a trace of the former status quo. Or it might cause

Her stay should be relaxed and pleasant and might even introduce a trace of the former status quo. Or it might cause confusion. Could go either way. I try not to think about it.

confusion. Could go either way. I try not to think about it.

3-20-05: *As I bake apple crisp and assemble split pea soup, I fret over the amount of time both parents spend napping during the day. Dad has problems with nighttime insomnia, yet takes as long an afternoon snooze as his schedule will allow. I am hoping that Julie's presence will interrupt the pattern.*

Maybe it's my ingrained personality, maybe it's the quirkiness of midlife brain chemistry, or maybe it's all the infuriating commercial noise about how you can attain true peace through pharmaceuticals. But finding healthy ways to maintain a sane perspective is tricky when life's dilemmas don't respond to textbook solutions.

Julie is my personal deliverance in the form of congenial talk therapy. Before she arrives, I promise myself I won't burden her with anecdotal horror stories or laments about daily hurdles. I won't prattle on that I sometimes feel afraid and immobilized, a martyr to my own physical and emotional frailties. That I won't blubber about being helpless to stop the decline.

Like a predictable sitcom, flip-scene to my first dog walk with Julie at my side. I hear myself yammering on about Zelda's poor eating patterns, her escapes into sleep, and her loss of logical reasoning power. About Dad's disconnecting and disappearing and his rejection of physical therapy to rebuild strength in his weakened limbs. About his too-casual acceptance of handicapped parking privileges and motorized shopping carts.

Julie is a violist with a world-class professional symphony orchestra. She knew what she wanted to do with her life by the time she hit ninth grade. She is kind and direct and honest. When she reassures me that I am "exactly the right person for this job," these are exactly the right words for the situation. My heart knows she is spot-on.

With confirmation that I am where I am meant to be, maybe I can steer myself out of Self Doubt Central. Oh, but beating up on myself proves to be so much easier than accepting that people vital to my sense of worldly security are slowly being ushered out of my life.

~~~~~

In my journal notes I declare that a mature person does not flap in the winds of circumstance. A mature person decides how an evening—or a day or a week—will go and then takes steps to make it so. But lofty aspirations are no match for the vicissitudes of human behavior, and soon I am on my knees pleading for the vision to know the difference between the moveable object and the brick wall.

When you step into another person's world as caregiver, you begin the delicate process of straddling two realities. This is where things get disorienting, where the lines defining personal space blur, and where outlooks may clash. It's a quandary beyond my ability to sort out. A person of faith cannot serve two masters. You either lean on the Lord or you cling to your own miserable means and stomp your feet at the unreasonableness of it all.

> A mature person decides how an evening—or a day or a week—will go and then takes steps to make it so. But lofty aspirations are no match for the vicissitudes of human behavior.

The struggle may continue—to keep your focus on the goal of giving comfort, your heart open to the joys of providing for daily needs, your mind grounded in the present and not sucked into a craving for the past—yet the Source of strength is always within reach. God's hand is ever outstretched. Remembering to grab on tight is the obvious solution that can get lost in all the washing up and putting away or the worry over missed meals and crossed signals.

And help often arrives in unassuming forms. After Julie leaves, Dad confesses that she gave him a stern lecture about making sure Zelda eats her evening meal. He reports this with raised brow and a sheepish smile, and I ask myself if he has been honoring Zelda's right to independence or simply entrenched in denial. Psychologist, evaluate thyself?

Chapter Four

You Has Your Ups, and You Has Your Downs

Zelda grew up with a hole in her heart. Not the congenital, physical kind, but rather a yearning sense of incompleteness that haunted her from preschool years into adulthood. Though she eventually filled that void with loyal friends and a family of her own, she continued to be burdened by the expectation, formed early, that disappointment is inevitable.

When Zelda, née Mary Audrey, was three years old, her mother gave birth to a second girl, Jeanette Francis—an answer to prayers for both parent and child. Young Mary was intrigued by the at-home delivery taking place behind closed doors in her parents' Beaver Dam, Wisconsin, bedroom. Overjoyed at the prospect of a lifelong friend and playmate, she gleefully entertained the baby—clanging pot lids like cymbals and making silly faces—and dreamed of all the things they would do together as little Jeanette toddled behind her like a devoted duckling.

Erysipelas is a bacterial strep infection that shows up as lesions on the skin but can invade the heart and lymph system through the bloodstream. In 1927, limited treatment approaches left infected infants and young children at great risk for complications. Jeanette

Francis was only 18 months old when she broke out in the strange, orange peel-like rash. Within days, the disease would rob the family of their joy and leave Big Sister an only child again.

Zelda's father withdrew in the face of this tragedy, but she and her mother remained close, comforting and amusing each other. "Chickabitty Shortshanks" her mother nicknamed her. And sometimes during dinner preparations a grand chase would ensue around the kitchen table, mother pursuing daughter, brandishing a raw chicken neck, as both squealed with delight.

As Zelda got older, her mother grew more protective, and Zelda chafed at the restrictions. By the time she turned eighteen, Zelda itched to test her wings with a move to Michigan to live with fun-loving Uncle Stanzie and Aunt Hannah while she attended Wayne University. Pulling against the reins of a respected, loving mother shaped within her a subtle determination not to be bridled or steered.

4-5-05: *It's late morning. Z stands at the kitchen counter using a corn-on-the-cob pick to eat a tiny portion of the banana I have sliced into a small bowl. She has already had one nap since I arrived shortly before ten.*

At noon, as she heads off to bed again, she stops in her tracks long enough to say that she wishes the aging process would "either slow way down or speed way up, one or the other." I hug her—a side hug, laying my left cheek on the top of her head—but she is unresponsive and holds her arms stiffly at her side.

I think she is miffed at my urgings to eat. But I get frustrated with her always leaving a portion of her half-sandwich for "later" when "later" never comes. It's just a few bites that would easily find room in what must be a perpetually empty stomach.

I understand the resistance. Who wants it implied that they don't have a handle on their own needs or how to meet them? As it is, Zelda's self-image is under assault from all directions. Made aware of a drip on the end of her nose, she mumbles to no one in particular, "Disgusting, just disgusting." With age, we attach new interpretations to things. Ten years ago, I didn't hyperventilate over misplaced sunglasses.

~~~~~

It's an exercise in vagaries, appealing to diminishing senses of taste and smell, sight and hearing. Even touch. But a person has to try. I draw on past observation. Dad loves chili con carne with chopped raw onion on top, and bacon in any presentation. Zelda prefers dark meat to chicken breast, which she finds too dry, and insists that the only apple worth sinking your teeth into is a Granny Smith.

You also dispel old myths like Dad's birthday tradition of pineapple upside down cake, which he apparently tired of long ago after too many years of repetition, but which I continued to proudly present to him every September 6 for as long as I can remember. Not this year.

But there are new favorites. Zelda swoons over my meatloaf patties: lean ground turkey, an egg, finely ground wheat cracker crumbs, soy sauce, micro-planed onion with juices, maybe a pinch of Chinese Five Spice. I pair them with extra-cheesy au gratins and pray for the best. Pray that Dad is tuning in after I leave for the evening. Pray that Zelda won't sleep through mealtime. Pray that my usefulness outweighs my pestering.

Dad's on a mission to reengage his own tactile senses, I guess. He responds to a cryptic ad placed by a masseur working out of a private residence miles away and blithely takes off for the afternoon—with no cell phone and no firm idea of what he may be walking into. Zelda and I are astounded. She worries that the ad could be bait, the destination a trap, and that Dad is not acting reasonably. She is right back in wife mode with her intuition activated and her gut in gear, totally aware of present reality.

I carry my concern with me as I clean. Since Zelda now sleeps in the guest room, the master—this large, oblong space with its oversized bed—has become my father's room. It smells of him. Of his hair and body oils. Of his medicated foot powder and Mennen Skin Bracer. Of his long afternoons sunk into the pillow cases. It's not Eau De Parfum, but it's not unpleasant either. It's simply the essence of him. As I drift into thoughts about how much I would miss that smell . . . the muted sound of his footfalls on the carpeted stairs brings me back to the here and now of having him as a focal point in my life. This he has always been. But I doubt that he knows how much so.

~~~~~

Household projects remain my touchstone, grounding me to the possible. I clean windows and scrape black, gold, and mauve art deco wallpaper off the walls of the lower-level bathroom. With Jack's help, I'll replace the cracked sink, the malfunctioning toilet, the gilt-edged vanity cabinet, the tiny mirror. Subtly marbled self-stick tiles will restore the worn flooring. Just thinking about the newness replacing the dinge lifts me.

But a project begun inevitably becomes a Pandora's box of unpleasant discoveries. The scraped walls require filling and spackling and sanding and more scraping. The floor replacement calls for leveling and laying down a base. All of this reminds me that I must stay fit and sound.

With a desk job, you can limp your way through the day without proper rest or hobbled by a minor injury. Not so with my current duties. Last month when I slipped on the ice walking Fergie and landed squarely on my left knee with a perceptible crunch, I erupted in spontaneous prayer: "Oh please, please, please. Don't let me break a kneecap; not now. I can't afford to be out of commission." No damage done, not even a bruise.

And when pain arises from an arthritic basal thumb joint, there is no way I'm buying into the slick sales pitch of an alligator-shoed orthopedist who wants to rush me into slow-healing joint-replacement surgery so he can fund another ski vacation.

And again, I hear the footsteps of time closing in as I nurse a bruised rib. I can't let a stupid stunt like leaning into the trash bin to recover a bundle of recyclables keep me from my scraping and sanding, my baking and cleaning. This work will not wait for me to rest and recuperate.

4-7-05: *Going on three and a half hours of sleep, I try to keep moving so I don't run down like a played-out windup toy. Chloé refuses to walk, but Fergie seeks me out for trot number three even though it's downright hot in the direct early spring sunlight.*

Back from our stroll, I dig out a floppy hat and dark glasses and pull decorative stones out of the front garden beds. The rocks Jack and I installed by request a few years ago now offend Zelda, so they must go.

Then I work on the deck—washing the furniture, tossing dead plants, setting up the umbrella table. Bringing things back from their winter neglect gives life to the view beyond the sliding doors.

Z sleeps, then joins me in digging out moss from between the deck slats until she tires and needs another nap. I worry about her lack of stamina. It is difficult to introduce physical activity when she is so often lying down. A body at rest wants to stay at rest, and inertia wins out over momentum.

~~~~~

As for those ups and downs, they rise and fall between the everyday plateaus.

4-11-05: *Lunch for two at LeAnn Chin's. Watching Z tackle simple tasks can be draining since her frailty makes even the effort of cutting up food excruciatingly labor-intensive. Then, after I remind her to grab the folded ends of the fortune cookie and snap it in two rather than chip away at the brittle edges, she coyly peeks at me through the hollow shell of pastry. Delicious.*

4-13-05: *Z heads for the bedroom for a nap, saying I should wake her if she sleeps too long. I suggest that I might find a trombone for that purpose, so she fishes a coronet-style kazoo out of the junk drawer and* *blasts out an animated tune.*

4-14-05: *Zelda says she wants to write to Gracie "sometime." I gather paper and pen and we get the letter written at that moment—and into today's mail. Follow-through and completion! This is huge.*

4-18-05: *Side-by-side gardening with Z. As I dig, she sows sweet pepper seeds and breaks into a few verses of "The Girl from Ipanema" and other assorted oldies. On my own, I would never give myself permission to sing like nobody's listening. How liberating.*

4-25-05: *Z and I visit a neighbor's garage sale in place of her morning nap. Haunted by images of B and Z's stockpile of boxed-up prints and shabby-chic frames, I cautiously dissuade her from purchasing a ratty-looking landscape. Back at the townhouse, I joke about not having added to the clutter, and . . . off we go, back to the sale so Z can gain possession of the treasure I had the temerity to suggest was not worthy of her attention. Defeated, once again, by my own flapping gums.*

~~~~~

We are gliding, blessedly, into milder weather. Zelda hates the cold and never felt more astounded at her good fortune than when a dedicated agent tracked her down as the beneficiary of an investment her father had made years ago. With this windfall, she was able to buy a modest getaway in Palm Harbor, to which she and Dad could escape for the harsh winter months.

Dogs in tow, they would pack their vehicle to the roof with anything they didn't have a duplicate of in Florida. A whirlwind surrounded these preparations with Zelda tweaking the to-do and to-bring lists and Dad plotting the route and prepping the car.

Occasionally his "we can buy one when we get there" practicality and her "waste not, want not" frugality ricocheted off each other, as in the Night of Many Leftovers, which lives on in family lore. Picture the weary businessman. He returns home at the end of a long, loose-ends-tying day, and is greeted by a dozen small tubs set out on the kitchen counter—remnants of the prior week's meals that his wife is determined to use up before they hit the road the next morning. His shoulders slump over the prospect of this highly eclectic meal and the flurry of cleanup activities to follow. He puts his hands on his wife's shoulders, looks deep into her eyes, and says pleadingly, "Let's eat out." She concedes. They eat out.

Once they reached Florida, their pace didn't slow. Dad worked from this southern base and traveled when he needed to see clients. Zelda became a volunteer docent of the Tarpon Springs collection of George Inness Jr. paintings and an active member of the women's service group at the local Unitarian church. Both participated in the Village Residents Association Coffee House.

That would be a coffee house—with entertainment. Dad might write dialogue for a mildly risqué playlet; Zelda had a gift for choreographing musical routines in pantomime. She made a convincing Groucho Marx, stomping around in a man's suit and oversized footwear, mouthing "Lydia, oh Lydia, that encyclopidia, Lydia the ta-at-tooed lady" through her false nose and mustache.

Photographic evidence of their lively former selves—from volumes of yellowing Polaroids to dozens of videos of their worldwide travels—is everywhere in the townhouse. These make for lovely hours of reminiscing or painful moments of longing, so it's not always safe to explore that territory. For the most part, the albums grow moldy, and the celluloid threatens to crackle with age and disuse. The main characters do not seem to notice.

4-29-05: *I spend 80 percent of the day cleaning the microwave and defrosting the refrigerator. Dad says, "I suppose it could use it." Zelda remembers doing it herself "not too long ago"—a highly fluid point of reference under our current circumstances.*

Next, I rescue the recently organized linen closet from its sprawl back toward chaos. Unlike bureau items have been laid on top of bed linens, and individual paper towels have been stacked across the front of one entire shelf. Oh, for a glimpse of the thought processes behind Z's detached gaze and distracted actions. But I will be very careful what I wish for . . .

What I may safely wish for is more opportunities to walk alongside and help gather up the edges of uncertainty that want to unravel around us.

Chapter Five

To Bend or Not to Bend

Being inflexible is a good way to get broken—if not into pieces, at least to the point of fracture. While I hate the idea of accommodating decline, sometimes I think Dad and Zelda have a healthier approach to adapting: a dash of denial, a smidgen of resentment, and a large dose of acquiescence. Meanwhile, I forge ahead, stubbornly committed to perfecting the imperfectible.

I dampen the bottoms of my feet as per the instructions on my Homedics fat-calculating scale and weigh in at 139.2. True charity radiates outward, not inward. But as hard as I try to redirect my focus, I am obsessed with stopping this weight gain and resuming the lunch-hour treadmill workouts I gave up when I left the workplace. Big bucks for an elliptical trainer at home. More attention to quality nutrition. Baked salmon and veggie stir-fry, low-fat breakfast bars and snack mixes made from scratch. I attribute part of my agonizing and overanalyzing to bad medicine.

In 2002, suffering from chronic fatigue and low blood sugar, my frantic search for drug-free answers led me to a holistic chiropractor's office in an elite Twin Cities suburb. I should have seen the flapping red flags when the good doctor drove not just one, but two, shiny new luxury SUVs. But I was so desperate for relief that even the mysterious practices of non-touch bodywork, contact reflex analysis, and a torturously severe elimination diet didn't break through my mental fog to flash an alert.

Seven thousand dollars into a supposed $1,200 program of weekly neck-cracking sessions and mounting dietary supplement costs, I took a hard look at six months' worth of credit card statements, cringed at my folly, and ducked out the back door of that posh establishment with my newly aligned spine in a slouch. I also refinanced my house.

Rational or not, I took away from this experience two unshakable insights: the idea that we're 90 percent responsible for our own ills, and a fear of food sensitivities. Both notions hover and haunt whenever I have a bad day. If only I could sort out which edibles to avoid and squeeze in a daily cardio session. If only I could convince Dad and Zelda to push back against their challenges. To move their limbs more and do memory exercises. I compile a library of resources—titles like *Successful Aging, Total Recall, Learn to Remember, Brain Builders, Age Right*—convinced that it can't hurt to try.

5-5-05: *As Z and I enjoy a long stroll on this glorious day, we encounter an enormous gaggle of geese. "They will scatter and fly away if you run toward them,"* she observes. I nod in innocent agreement, hands clasped behind my back, gaze fixed on the route ahead. A split-second later, *Z veers off the path at a gallop, flapping her arms wildly, and charges the grazing flock. Point demonstrated, as the thunder of beating wings sends a thrill up my spine. I guess there's more than one way to do calisthenics.*

~~~~~

Dad and Zelda chose well in selecting their downsized retirement home. The townhouse is less than two miles from the freeway entrance and, from there, only fifteen minutes from either downtown,

Minneapolis or Saint Paul. Yet it's nestled in a verdant oasis of hills and ponds and wooded walking trails that insulate it and make it seem closer to sedate countryside than teeming shopping malls.

The housing layout is mostly four laterally attached two-story homes, each with a deck extending over a generous two-car garage. The place was more than twenty years old when Dad and Zelda moved in, and they've lived in their unit for thirteen years. Being surrounded by other people lends a sense of security. And while the building exterior is well maintained, the inside reflects years of wear. I want to boost everyone's morale by refreshing the decor. But is it an insult or a gift to offer such unsolicited improvements?

Dad and Zelda have different ideas about these things. It may be his castle, but Dad is more than happy to let someone else make it a home. Zelda was a nest-builder. Sound, traditional cooking was her forté; housekeeping and decorating were her proprietary realm.

When she first began to lose her grip on these skills, Dad urged her to let Merry Maids come in and help out twice a month. The "helping out" part was semi-tolerable for a few weeks. It was the "coming in" that troubled her deeply. "I know you want this," she mustered the determination to tell him. "But I really, *really* do not." She had given it a try, but the thought of some stranger peering into the nooks and crannies of their personal spaces repulsed her. That it's me now poking around seems to be OK. Or . . . mostly OK.

~~~~~

Abstract attempts to blend self-interest with mission get shifted to the back burner when life keeps happening while you're still drawing up a plan. No matter how many buckets of sweat and tears you contribute, there's no guarantee you can come up with enough patching plaster when things start crumbling around you—metaphorically or otherwise.

5-9-05: *I no sooner return from taking Corine to her doctor's appointment and then dashing over to B & Z's to start my day with them than*

Dad announces that Jack called to ask me to drive him to the eye special-ist. The intra-retinal bleeding has worsened. He can no longer see well enough to function at work.

I walk the dogs, then hurry over to transport Jack to his emergency appointment, where Dr. R schedules him for surgical removal of all the vitreous fluid in his left eye. Some paperwork and a few telephone calls and—boom—he is on six weeks of paid leave. Thank God we opted for short-term disability insurance. So far, his employer seems supportive. But I guess the company has no choice in the matter.

~~~~~

The nice weather brings more opportunities to get outside and fill our lungs with warm spring air. It seems to entice Zelda and reenergize the pups.

5-11-05: *I look like a human Maypole as I juggle two leashed dogs that are zigzagging crazily back and forth. Observers must wonder if this is some bizarre rite of spring. Ye Olde Elimination Ritual, wherein the celebrant passes a loaded bag of puppy poop back and forth over her head in a random, swaying motion. And, for a finale, prances backward into the nearest arborvitae bush.*

"Maybe I could try driving again," she ponders aloud. I am struck numb. Paralyzed in mid-motion. Holding my breath for the response. "Sure," Dad answers cheerfully.

Dad tends to keep going regardless of the season, but then he hasn't had to give up the golden key to mobil-ity and independence—driving. Zelda hasn't gotten behind the wheel in more than a year. Being self-honest to her core, she realized long before the mild tremors and spells of forgetfulness got worrisome that her reaction time was slower. She may have strained the state patrol's radar equipment along their route to Florida over the years, but she wasn't going to risk becoming a news blurb in the local paper because of a slow braking foot.

Today she is mourning that loss of freedom. "Maybe I could try driving again," she ponders aloud. I am struck numb. Paralyzed in mid-motion. Holding my breath for the response. "Sure," Dad answers cheerfully. "You could start out right on the townhouse grounds to see how it goes."

What is happening here? Have I been transported to a parallel universe? Does he actually think this is a good idea, or has indulgence become reflexive? It seems they are both gung ho for this proposal, but what else could he say? There is no better reply.

Reassured by the possibility, Zelda never raises the subject again.

There is an edgy comfort in the realization that fading memory can sometimes be a blessing. But it's a daily lottery that doesn't always pay out in your favor, and knowing how it weakens its victim sets my defensive instincts at full throttle.

5-13-05: *I spackle the remaining bathroom wall, walk the dogs twice, and drive Z to the Bibelot Shop to search for a gift for a friend. Next, lunch at our favorite Chinese buffet. Today she seems dazed. I worry about her absent look and her robotically marching in the wrong direction toward the exit rather than the chow line. But during our one-to-one seated conversation, she does quite well.*

Still, I feel protective of her and watchful, emboldened to confront a boisterous Neanderthal holding forth a few tables away. "Do you think you could manage not to use the F-word eight times in every sentence?" I suggest, forcing a smile. "I'm here with my 82-year-old stepmother, and we would both really appreciate it." Apparently stunned, McPottymouth blinks twice in response, and I escape without bodily injury.

At the grocery store on the way home, Z stops mid-aisle, looking for . . . I'm not sure what. I suspect she isn't sure either.

~~~~~

Walks continue to provide diversional therapy.

5-16-05: *Today, with bud-plumped foliage offering the promise of* *summer blooms, we take extra-long dog walks and complete a full one-miler with Z. She detects a pug-nosed gremlin face in the bark of an oak tree. Cavorting squirrels get nicknames, Otto and Olivia, after characters she remembers from a story read decades ago.*

Lots of encounters with the doggie set, too: Pippin, a suave Cavalier King Charles Spaniel; the twin Sheltie whirling dervishes, whose owner can't risk pausing for fear of being swept off her feet; adorable Daisy, an appealing little Yorkie Poo who is a miniature teddy bear covered in black curls and bounding with puppy energy. Z observes and coos mechanically but does not make contact.

Zelda has been a committed pet owner all her life. Her most cherished childhood gift was a Boston Terrier puppy, Dixie Dot, a constant companion and always willing playmate. In adulthood, there were the cats Katie and Sam, followed by Cali and Max; perceptive Phoebe, a Rat Terrier mix; and the incomparable, devoted Sally Dog.

Sally had been discovered beside a friend's driveway, cruelly discarded by a passing motorist. Looking like a pile of dirty rags, she uncomplainingly curled up in a safe, sunny spot and waited to be rescued. Dad and Zelda's was the perfect home for this appealing little canine adoptee, and a supremely grateful Sally spent every possible moment cuddled up to one or both of them.

Zelda used to tell inquirers that the wee hairy mutt—all scraggly, crimped tufts of black fur with a licorice drop of a nose—was a Mount Ararat Goat Hound. Well, she could have been. Who knows what one of those creatures would look like, anyway?

One thing was certain: Sally loved sweets. Once, when her two best buddies were out for the evening, she climbed a chair to mount the horseshoe-shaped kitchen counter, then traipsed across stove, cutting board, double sink, and dishwasher to reach an irresistible box of Fanny Farmer chocolates "hidden" on top of the refrigerator.

Dad and Zelda returned home to piles of soggy brown candy papers and a stomach-dragging, shame-filled pooch casting mournful, wordless apologies in their direction with her liquid brown eyes. All three survived the event, and, by the next morning, there was little

Sal, dragging her leash in her mouth, begging for a romp outside.

These days, Zelda can't recall that remarkable incident, and her life-long loving connection with furry critters seems thin, insubstantial. An arm's-length sort of relationship replaces the former bond. The two little girls currently in residence are no match for Sally, but they have always garnered Zelda's affectionate attention. Now, not so much.

I fend off negative thoughts. Seize the comedic as it whizzes by. Everyday Zeldaisms help. And they prove that wit can survive even uncooperative synapses and blocked neural pathways.

~~~~~

So, how to adapt but not surrender? I fend off negative thoughts. Seize the comedic as it whizzes by. Everyday Zeldaisms help. And they prove that wit can survive even uncooperative synapses and blocked neural pathways.

5-18-05: *A truly dreary view out the wide expanse of sliding glass doors—gray and rainy and blustery. A high of only 42 degrees. I feel wretched—headachy, queasy, lethargic. Immediately, I jump to condemn last night's snack of fresh strawberries. Or was it that lunchtime can of Diet Pepsi?*

It doesn't help that Z had a bad start: forgetting that she'd taken a morning nap; asking me about retrieving the mail after watching me do just that; needing to be called by name to stay connected with the discussion. I pray that this is an isolated backslide.

Sanding the respackled bathroom wall, cleaning up that gritty mess, then laying down a heavy coat of primer. These things help me refocus.

Next, I treat a water ring on the coffee table with mayonnaise—a trick Z taught me during her antiques-collecting days. Here is little Chloé, following up on my efforts with a thorough surface-licking. Laughter all around lifts spirits and fires Z's imagination. She decides we should christen the new bathroom with a name or title. Maybe even install a plaque. "El Smello Baddo," she declares, then giggles. "I shouldn't say such goofy things." And here I stand, longing for more goofiness.

The pull toward discouragement can be harder to resist as you move from day into evening, from crazy-busy to not knowing what to do next. Layers of concern, pushed off like too many blankets during hectic daylight hours, seem to calcify into a sort of shell. Not the protective kind, but the kind that makes it hard to rally.

5-23-05: *Ever since Jack's eye surgery last Thursday, he's been chair-bound, nursing a pain in his gut. Probably the antibiotics. This morning, he has a dental consultation for a chipped tooth. Probably mere coincidence. Why does it feel more like piling on?*

Dinner is excellent leftovers from our going-away meal with Pastor's family: marinated beef tenderloin, princess salad, roasted peppers and asparagus, Hasselback potatoes, tweed popovers. But when the pastor's eleven-year-old, our little buddy Jesse, bikes one last time past our living room window today and turns to wave, I have to blink back tears. He has been our surrogate grandson, our Taco Bell lunch partner, our pew-sharing source of delight since he was six. The thought of his moving to Wisconsin renders me breathless.

Then news of a visit from Joan disrupts my plunge into a culvert of self-pity, mid-dive.

~~~~~

Joan is Zelda's second-oldest. She is her family's glue. She keeps the sisters connected and lives close enough to her mom to visit frequently. A longtime University of Wisconsin employee, she's known as "the heart of the German department" by her coworkers. Joan would be the one to bake apricot coffee cake to share with coworkers and invite retired professors to holiday dinners. The one who visits old family friends in their nursing homes and is her aging father's health care advocate, chauffeur, and household manager.

Saint Joan. This we call her without a trace of mockery. My own father is not easily impressed, nor is he often a repeater of stories. But I have heard more than once his account of Joan hopping out of the family van to help a motorist push his car out of a snow bank and then hiking the rest of the way back to the townhouse. In a blizzard.

Joan is competent and take-charge in a manner that Zelda accepts as the expression of love that it is. Why should I feel intimidated by this paragon of virtues? Let me count the whys . . .

Find incentive, where thou may. Perhaps what I lack in self-confidence, I can make up for with dynamism.

5-25-05: *I scurry like mad to prepare for Joan's visit: install a paper towel holder in the kitchen and reseed the doggy-ruined patches of lawn by the front sidewalk; wash dishes, vacuum, dust; clean out the refrigerator and mop the hard surfaces; do a second dog walk; feed the pups.*

Z has begun this last task. She refills the pet food bowls, gets distracted by conversation, and stands while holding them thirty-six inches above the bobbing, frustrated heads of the intended recipients. Chloé and Fergie break into a frenzied dance at her feet, but she is unaware. I casually slink in to relieve her of the now-forgotten doggie dinners in her hands, set them before the anxious pups, and keep talking as if I hadn't just brazenly intervened.

I finally leave around 4:50, frustrated by having to move linens to their proper spots and clear away newspapers, litter, and clutter. Twice. It's as if I am the only one in prep mode for Joan's impending visit. Well, duh. I remind myself that neither Ma nor Pa was particularly concerned about such minutiae in the past. Draw a thick, black line between what I'm doing for their benefit and what I'm doing for my own. And suck in a deep, regenerating breath.

Refreshed, I recall arriving at their door last Friday morning, Zelda welcoming me with a beaming smile and saying, "You are my

It's as if I am the only one in prep mode for Joan's impending visit. Well, duh. I remind myself that neither Ma nor Pa was particularly concerned about such minutiae in the past.

sunshine," and I want to weep at the sweetness of it.

~~~~~

Zelda loves the shaggy little yellow stuffed ducky I gave her for her eightieth birthday and keeps it displayed, legs a-dangle, on the bureau in the dining area. She thinks he looks like a cross between a monkey and a waterfowl. I say, "It's true. Ducks don't sit like that." She responds, "It depends on how they feel!"

This whimsical attitude accompanies me as I guiltily sneak into the obscurity of the garbage bin a gruesome, decrepit rubber Halloween mask Zelda had been reluctant to part with. I sense the crumbling latex monstrosity glaring at me in reproach and slam the lid shut with a snort of sheepish laughter.

My husband's gift for lightening the moment also comes to mind at helpful times. At Jack's follow-up appointment, the vitreo-retinal specialist discovers that excess bleeding in the post-op eye is causing a high intraocular pressure reading. It should be 20, not 44. The doctor prescribes more drops and performs an ultrasound. Waiting for the results, Jack wonders out loud, "Should I ask whether it's a boy or a girl?"

Chapter Six

Remembrance of Things Lost

We all know people who take good care of their health and others who try not to think about such things. In most couples, it's the wife who clips the articles by Dr. Oz and actually listens to those Medical Minute PSAs that flash by between segments of the nightly news. The wife who leans on her spouse to skip the loaded baked potato in favor of a spinach salad or leave ESPN behind long enough for a power walk. Dad and Zelda glide easily into this profile.

When I look into the causes of the cerebral cortex degeneration that leads to dementia, I find a roster of likely suspects: obesity, high blood pressure, mini-strokes, prolonged stress, sedentary habits that lead to impaired circulation. Fifty years ago, who knew about shortened telomeres or the dramatic benefits of exercise in preserving blood flow to aging brains? And only in the last twenty years have scientists identified specific minerals and vitamins with protective potential and stepped up investigation into micronutrients and phytochemicals.

Dad still operates on 1950s data. Zelda was only fifteen when she took charge of her own diet, conquered her sweet tooth, and overcame adolescent pudginess. She smoked for a few years during her twenties but dropped the habit with her first pregnancy. And she maintained sensible health practices through adulthood. Gardening, dog walks, pedaling her three-speed around the neighborhood. She even took on the arduous challenge of cross-country skiing one winter.

In fact, her approach to wellness reads like a checklist from the Mayo Clinic Dementia Prevention web page—from lifelong learning to hearty social connections to growing her own vegetables to judicious use of dietary supplements to abandoning toxic relationships. Among her generation, she embodies that unfortunate perverse exception of genetics overriding diligence.

My awareness of this taints her struggle with the reek of injustice.

6-1-05: *I tidy up and walk the dogs, then prepare to take Z to Rosedale Mall to shop for warm socks. She stands at the top of the stairs dressed in slacks, T-shirt, wool sweater, and windbreaker—ready to head out into the 78-degree day—and wonders aloud where her purse is.*

When I gently point out that it is already hooked over her shoulder, she leans her head against the wall and closes her eyes in despair. How do I reassure her that these things—like searching for glasses already perched on your head—often happen among the general public when she is convinced of the singular incompetence of this population of one?

My father's lifestyle history reads quite differently. Jack says Dad reminds him of Gary Cooper—a portrait of the post-war modern man, droll and enigmatic. My iconic mental picture is of him sitting on the couch before dinner with a *Time* magazine propped on his knee and a martini in his hand, a cigarette sending up spirals of wispy smoke from the ashtray beside him. He amused himself with the occasional round of golf or game of badminton, and he might mow the lawn on weekends. But he would always rather play bridge than tennis, and I can't recall ever seeing him toss a baseball to my brother, who probably wasn't interested, either.

Papa was slim by nature. He had to gorge on bananas for weeks to get his six-foot frame up to the 140-pound minimum-weight requirement for Navy enlistment (1942). He liked salted cashews with his cocktails but chose black coffee and another cigarette over dessert. His love for raw oysters aside, he was basically a meat-and-potatoes, lasagna and spaghetti, chili dog kind of guy. A wedge of lettuce? Merely a vehicle for a large ladling of bleu cheese dressing. Green beans and corn? Maybe. Alfalfa sprouts and zucchini? Not likely.

No one was more amazed than he that his habits didn't catch up with him until his seventies, when he was diagnosed with early-stage lung disease. It was that condition that prompted the one and only Zelda blowup in the annals of their joint history. Passively disregarding his health was one thing. Committing suicide by nicotine was another.

Chloé Victoria was fairly new to the household at the time, and Dad had sworn off cigarettes at his doctor's urging. Zelda was enjoying cleaner indoor air and a huge sense of relief. When weeks into the program their playful puppy triumphantly emerged from the bedroom with a pack of stashed Marlboro Lights clenched in her teeth, the spit hit the fan—big time.

Chloé had dragged Dad's underwear out of the dirty clothes bag in the past to keep herself comforted while they were away. But that was merely embarrassing if you were bringing friends in for coffee after an evening out. This exposed deception was the match that lit Zelda's fuse, and there was no excusing it away. Forget the '70s Fritz Perls poster that hangs on their basement wall:

> *I do my thing and you do yours. I am not in*
> *this world to live up to your expectations,*
> *and you are not in this world to live up to mine.*[1]

Dad was darned well going to live up to Zelda's expectations on this one. In all else, he could do his own thing.

~~~~~

I honk more often at other drivers these days. And come dangerously close to exploding out of my own flesh in a guttural, *Alien*-like scream any time onlookers register disgust over Dad's gagging cough or Zelda's vacant stare. If I keep chugging down this track, I'll soon be screeching at passing cars from some street corner.

> I come dangerously close to exploding out of my own flesh in a guttural, *Alien*-like scream any time onlookers register disgust over Dad's gagging cough or Zelda's vacant stare.

One comfort has been Dr. A's extremely helpful prescription for an acetylcholinesterase inhibitor, Reminyl. This godsend gives us a shot at keeping the enzyme AChE from blocking neural synapses that we are trying to keep active and firing. Missing a dose has striking consequences. After innumerable reminders, Zelda might continue to be confused about what day it is and fret inconsolably over having the date straight for a doctor's appointment. ("You were here when I did the arrangements, weren't you Suz?")

And the dulling effect of a missed pill is immediate.

6-6-05: *As I arrive at 10:15, Z is beginning to wade listlessly into the day. As I return from walking the dogs, she is slowly pouring herself a bowl of Sugar Crisp. Dad says she went to bed at 8 p.m., slept through until 9 a.m., and didn't get her evening meds last night. In the movie theater of my mind, I grab him by the shoulders and shake him until his teeth rattle, demanding to know why he doesn't pay more attention to these things. In the cinema verité of my life, I shrivel with cowardice and choke on swallowed fury.*

Z doesn't want to leave the house but finally agrees to a trip to the library. Once there, she shares charming off-the-wall observations with the woman checking out her books but dithers trying to dredge up her library card. Meanwhile, the oily-haired cretin in line behind us gets his enormous paunch in a fidget over having to wait for her to sort things out. The urge to lunge at him feels instinctive. Again, the film reel spins in my head: I stand rigidly erect, slap the evildoer with an empty glove, and dare him to a duel at dawn in valiant defense of Zelda's honor.

Desperate to understand these impulses, I inventory all the stressors surrounding me, things like Zelda's negativity. She remembers rainy days in exaggerated detail but doesn't recall all the sunny days in between. She looks at a relaxed Fergie, asleep on the couch, and pronounces her sluggish. Notes a perky-as-ever Chloé but observes that she may be "at the end."

Add to the list a looming six-hundred dollar van repair, 50 percent due on major dental work, Jack's not yet being able to make out the big "E" on the chart at Dr. R's office, and milking the budget to take Dad and Zelda to Olive Garden for dinner—atonement for stealing time from them to tend to Jack and mother-in-law Corine.

Why are some people so much better at handling life's pressures? I hold myself up next to courageous, gracious individuals of note. Do they ever suffer private moments of collapse? Still, private is so much better than public.

~~~~~

The distant past for Zelda is acid-etched in concrete. Consequences have played out and require no further analysis. What she can draw up from the well of ancient memories rests on solid ground—a distinctly defined bit of history, reliable and reassuring. Sometimes access is impeded. But when the haul is a good one, it can be startlingly rich in detail.

This month she seems particularly engrossed in "then." She recalls that it was the Jewish boys who asked her to dance at high school gatherings and remembers a compendium of statistics from the night her baby sister was born. A wail from the master bedroom. Questioning her aunt, "Why is Mama crying?" Her aunt's response: "That's not Mama. That's the new baby." Zelda talks of Miss Feegle, the LPN in attendance, a kindly woman with a stocky build who told of opening a storage trunk at her home only to find that mice had gotten into it.

Months later, there was the dribble of green juice down baby Jeanette's chin as she gummed homemade spinach baby food.

The family cat was named Katrina, Trinny for short, and the main meal of the day was at noon, with perhaps potato salad and green tea for supper. Around her family table Zelda learned that an early ancestor named Drowne made the gilded grasshopper weather vane that sits atop famed Faneuil Hall in Boston. Playing with neighbor children, she became 1930s movie sweetheart Janet Gaynor and imagined costar Charles Farrell as her pretend boyfriend.

She takes me back to her teen years with talk of her mother's cousins and gatherings in a large Wisconsin kitchen where family members played accordions while guests danced the polka. Even her dad joined in.

As upperclassmen at the University of Wisconsin-Madison, she and her friends formed a club based on the 'Lil Abner comic strip. They met at Liz Waters Hall, which looked out over Lake Mendota. A lost and distant expression steals across Zelda's face as she recalls that Bebe and Moonbeam both died too young of cancer, and she quotes the letter she got from Bebe's husband, Mr. Rush, announcing the sad news of Bebe's passing. Amazingly, what follows next is the family history of this same Mr. Rush and his Polish immigrant parents.

But the present, for Zelda, is fuzzy-around-the-edges and her interpretive tools have been corroded by time.

6-7-05: *Z hums a made-up march to power a short afternoon stint on the weight machine. Afterward she and I talk for ninety minutes nonstop as her emotions gently rumble to eruption. She is deeply disturbed over Dad's audacious comment about his reason for getting married. ("So I could have regular sex!") He offered this lightheartedly in the context of a discussion about first marriages, but she latched onto the crude implications and generalized from there. You don't have to have dementia to identify with her hurt.*

She is equally upset that he uses a contraction of his female counselor's first and last names for his online password, thinking this means he

> You don't have to have dementia to identify with her hurt.

has changed their email address from BilnZel. He admits that the password choice was a dumb move. It's not like she is thrilled with the counseling idea anyway, or the fact that he is undeniably more upbeat on the days when he sees this "other woman."

By conversation's end, Z has decided that both she and Papa would be better off if they hadn't married, that he would rather be with someone "more attractive and more with it." This sad conclusion segues into a story about a "funny old man" at their local Unitarian Society who, on two different occasions, kissed her hand as he was leaving the meeting place after services. "He saw something there," she says, tears welling up and spilling over.

~~~~~

Dad is not insensitive by intent, but he has always had a devilish sense of humor. His tendency toward shock-value pronouncements is further unleashed by a jigger or two of gin. Those jiggers are less likely to find their way into his system these days because drug interactions and an aging metabolism render their effects less pleasant. A beer with lunch is now the standard, the Churchill martinis a mostly discarded pre-dinner ritual. Still, his inhibitions seem distorted—a by-product of whatever obscure physiological mysteries his own body harbors.

He does try to make amends. Brings home a book from Barnes & Noble that he purchases just for Zelda, saying, "See, I do think about you."

Zelda's first response when he says, "I bought you something," is "What is it, a fish?" When he says it's a book she replies, "Well, that's better than a fish."

And when she finds out it's *Zorro* by Isabel Allende—one of her favorite authors—her trust is restored, and they exchange makeup hugs in the hallway.

Zelda's sense of humor is altered, too, knocked atilt by quirky brain cell activity. But it often delivers her from the edge of the pit of hopelessness she sometimes teeters over. She may almost close the garage door on me, unable to take in things beyond her primary focus at a given moment, but she can still expand her thinking to find the humorous nub of a thing. Or create one.

6-10-05: *At WalMart, as we buy paint for the bathroom, the guy mixing the tint refers to us as "young ladies," and does so with a smirk. "Smar Tass," says Zelda under her breath as we leave his range of hearing. On the way to the car afterward, I ask if she wants me to put her purse in the trunk along with our shopping bags. She declines. "No. I should keep it with me. It almost feels like it's part of my gall bladder."*

I raise a hand to point out the neighbor's potted plants, and Zelda admonishes, "Be careful how you wave. You may be inviting them to visit without knowing it." I grab for a Kleenex to sop an emergent nose drip, and she hollers with full onomatopoeic effect: "Honk!" If we discuss her shakiness after exercise, she asserts, "What I need is a good bowl of dog food." After a skimpy meal, her innards thunder and roll. "Can you hear it? *Aaaack, urp, rumble.* My stomach is behaving very badly."

Chloé is addressed as El Barko or Hi Ho, Hi Ho, Great Irritant. Prunes are intestinal Brillo Pads. Post-meal fullness brings on a tummy patting: "I feel like there's someone living in there."

Outings supply more source material. "You don't know the name of that plant? That's the clapasillis. My goal is to teach. I take my torch on my horse like Paul Revere and travel the country over. Yes, the clapasillis is a very rare plant not known to many, but it has a nectar that can be withdrawn that will send you to the moon. You'd like that."

While touring the aisles of the grocery store, I might hear a soft, vocalized "shoo, shoo, shoo" noise paced along with her footsteps as she pushes the cart along. Then maybe a high-pitched "toot-toot" as she approaches close behind a snowy-haired chap, apparently beeping to clear the way. If I look at her and smile, she innocently purses her lips for my benefit.

~~~~~

6-13-05: *I return from the morning dog walk to find Dad gone, the kitchen faucet running, Z asleep, the dog bowl blocking the path to the dining table, and a note in Zelda's handwriting: "5:00 Monday OK." What does this mean?*

Meanwhile, Zelda leaves some clues about the workings of her mind via multiple drafts of a Father's Day poem:

Papa dear we've come to say, we love you on your special day. Yes we do, we dooly ooly. Please know we're glad to live with youly Signed wise doggy Fergie, loud dogo Muttysky, and Ma Ma Z.

She gives hints about the workings of her body, too—paradoxical as they sometimes are. We are hanging clothes in her closet when she says, "I used to be able to do this." She then proceeds to lift her left leg straight out, waist-high, in front of her and touches her big toe with her outstretched hand—and then does the same with her right leg.

~~~~~

6-19-05: *Father's Day dinner at my house. Grilled T-bones, crusty baked corn pudding, balsamic-dressed tomato salad. Grilled peaches with vanilla bean ice cream to finish. Z is so herself—alert, conversational, tuned in—issuing not one non sequitur to be politely ignored by fellow diners.*

Back at her house, where the burden of expectations encumbers, where she feels she should be on top of things and know what's what and what's where, she chaotically searches for a box of Honey Bunches of Oats. Together we discover it and other grocery items on various surfaces in the garage and on the lower level, a Hansel and Gretel trail for the forgetful wanderer.

Later the same day, I find that rediscovered box of cereal in the refrigerator along with the single portions of stew I had left for their Saturday dinner two weeks ago. Missed weekend meals get added

Later the same day, I find that rediscovered box of cereal in the refrigerator along with the single portions of stew I had left for their Saturday dinner two weeks ago. Missed weekend meals get added to the worry list.

to the worry list. It's no wonder the panties Zelda has hung up to dry on the stair railing now display a knotted shoestring—an improvised waistband cincher.

6-21-05: *Z looks, from behind, like an Auschwitz survivor—stooped, emaciated, clothing barely suspended as if draped over a fragile wire hanger. I cook her a soft-boiled egg only to find that she has climbed back into bed. An hour later, we reheat the egg, but it goes tepid while she toasts half a slice of bread. Finally settled at the table, she hops up again to dilute her orange juice with water. Now everything is stone cold.*

Sipping, instead of drinking, a canned dietary supplement makes things worse. She doesn't take in enough of the liquid to do her any good, just enough to dull her appetite for real food—an appetite already corrupted by a return to her childhood love of sweets. If she can't finish her soup at lunch but then wants to sample the Cocoa Puffs and half a monster cookie, I am stymied in my response. Unaware that she has skipped the main dish, she sees no harm in pleasing her senses at this moment.

I may be forced to cater now and then, but I hate the idea of aiding and abetting.

6-23-05: *I enter the kitchen to tidy up and discover a gosh-awful-looking bowl of gray-brown goop hiding under a saucer. Z explains that she couldn't find any oat bran for breakfast, so she crumbled a chocolate-coated granola bar into a bowl and poured Ensure over it. After our pre-lunch walk, she says she feels strangely shaky. I would be flat on my face.*

~~~~~

"The fabric of our days," reads an entry in my journal. Sounds like a Cotton Council commercial. But in Bic-blue ink, scribbled drowsily on off-white pages, it's meant to capture the contrasting wefts and warps that interlace throughout the month.

Chloé and Fergie bark madly to go out, then immediately demand to come in. Oddly refuse to walk in the nicest of weather as if insecure about the changes taking place around them.

Zelda disappears into the bathroom to apply eye drops. "I'll be back in a flash." Fifteen minutes later, she stands searching the bedroom closet for her wedding band.

But woven through it all are fragments of froth and good fortune. I gasp as Zelda drains a sink full of freshly drawn hot, sudsy water. She responds, "What's wrong? I thought perhaps that baby alligator had risen up out of the garbage disposal again."

I say, "Yes, as it does every Thursday at about this time."

She says, "With its pointy little teeth."

On the home front, Jack's eye improves, and his prognosis is good. And I enjoy patches of relief from chronic headaches and fatigue.

6-28-05: *Accomplished enormous amounts of cleaning, laundering, cooking, and gardening at B & Z's as I Energizer-Bunny my way around their place on the wings of high spirits.*

Chloé and Fergie, The Hairy Squatter Brigade. These masters of the art of Walkus Interuptus stop to sniff, snoop, or poop every twenty paces. And based on their output during our post-weekend strolls, I am convinced that the pair of them practice anal retention on Saturday and Sunday. Guess I'll have to make sure to never miss a Monday dog walk; wouldn't want to be responsible for their exploding.

Chapter Seven

In Search of the Holy Grail

7-5-05: *Yesterday, an indoor picnic at our place to celebrate Z's favorite holiday, the Fourth of July. The aroma of saucy, oven-barbecued ribs and garlicky, foil-wrapped potato wedges infused the air and prickled the senses. Today, back to the regular routine.*

I arrive at the townhouse and prepare the dogs for their walk. As I labor to untangle the leashes, I hear a knocking on the entryway wall that abuts the guestroom. It's Z, rapping out a syncopated greeting. I knock-knock back.

Later, I talk her into running errands instead of heading back to bed and, at one stop, leave her in the car briefly while I pick up a new paint brush. When I return, she pretends to be out cold—head propped on the seat back, mouth agape, tongue hanging out to the side. With a quiver of her lip, the hoax is exposed.

To wrap up the trip, a carryout salad for me and McNuggets for Z, plus a rental of Harry Potter and the Philosopher's Stone. *Better than sleeping the afternoon away.*

~~~

Fluctuations in mood. They're intrinsic to the human condition. When a cognitively able person gets angry or sad, the feeling usually fades once the cause has been addressed. You talk it out, reason it through, or confront it. Maybe you distract yourself with an uplifting activity. But if you're operating under a shadow of fear, paralyzed by the mounting sense that you can no longer manage any of those approaches, the rules of the game may as well be written in hieroglyphics. Unresolved feelings stay intense, last longer, and pull the sufferer deeper into that shadow.

Zelda is stepping into the darkness more often this month. Troubling emotions pop up from nowhere like the pesky, evasive rodent in a Whac-A-Mole arcade game. Add to that the blurring of time and space, and her internal clock becomes as difficult to reset as her emotions. A plan made on Monday gets sucked into the thin air of the stratosphere overnight, so that Tuesday begins with no blueprint, no to-do list, no road map. No wonder she gets angry. How can you trust a world that is zipping along full speed and leaving you behind its wake?

7-8-05: *Difficulty in dystopia. Dad had drawn a "P" on his left thumbnail several days ago—a reminder to have patience. When Z saw it yesterday, she was wildly certain that the "P" must stand for counselor Pat, whose company Pa presumably prefers. It's junior high with crow's feet and pill-minders.*

Depleted from running interference against her desire to see Dr. A every few weeks, I have migraine aura two days in a row. That's rare; I can usually stave off these vestigial symptoms with quiet time in a darkened room. But by the second day, I am low on resistance. I tense up over Z's obsession with Dad's bad joke about the advantage of marrying an only child so you don't have to share her inheritance. Maybe I need to paint a "P" on my left thumbnail.

~~~~~

You don't want to press too hard against the will of a person whose view of the world you can't begin to conceptualize. Urging Zelda to buy just one fresh, pretty five-dollar guest towel for the newly redec-

> You don't want to press too hard against the will of a person whose view of the world you can't begin to conceptualize.

orated downstairs bathroom seems at first to be an innocent miscalculation. As it turns out, my method is stupidity in action. "Oh, c'mon," I coax playfully. "Let's loosen up and have a little fun."

Maybe if we hadn't had that minor wrestling match over ditching the disintegrating bath mat with its rubber backing crumbling into black powder all over the pristine new floor. Her independent streak now hemorrhages into obstinance, and she is not about to surrender. I rub my own nose in the obvious: she is already relinquishing so much to my management. *P.*

~~~

Experience is a hard teacher because she
gives the test first and the lessons afterward.[2]
–VERNON LAW

So what's the deal? Have I been cheating on the exam? Nodding off over the essay questions? Apparently so, because enlightenment continues to elude me.

When Zelda suddenly flares at the idea of auctioning off a table she had agreed to sell the day before, I forget every one of my own insights. When she bristles, goes dark and brooding after overhearing Dad say he doesn't want her to postpone her dental appointment, I blank out on a response.

Then, when she exits the dentist's exam room and hisses, "I am seething," I cringe and brace for the worst when I should be softening my eyes and preparing to empathize. Dr. O wants to talk to Pa about repairing Zelda's lower front bridge, but because Dad is at a counseling appointment instead of at the dentist's office with us, she is furious. Fuming. Incensed.

I paste composure on my face and falter over my own words trying to rosy things up and cast Dad in a better light. I mention that her own daughters think he is doing an admirable job of dealing with their changing circumstances. Suggest that he is getting the counseling to improve his role in their relationship.

Zelda focuses like a laser on comment number one, draws every muscle up stiff and taut, and accuses, "You mean he's good to put up with me?" I then spend a tearful hour over grilled chicken sandwiches at Wendy's trying to undo the injury. If only I could think things through and not spring impulsively into verbal tap-dancing mode. If only I knew how to cram for the pop quizzes. *If only.*

~~~~~

Dark moments aside, Zelda's innate sweetness leads her to agree to many things. "If you say X, then I'll do X." But resentment creeps into her tone, then gets tucked back under the skin to fester. A hearing-impaired husband with his own aging pains is not as tuned in as he might be, either. These days, his instinct for self-preservation butts up against hers with regularity.

7-11-05: *I arrive at B & Z's around ten. Z meets me at the door along with the dogs, which is not common; most often she is back in bed by now. Papa is going to see Mary M, who is recuperating from heart bypass surgery, she announces. "When I said I wanted to tag along, he said that would make the visit 'too busy.'"*

Her assessment of his explanation: "Busy, schmizzy!" She is enormously offended. I say I would be, too, and encourage her to tell him that he hurt her feelings, reasoning that once he knows this, he will reconsider.

Z confronts him at the computer, tells him exactly what she told me. He replies, "Well, you can feel any way you want, but . . . " By the end of the conversation, they are speaking cordially. And when he returns from his outing, he is kind toward her and she is playful toward him.

Meanwhile, I am sockless. Blown right off my feet, those anklets. This is our new Realville, I guess. But I'm having trouble keeping up with all the reconstruction.

~~~~~

I was raised in the Protestant tradition—mostly Presbyterian and Methodist. I think Dad went to church because it was important to my mother. And because it was what middle class suburbanites did in the post-war, pre-counterculture years. He also enjoyed the stimulation of monthly Bible study sessions that revolved from one member's living room to another and welcomed challenging questions and intellectualized answers. He accepted deacon and elder positions, contributed to building funds, chaperoned youth outings and summer camp. All of this suited his personality as a doer, an achiever, a contributor to society.

My childhood take on faith was to look forward to Christmas as a hallowed, glowing, transcendent festival that illuminated winter's darkest hours; to relish Easter as a bright, cheerful celebration of renewed hope, ushering in spring; to be inspired and transported by the lyrics of "Go Tell It on the Mountain" or "Were You There When They Crucified My Lord?"

I also prayed regularly, offering up concerned pleas for the protection of those I couldn't imagine life without. I was blessed in those days with a tender heart and an awareness of how fortunate I was. But my beliefs were built on a shallow understanding of God's Word. Along came the tide of the swinging, secular '60s—and it washed the shifting sands right out from under every member of my birth family.

As each of us drifted away from organized religion, my mother became reclusive, my father left their twenty-eight-year marriage and the firm of consulting psychologists he'd been with for nineteen years, and my musician brother got sucked into the world of sex, drugs, and rock 'n roll. As lost as any of them, I stumbled through the exit-less maze of rebellious unbelief for almost two decades before God led me home to His truth through a high school reunion encounter with my now-husband Jack.

Today my relationship with my Creator is deeper, more soul-embedded, better informed. I study His Word, seek out His will, and research His promises. I trust that He indeed works all things for the good of those who lean on Him. I know that He sees the entire vast landscape of butterfly-effect interactions beyond the teeny corner of existence that I inhabit. And I believe with absolute assurance that He has a plan for us. Absolute assurance.

Where I wade into the bog of anxiety is needing to know this very minute just what that plan is.

~~~~~

The more Zelda insists, "I just need to rest my bones," or rejects a repair of her lower partial plate because "It's expensive and I'm so old," and the more often her hand tremor surfaces or her memory lapses, the more I assume we're not doing enough to fend off the enemy—whom we have met but not yet identified. I request referrals to a dietician and a physical therapist. Persist in trying to connect through conversation, to stimulate through trivia challenges, and to track down simpatico local specialists.

When I can't ferret out the secrets to making things better, I start to thrash around for answers, to seek out superheroes who have powers beyond my own pitiful repertoire. There is a place that Zelda has heard about in Wisconsin, the Marshfield Clinic, where people seek help when other sources have failed them. A reputedly caring place where geriatric patients are treated with respect and optimism and given a plan. We will go there, and they will pull from their chest of treasures a magical talisman that will generate the miracles we crave.

OK, so maybe those florid sentiments belong entirely to me. But everyone in the household is on board for the quest, and making the appointment gives us all something to hang our hopes on and propels us through the month.

7-20-05: *Z and I go grocery shopping while she nurses a bout of constipation and comments that we must be sure we have our "gizzard girdles" on before we set off. Further, she reveals, she discovered some vegetable laxative she didn't know she possessed until it stood up, waved, and said, "Hello, I'm your happy plumber!"*

Also today, a jaunt to the Como Zoo. Having been back and forth a few times about whether to make the trip, Z arises from a short nap imbued with a mood to sally forth. As we leave, she skips over to Dad's chair, kisses her fingertips, then transfers the kiss to his lips.

~~~~~

I shall never fathom the cruelty of some of my fellow humans. Encounters with these incarnations of ignorance leave me grateful that the same illness that robs Zelda of appreciation for the avian symphony surrounding us on our walks also protects her from occasional eruptions of sheer ugliness.

7-22-05: *Ambling along the townhouse trails this morning, Z and I encounter the resident handyman tooting around on his little put-put as if he were actually tending to landscape maintenance. "Is she easier to walk than the dogs?" he bellows over the buzz of the motor, an idiotic grin smeared across his face. "At least you don't need a leash."*

There is no place to duck for shelter from this verbal assault. I yearn with all my depraved little heart to strangle the creep with his own garden hose. If I thought a bucket of water would dissolve him into a gelatinous puddle of half-witted meanness, I would scale a ten-foot retaining wall to get to the outdoor spigot. But it's too late to escape. The acid phrases have been spewed,

There is no place to duck for shelter from this verbal assault. I yearn with all my depraved little heart to strangle the creep with his own garden hose.

and the injury lingers even after the shuddering subsides.

Instead, I twitter out a nervous laugh, tell Z he is stealing her line, and pray that she is as unscathed by the unfortunate event as she seems.

This is common lately: Zelda connects with the outer world only in brief flashes. So she has repelled today's insult without injury. Instead, she digs up inner resource material for conversation. She's not ready to accept the explanation that, no, a new tape inserted into her boom box will not erase the one she had played earlier. But she vividly recalls the anguish of being asked to an eighth-grade dance only to have the young boy cancel his invitation days later.

~~~~~

I could probably use a smidgen of Forrest Gump's serene philosophizing about now, but it occurs to me that life is more like a bowl of Bertie Bott's Every Flavour Beans than a box of chocolates. Tucked right in there with all the sugary delights—the blueberry, the banana, the marshmallow—is the jolting presence of rotten egg, earthworm, and earwax.

The selection's looking a bit picked-over at the moment. My mother-in-law butts heads with her endocrinologist over the prospect of a risky parathyroid surgery. Hints that she and the homestead we share are being short-changed as a result of my demanding daytime commitment. A return to work has Jack grappling with his job requirements, bouncing blood sugars, and uncertainty about his vision. Zelda continues to fixate on the negative. And Dad, burdened by the decline within his household, acts dismayed that I am not able to be here on Saturdays, too.

I can stomach this, I tell myself. But, of course, it's not only the immediate and the tangible I'm trying to digest. It's the whole complicated history-reliving/future-catastrophizing package that gives me the wobblies.

~~~

My father was my idol growing up. He overcame adolescent turmoil, educated himself well, achieved career successes, volunteered his time generously, and used his talents brilliantly. He was a supremely thoughtful gift-giver who planned memorable family vacations. Washington D.C., New York City, a stay at the Disneyland Hotel in 1961. The Grand Canyon and the Lowell Observatory in Arizona, Lily Dale in upstate New York, Ruttgers Resort in northern Minnesota. Camping in the Porcupine Mountains of Michigan and a weekend at the Palmer House in Chicago.

He was also bright and well-read—a sort of Renaissance man for the twentieth century. In my youth, he could answer virtually any question I could come up with, whip up a mean omelet and impressive hand-cut French fries, take and develop professional-quality photographs, and recite Ralph Waldo Emerson at length. Later, he taught himself to restore an old Rambler convertible and re-cane furniture by hand. And all along he published journal articles and letters to the editor, crafted puns with the best of 'em, and completed *New York Times* crossword puzzles in ink. Being his daughter was—for many years and to my shame—enough of an accomplishment for me.

Most young adults will have long since ushered an idealized parent down from the pedestal. It is the kind, mature thing to do. The alternative is to maintain the fantasy well past your Tooth Fairy years.

I regret having done my father this disservice. All those years of sticking my fingers in my ears and looking the other way—la-la-la-la—whenever he erred or offended. In his mid-eighties, the descent from the pedestal is a much more awkward event.

If we can get some help with Zelda's concerns and focus on building each other up, what a healing cupful that will yield. It's intoxicating to think that Marshfield holds potential for meeting these goals.

~~~~~

I wish I could capture—like sunshine in a jar—the delight of my daily dog walks. I would release it in Zelda's direction whenever she gets crammed into one of her dim corners. I give up on arguing the case that ninety pounds may be dangerously low for one who once weighed a healthy 115. ("But I am quite short," she will say.) Or insisting that she worked hard for years, invested wisely, spent cautiously, and deserves to savor some small luxuries even if—especially if!—she "might not be around six months from now," as she insists. But, in general, I believe that some opinions are still worth advocating.

My father had to scuttle his dream of pilot's training in the Navy when medics discovered a tumor on his right mastoid process. Corrective surgery in his thirties left him with only one eardrum. Zelda has lived with his hearing deficiency for over thirty years. Still, I must remind her of it when she speaks to him in her newly diminished voice and he doesn't hear her, and she recoils angrily into the conclusion that he's ignoring her.

Her leaps to assume the worst land her oceans away from the warm letters of their courtship when the wonder of finding her one true love animated every ardent emotion she poured out to him.

7-28-05: *"Do you want to go for one last walk of the day?" I ask Chloé and Fergie this late afternoon. "Does a fly want a piece of cake?" Zelda chimes out in response. On our stroll, the pups and I meet Bailey, an eight-year-old golden retriever with hip dysplasia who was adopted from the humane society and is incredibly easygoing until she sees men's work boots or very small children.*

We also meet Cayman, an engaging collie-shepherd mix named after the resort island where her owner found her orphaned twelve years ago; Parker, the misnamed shih tzu—a barker whose "mommy" asks the impossible of him with perpetual shushings; and the three white Bichon fur balls, Charlie and company, strolling with their stylish, silver-haired mistress.

Then there is sweet, excitable Max, owned by an equally sweet, pleasingly plump neighbor lady. Max is a predictably pudgy cocker who wants so dearly to get close enough to give sloppy kisses.

Attempts to relay to Zelda accounts of our traveling puppy pow-wows are hard on both of us. She simply cannot pick up on my elation, can't tap into the place within where feelings of canine connection used to reside. Seeing the empty look on her face as I lay the opportunity before her drains me of my joy. So this loss gets added to the debit side of the ledger, and we move on. Finding new sources of pleasure may be challenging, but surely it's not impossible.

~~~~~

Zelda dips washcloth compresses into heated water to treat her reddened eyes (then wants to use that same water to pour into a glass of Metamucil) and takes her evening medication at noon. Perhaps not a ripe time for completing the Marshfield Clinic pre-visit health history form.

Although the effort of scouring her memory for medical details leaves her "shaking all over," she soldiers through. As her steady-handed secretary, I decide when a reasonable estimate will grease the process and not adversely affect the final results, and—voilà!—every blank gets filled. This has to be a good omen for our noble mission, the transcriber giddily proclaims.

Chapter Eight

Off to See the Wizard

The trouble with bubbles of optimism is they tend to burst the moment they bump up against the ordinary state of things. If these preparatory weeks are any indication, there may be a few loose bricks in our path to the Land of Oz.

In the '60s and '70s, when nurse's aides were still responsible for full patient care, I worked in several hospitals and nursing homes. At the beginning of every shift, we would have a short meeting. Diagnoses were reviewed, patient needs were outlined, and we were forewarned of any erratic behaviors. Expectations were clear, and first-rate training prepared me to handle my duties with confidence.

In 2005, I step daily into a minefield with no markers. Oh, Dad occasionally comments if he and Zelda have had a really bad night. And on her more connected days, Zelda may hint that she feels hovered over. But on not-so-good days she consults me for guidance at every turn. It isn't always clear in which mode we're operating until it's too late and I have overstepped. "Oh, I was going to mop the floor, so you don't need to wipe up that area," I might say, then have to apologize later if she's taken offense. Rescued dish sponge, ruined rapport.

It might be easier to hack my way past these unknowns if my own passions weren't so easily inflamed.

8-2-05: *The hemoccult kit for Marshfield sits on the table as Z and I* *settle down to lunch—a reminder to complete the three-day stool collection test next week. I make small talk about the instructions not yet in effect. "You won't be able to have red meat once you start the sampling process." She misconstrues and immediately wraps her sandwich in a used napkin and stashes it in the freezer.*

Such a lovely piece of expensive tenderloin on nice crusty artisan bread, which I had brought from home, prepared, and shared, only to have her take one bite and then reject—all based on a clouded perception of the concept "later."

I suck in a deep, calming breath and try again to explain the timetable. She is unreachable. A wall of stubborn resistance rises before me— the set mouth, the angry scowl, a stormy look about her eyes—and my own emotions mount in response. My esophagus burns, tears brim. Why does being misinterpreted like this pull lava-hot bile up my craw to lodge and gurgle away?

And the moment refuses to pass. Zelda forgets the context and frames the misunderstanding as my forcing her to eat. Describes it as the worst confrontation she has ever experienced. I know this is unintended hyperbole, yet I feel sickened and shaken. Even lose sleep, reliving it all in my head. We once had such an affectionate appreciation for one another. Kindred souls, she had christened us. In introductions, I was her "fifth daughter."

In these present edgy days, this minor incident produces a cloud of gloom that leaves her stiff-necked and cold. Follows her into tomorrow, overshadowing even the arrival of her daughter Julie and a trip to the garden center.

8-4-05: *Acting as if I were holding a gun to her back, Z marches stoically among the potted foliage as if she never had any input into the plan to shop for plants. I ask, "What color do you like?" and she responds, "It's not really my choice to make."*

Later I learn she's been complaining to

With my stepsister here to stand in, I will take Friday off—and hope that three days is time enough to heal these wounds.

Julie that she gets dragged places she doesn't want to go, forced to trudge around when she doesn't feel up to it. With my stepsister here to stand in, I will take Friday off—and hope that three days is time enough to heal these wounds.

~~~~~

I enter cautiously into preparations for our Marshfield trip—a 165-mile journey into the emerald green expanse that is Wisconsin. Zelda's nervous preoccupation with keeping tabs on Julie within the house adds yet another layer of anxiety to muck up the tenuous tranquility of the family circle. I find clean underwear and used Kleenex squirreled away in the linen closet. Note that Zelda is especially unsure of her pill-taking schedule and of the time and date.

"I'm all packed," she assures, turning down my offer of help. In her small bag: one pair of panties, her glasses, two dozen maxi pads, and a comb. No toothbrush, no change of clothes, no pill bottles, no eye drops, no PJs. A reverse sneak thief, I stow away all of the above, then bate my breath waiting: Will she detect interference?

Seated at the lunch table with Julie and me, Zelda asks, "Where is that giraffe going to go?"

Puzzled, I ask back, matter-of-factly, "Which giraffe is it that you are referring to?" Brief pause.

"The one with the red nose," she says, returning to reality with a smile of comprehension. The odd moment becomes a small private joke, and we are on track again.

Julie heads home, and the next day we are on the road.

8-11-05: *An hour into our trip, Z mischievously queries Dad: "Would you like for me to drive for a while?" Somewhere around Menomonie as we transect stretches of velvety farmland in all directions, she volunteers, "If you drive for twenty miles, you'll come upon Stratford and my true love with his cats and dogs." Dad is oblivious, his good ear exposed to the ruffling wind outside his open window. "Aha," I reply, sage-like but baffled.*

We arrive in one piece, following the exhilarating experience of passing semis on two-lane country byways, and check into adjacent rooms at the Baymont Inn. Then it's off to Applebee's for riblets and cole slaw, sautéed shrimp on a bed of almond-studded rice, and walleye with crisp-fried red potatoes.

With her short legs and full tummy, Z has trouble exiting the oversized banquette booth. She stops mid-effort, saying, "I feel like somebody's demented grandmother," then breaks into a laugh and adds, "I am somebody's demented grandmother!" It's a hearty, deep-felt laugh—the sound I hear in my head when I relive our earlier escapades—and the moment is golden.

10:30 p.m. I am changed and settled, dappled and drowsy and ready for sleep. There is a knock on my door. It's Dad, asking to borrow toothpaste.

~~~~~

In one delicious paradox, being away from home seems to reorient Zelda. I had feared the opposite. Virtually took it for granted. At 9:30 a.m. on Friday, August 12, we sit at a table in a small conference room at the Marshfield Clinic waiting for the primary physician to meet with us. Dad reads the *Marshfield News-Herald* and sips black coffee from a white foam cup as Zelda leans close to my ear. "I'm tired," she whispers. "Maybe we could tiptoe out before the doctor gets here." Diverted when a piece of medical apparatus whirs somewhere in the distance, she quips, "Sounds like a circus of trapped cicadas."

Having opted not to escape the premises, we spend thirty minutes with Dr. K, who explains all that lies ahead. A complete physical to rule out any underlying conditions. Blood tests to check for abnormalities and evaluate current medication dosages. An appointment with a physician assistant with specialized training in neurology who has been with Marshfield's Memory Disorder Clinic for thirteen years. Retention tests and cognitive assessments.

Zelda is a trooper. She tolerates all the indignities and discomforts of a thorough workup with Zen-like calm and appreciation for the warmth of these competent professionals. Their gentle but non-patronizing manner. The trust-inspiring explanations. We are all impressed. Big City medicine in a small-town setting and then some. A staff member had met us to greet and guide before we even got through the clinic's front door. As the day wears on, another pastel-clad employee whisks out a wheelchair for Dad, whose legs are giving out as we traipse the miles of hallway between exam sites.

And we learn so much. The tremors look more like Parkinsonisms than anything else. There is no evidence of Alzheimer's. A whole laundry list of symptoms is explained by late-onset, slow-progressing degenerative central nervous system disorders—from the Dopamine depletion that can cause both depression and a masklike flat affect, to slowed movement, fatigue, and disturbed thought processes.

I have to get all this down in black and white before I forget a single detail.

From: Milton Williams
To: Deb, Joan, Julie, Rob
Cc: Barb, Mary Kaye
Date: 8/15/05 - 12:12:45 PM

Hello, all -

Suz here, writing at Dad's computer, with a summary of our trip to the Marshfield Clinic last Friday.

We found an exceptionally caring and patient-centered staff at the clinic. But first and foremost, we obtained a primary diagnosis of late-onset Parkinson's disease, which is slow-progressing and explains Zelda's every symptom, since it can cause . . .

- A mild form of chemical depression, resulting from the same depletion of Dopamine and neurochemicals that causes rest tremors.

- Bradykinesia (extreme slowness of movement) and hesitation.

- Weakness, fatigue, and tremor (which affect handwriting and cause stooped posture and balance issues); rigidity and range-of-motion limitations; and changes in gait, all which appear early on, but are not progressive or disabling.

- Hoarseness and a soft speaking voice.

- Irregularity and abdominal distress or bloating; loss of weight; muscle cramping; bladder urgency.

- And finally, dementia or mental confusion in 40-50 percent of all elderly Parkinson's patients, and defined as changes in memory and cognitive ability sufficient to have an effect on daily living.

Zelda/Mom is relieved to have so many seemingly unrelated symptoms explained, and we were all extremely happy with the quality of the time the staff spent with us and their willingness to address all of our concerns at length.

Before leaving Marshfield, we were referred to a Twin Cities dietician and got an immediate start on a chewable, chocolate-flavored calcium supplement—easier to ingest and digest, and not likely to cause constipation. Because Zelda's rib aches are due to postural changes and rigidity, we also came away with a booklet of exercises to help with the movement and muscle-contraction issues.

The loss of taste and smell is probably irreversible, but we will focus on food presentation and pleasing textures to compensate.

Dr. K, an internist, encouraged us to find a Parkinson's specialist and recommends cognition exercises and social stimulation to address memory problems and emotional well-being, with the caveat that too much stimulation can result in the kind of negative stress that causes more confusion and anxiety. He also recommends against starting any Parkinson's medications because they can worsen memory problems and because of the slow progression of the disease in Zelda's case.

Hope this is helpful in bringing everyone up to date. Please let me know if there is anything I have failed to cover here.

Love to you all. I really appreciate your input and support.

~~~~~

I've never been more in awe of Zelda. She certainly didn't choose to have this condition or do anything to bring it on. ("This is how I wanted to get old," she says wistfully from time to time.) But she was willing to extend herself in search of answers and inspired Dad and me to stretch along with her. I think we would all prefer to continue long-term care with Dr. K and his crew, but we do feel less like we're taking squirt gun shots at a vaporous intruder now and are better armed to confront the monster in the closet. Maybe even teach it some manners.

> We do feel less like we're taking squirt gun shots at a vaporous intruder now and are better armed to confront the monster in the closet. Maybe even teach it some manners.

Back home we ride the Marshfield high into the weeks that follow. Zelda and I do chair exercises from the Parkinson's book and walk a fair distance around the grounds. As we near the pond, I spot a solitary duck at the far edge of the water and comment that it's odd to see just one, that they usually hang out in groups of two or more. Zelda offers that the second duck must be "out on the town, because ducks will be ducks, you know."

Later, we practice the heel-toe walking method prescribed in another pamphlet. Soon Zelda is rhythmically dragging each foot before planting the heel down—shuffle-brush-thud, shuffle-brush-thud—and inserting a little bounce between each step, the prelude to a rousing round of "The Old Gray Mare, She Ain't What She Used to Be."

Incrementally, we settle back into a weekday pattern that requires daily tweaking based on external and internal events. The observable and the subliminal. The seen and the unseen.

Mostly self-contained and taciturn, Dad cranks out the occasional opinion piece and signs up for Lifelong Learning Institute courses; treks off to the library and other places unknown; schedules 7 a.m. dental appointments for himself. Zelda makes multiple mini-lists of things to discuss with Dr. A, then scatters them like ersatz rose petals all around the house; recreates, like living art, her impression of a teenager's bedroom—outfits strewn over any available surface; and keeps me guessing as the bowls for dishwashing and dish rinsing migrate from day to day in an oversized version of the shell game.

I find crumpled paper towels hung over the wrought iron stair rail, being dried for future reuse. And like a cartoonish science experiment, the refrigerator contents once again expand to produce intriguing results: a dab of tartar sauce in an uncovered coffee cup, its skin thickening with each passing day, sits next to a two-bite portion of petrified breaded fish. A munchkin entrée gone horribly wrong.

8-17-05: *I offer Z her trench coat so I can sneak the pink windbreaker into the wash while she and Dad are off bringing Dr. A up to speed on our Marshfield trip.*

Dad waits, uncomplaining, as Z decides she must brush her teeth with baking soda "to counteract the acid" before they leave the house. The phone rings. It's Rob calling from Michigan to announce that she and her longtime boyfriend have just returned from some exotic port where they got married under palm branches and tropical blue skies. And where there have been recent accounts of violent crime and kidnappings.

The sound of the long-distance voice diverts and envelops Z, and her eyes well up with worry over what might have befallen her oldest daughter and her groom so far from home. She will be late to her appointment. But my anxiety over that fact is just one more waste of emotional energy.

~~~~~

I research fixations in dementia and confirm that they are common—the immediate and specific focal point of a general need for reassurance. My nursing home experience taught me that certain bodily functions fascinate more than others.

The stool collection process for Marshfield has set up a bowel obsession in Zelda—an unflattering senior stereotype that I know she would rather not be living out. Consuming fiber supplements becomes a secondary preoccupation, and she acquires fluency in the exotic vocabulary of purging agents. Reminders that constipation goes along with Parkinson's do not deter her from wanting another consultation with Dr. A.

8-23-05: *Z intercepts me after the first dog walk of the day distressed about not being able to "go" and reports that she had a double dose of Metamucil for dinner last night in place of the chili I made. Today, she starts a second cup of Metamucil before noon although it's taken hours to get the first one down, and I find another dose so long neglected that a spoon stands up in it. You'd have to slice it and chew it, like Jell-O Jigglers for grown-ups, and then wait for what would no doubt be an undesirable outcome—no word-play intended.*

Later, we have trouble getting out the door for a walk to "get things moving," as she answers a dozen false alarm bathroom calls. She's never had an accident of that nature yet is terrified that today might be the day.

I prepare a slice of whole wheat toast with peanut butter for her, but she worries that the gooeyness will somehow gum up her internal plumbing. I remind her of Dad's standard advice to take a book in and sit for a while. She eventually eats but declines to retire to the reading room and ultimately admits to having additional successes following the one on Friday, which I had helped her celebrate.

I talk her out of seeking professional help for her current distress until we've got some real food roughage into her and tried walk therapy—the natural approaches she would have relied on in the past.

And I wonder: is pleading for a BM a proper use of prayer?

~~~~~

Even with a fresh batch of resources to draw from, I still get sidetracked by my need to logic things out. When Zelda launches into a rant about the osteoporosis medication "fraud," the obscenity of the price of a single pill, and the possibility of the doctor getting a kickback for each prescription, I try to placate with explanations. The trusted Marshfield doctor did validate the need, after all. And isn't the cost a fair trade-off for the inconvenience of ending up in a wheelchair? Then there are the millions of dollars a drug company spends on research and development before that first pill rolls off the assembly line.

This time Zelda hears and absorbs. "Should I put a sign on my back that says 'stubborn old hag'?" she asks.

"No," I advise. "Have it say, 'independent thinker.'"

It's a moment of clarity for both of us. And when, later in the day, she kids that she heard Chloé singing, "They're coming to take Ma away—ha ha—to the funny farm, where life is beautiful all the time," a take on lyrics she found amusing in 1975, and adds, "Little did I know . . ."—well, her sad burden claws at my heart.

Yet with all of this deeply significant reality swirling around me, I am entirely capable of developing fixations of my own.

8-31-05: *I am disgusted. My weight has now crept up to 140—140.8 to be exact. And yes, I know that's small potatoes in the vast cauldron of worldly troubles. But after ten days of no exercise during a disastrous attempt to switch to bio-identical estrogen patches, I get sucked into the quicksand of depression via my own personal catch-22: I'm too lethargic to exert myself even though physical activity is what pulls me out of the black hole of funk and low energy. The body in a slump stays in a slump and can't get the motion thing going.*

Today, a movie theater outing with Ma and Pa. We'll see The March of the Penguins together. A little delight for us all, I am thinking. Think twice. That's how many times I walked out of the screening infuriated.

Frame after frame of raw realism against a backdrop of frigid surround-ings portrays only despair and utter hopelessness.

What the heck, I'd like to ask the reviewers, is "touching and inspiring" about a relentlessly tedious and often futile dreary annual trek across frozen surfaces, only to watch your young be scooped up by predators or freeze to death at the accidental lapse of a parent's attentions? "Love finds a way"? Sentimental rubbish. Try "biological necessity driven by base instinct"—to which moviegoers inexplicably flock in droves.

Perhaps the general viewing public was as misled by those cheery little previews as I was. There is—maybe—ninety seconds of smile-pro-voking substance here. I am blue from the stark, white chill of it all. I feel lied to and angry, more depressed than when I walked in. Z's assessment is succinct and accurate: "Cold and ice. So much cold and ice."

Sour notes. I hate to end a month seeded with successes on sour notes. Tomorrow brings a fresh page on the calendar and a shot at a good night's rest with my trusty old bottle of estrogen pills back on the bedside table. A nightcap of Kipling can't hurt, either.

> "If you can dream and not make dreams your master
> If you can think and not make thoughts your aim;
> If you can meet with Triumph and Disaster
> And treat those two imposters just the same.
>
> "If you can make one heap of all your winnings
> And risk it on one turn of pitch-and-toss,
> And lose and start again at your beginnings
> And never breathe a word about your loss.
>
> "If you can fill the unforgiving minute
> With sixty seconds' worth of distance run
> Yours is the earth and everything that's in it . . . "[3]

And, what's more, I'll lasso the stars and sun.

Chapter Nine

Ob-La-Di, Ob-La-Da, Life Goes On

Dad and Zelda had been married six years when I moved back to Minnesota—newly divorced, jobless, and without a place to live. They welcomed me into their home and propped me up through some perilously shaky attempts to get a foothold on maturity. Zelda and I cooked and baked together, and the three of us spent long evenings playing Scrabble or Facts in Five. Or we would settle into our favorite living room chairs to read and share quiet observations on the state of humanity, a fire snapping and popping in the hearth nearby. On weekends, we might breakfast out and then hit estate sales in search of obscure treasures.

Back in the warm cocoon of family, I felt cloaked with a sense of security I hadn't enjoyed since my home life started to deteriorate in my mid-teens. Dad provided for the household and took care of all things mechanical. Zelda nurtured and befriended, nudging me out of my shell of introspective self-loathing. I wasn't a loser in their eyes. Just someone who needed time to heal and a fresh run at being a grownup.

At twenty-eight, I was grateful for the opportunity to stop worrying about the future and step into a quasi-parental relationship with these two hardworking, responsible types. Life with Dad and Zelda was a serene refuge from the mess I'd made of my own existence as an underachieving college dropout, imprudent in the ways of love. Pulling on the emergency brake, I leaned on their cordial companionship as I groped my way to my own sense of purpose.

Thirty years down the track, it's payback time. They were patient and giving in my hour of dependence. I draw on that. And yet the present continues to be a breath-snatching house of mirrors where each turn can thrust us into confusing confrontations with our own reflections.

9-1-05: *I get to the townhouse and find the front door unlocked, the van and its owners nowhere to be seen. By the time I've walked the dogs, B and Z are home again. I won't risk upsetting them with the unsecured entryway report.*

Mere minutes after their return, Z announces that her purse is missing, and she and I begin a house, garage, and vehicle hunt. We finally have a system in place where I am tracking her medications, but she refuses to take her morning Reminyl until she has found the purse.

Z is virtually standing on her head in the back seat of the Toyota when I locate the mislaid handbag in the upstairs bathroom wedged between the toilet and the tub. This discovery troubles her to the point of anguish. Dad uses that bathroom, not her, she insists. She can't believe she went in there at all, much less long enough to leave anything behind.

Ignoring the faulty premise, I explain, "Dad wouldn't have any reason to be toting your purse around." She returns the glower of the offended. Bite my damnable tongue.

Later, I round the corner to catch her taking pills 1-5 instead of pills 1-4, which is the daytime dosage. Crash goes the tracking system, and I blurt out a correction in frustration.

"Better I should just move on," Z responds solemnly. Shame on me. Again.

~~~~~

Sunday, September 4. We observe Dad's 85th birthday two days early so we can gather our sparse family at my house for a joint celebration. His only grandson, Rich, and his only granddaughter, Rachel, attend with their spouses, Jenni and Rick, respectively, and with his three great-grandchildren—nine-year-old Skye, six-year-old Maeta, and five-year-old Dylan. There is kid-friendly grilled chicken, beef kebobs for the big guys, double-deviled eggs and potato salad, at the guest of honor's request. And for dessert, chocolate strawberry shortcakes— the youngest diners devouring the gooey, chip-studded pastries like cookies and the rest of us piling on ruby red sliced berries, dripping with their own sugared juices, and large, fluffy mounds of freshly whipped cream.

There was a time when this date would have been marked by a cookout on Dad and Zelda's deck, planned and catered by Zelda. For his seventieth, she organized a surprise party with three dozen friends and family members announcing their arrival via an improvised marching band. Drawn to the front picture window by the hullaba-loo, an astonished Papa watched as the motley crew of kazoo-tooters and cymbal-clashers, led by an earnest percussionist thumping a large bass drum, made its way down the street and through the front door.

I wonder how Zelda approaches this current milestone. Does she sense how different it is from earlier occasions? Or does the here and now have its own little compartment in her brain unrelated to mem-ories of birthdays gone by? It seems to depend on the day and the barometer and the pill-taking schedule. But perhaps those are just coincidental, tangibles that mask the perplexing unknowns. On this day, she is not sharing her thoughts.

And seventy-two hours later, any ponderings on the subject will have washed away like those love letters '50s crooner Pat Boone once traced into the impermanent sands of melody, more practical cares having elbowed their way to the forefront.

9-7-05: *On this mildly gray and drizzly day, I let myself in at B and Z's to find the Ethan Allen love seat dismantled, a frying pan lid resting on one of the displaced cushions, Dad in the upstairs bathroom, and Z asleep on the downstairs futon.*

Set at the peninsula end of the kitchen counter is a bowl of Grape Nuts drenched in milk with a dog biscuit crumbled on top. I never do find out what was going on with the couch. Or with the Frankenbreakfast.

At lunch, Z defends against eating all of her freshly made hot ham and cheese croissant, saying, "I always finish it later." (I always throw away petrified half-sandwiches later.)

~~~~~

It's hard to estimate the ripple effects that our stumblings through this misty Other World create. I know friends are dismayed that they can't take Zelda to lunch without fearing an hour-long, off-the-wall tirade about how Dad sold the house on Lindy "out from under" her when they know it was she who campaigned for that move. I know the stress seeps into my pores and abrades my easily frayed nerves. That it drives Dad into himself or out of the house more often than he might ordinarily withdraw from us. And I see the strain erupt between the household's residents.

9-12-05: *I step outside to walk the girls, but sputtering rain makes them dart in zigzags, trying to decide whether to venture forth. We barely reach the first grassy ridge before a thunderous clap of lightning sends all three of us scampering back to the front door. Once inside, Fergie attacks Chloé, snapping and snarling as if the whole frightening incident had been Chloé's fault.*

Z enters the living room wearing black socks but no shoes, voluminous denim culottes, and a misbuttoned maroon mohair cardigan. A hankie peeks out of the cowl of her turtleneck and her hands tremble as she stoops to lean on the coffee table—"drained," she volunteers, from cleaning up coffee grounds after Chloé got into the trash last night.

    9-15-05: *I sit in the under-lit, closeted corner that is Dad's office, rehashing my bumbling of yesterday—when I found it necessary, for some reason, to point out that we still need orange juice. That what they bought on their last joint shopping trip was orange-flavored Sunny D. This causes Z to say, "Well, that's a good demonstration of my condition," and Dad to bark, "Well, somebody's got to drink it."*

~~~~~

The "life goes on" part of things hardly has a singsongy kind of predictability to it, but it does have a rhythm that carries us back and forth between old practices and new. Zelda suddenly feels compelled to make soup. Into the pot go doggie-bag barbecued ribs and chicken bouillon, cubed chicken breast, rice, and cream of mushroom soup. As she stands at the stove stirring the muddy concoction, I see the Campbell's lid bobbing around with the other ingredients. Shock paralyzes my tongue—an unexpected blessing.

We three set out to browse the shelves at Barnes & Noble. An hour later, Zelda insists we've been there mere minutes when it was she who complained on the ride over that she shouldn't have let us talk her into going. Dad buys *The New Rules* by Bill Maher. I buy *Useful Idiots* by Mona Charen. Some consistencies hold.

Back home, Dad and I discover individual cans of Boost chocolate drink scattered around the garage—Zelda having seeded the area with them, motivated by a fleeting impulse that eludes retrieval or analysis. Dread seizes my chest, annihilates my post-Marshfield composure. Sends me scurrying to the Internet for data on treatable conditions that share her symptoms. Maybe our trip to the neurologist will uncover normal pressure hydrocephalus. The description fits. And it's a condition with remedies.

But that appointment is two weeks away. Today, Zelda staggers into the kitchen. Says she is short of breath. I offer a soothing back rub, but there is so little meat on her bones that this soon becomes uncomfortable for both of us. Breathing exercises are a better idea. They refocus the mind and relax tensed muscles. And we can do them together standing on common ground.

Back in our separate worlds, Zelda makes long, slow visits to the bathroom, with ten-minute lapses between toilet gurgle and reemergence. Talks into her chest in a small voice but sternly upbraids me if I call to her from twelve feet away. "I can't *hear* you," she scolds. "Are you speaking to *me*?!" Or she stands in the hallway looking dazed and cries out, "Where are you?" as if her not being able to track my voice were a major act of rudeness on my part.

I so want to not view her as a child. I want to respond to her on her own terms, to help her maintain her self-respect. But when emotion reduces me to a gelatinous pool of wax, maintaining my own decorum becomes hard work.

9-16-05: *Mary Kay was scheduled to pick up Z at 9:30 this morning for a breakfast date. Dad tells me Z was completely dressed and ready to go when he got up at seven, and I want to cry at the heartrending sweetness of her being so eager and so uncertain.*

Later, Z and I walk three-quarters of a mile over hills and alongside ponds. We stop often to take in the glories of this sun-drenched, 76-degree day—opulent splashes of amber, bronze, and persimmon punctuating the autumn landscape; lush pots of creamy asters and myrtle green ivy grouped for maximum effect.

She tells me there is a communal approach to gardening here. That townhouse residents with itching green thumbs join together to plan and cultivate designated areas. And to work botanical magic, it would appear.

As we pass a neighbor's elevated deck, Z comments that she thinks she might have seen a gnome rappelling down from the balcony to greet us. "*What does one say to a descending gnome?*" *I ask in response. She, however, is keeping that information to herself.*

~~~~~

I sometimes wish I could have eyes here twenty-four hours a day. Make that semi-wish. We seem to be a trio of old dogs trying to learn new tricks, Dad and Zelda and I. Obviously, I have to unplug from that process from time to time. But I also need to know that it doesn't stop being a process when I walk out the front door. That I have set wheels in motion, and the momentum has a shot at carrying things through until the next morning.

9-19-05: *I read Ogden Nash to Z, then try to help her memorize a two-line verse: "In the world of mules, there are no rules." She is keen to participate but consistently substitutes the word "day" for "world," or says "jewels" or "tools" instead of "rules." She can't follow the logic of the word pattern even when I break it down and explain it.*

Weakened by the short drill, she asks to wait for a day when she feels more "with it." I so want to offer stimulation. Am I expecting too much? Isn't prodding her at least better than a retreat into expecting too little?

Later, we sort through her collection of quotations and anecdotes. She asks, "Who is Albert Schweitzer?" Can't recall ever knowing a couple named Hodgson whom she and Dad met on an elder hostel trip and have socialized with many times.

Chink, chink goes the crumbling of her life's memories, clunking into tiny piles of rubble at her feet.
And none of us can sweep fast enough to keep things tidied up.

Chink, chink goes the crumbling of her life's memories, clunking into tiny piles of rubble at her feet. And none of us can sweep fast enough to keep things tidied up.

Human interaction is stimulation of a more low-keyed variety. Maybe the kind that coaxes out Zelda's gregarious side—the side that once donned period costume, memorized the complete history of the Alexander Ramsey House in Saint Paul, and led tours of the restored Victorian mansion that had been home to the first governor of Minnesota Territory.

We sit sampling coffee and pastries in an upstairs conference room at the Como Park pavilion. It is our first Parkinson's Support Group meeting. We listen as the fifteen or so attendees share heartening tales about dealing with disabling tremors for many years, yet still dancing for exercise whenever they are able.

When it's Zelda's turn to introduce herself, she defers to me as her spokesperson. Dad has come, too. I think he is bored and antsy. He is tough to entertain. But I like the warmth and enthusiasm of the mildly self-congratulating group leader. And the feeling that we are doing something to cope.

Coping. The act takes on a whole new dimension when you discover the dog food bowl on the bedroom dresser and a cereal bowl where the pups eat their meals, and find yourself speculating about who had what for breakfast. Or you come across a Band-Aid stuck to the hall railing—fully plastered on as if placed with meticulous intent—and wonder which member of the household now walks around with an untended wound.

9-23-05: *Following a night of severe thunderstorms, I arrive to find Papa still in bed and Z unable to put a sentence together. She starts to express a thought but can't stay tuned in long enough to finish. Another medication system breakdown?*

She naps, and I am awash in a shameful sense of relief—as if I were a fourteen-year-old babysitter again, thankful when my difficult charge finally drops off to sleep. But remorse doesn't keep me from holding my breath, hoping that the dogs' yapping won't awaken her. I am a swine at soul level.

In more cogent moments, Zelda confides that the counseling issue is partly resolved, but she would like me to research the credentials of Dad's therapist. I suggest couples counseling since their relationship suffers over his one-on-one arrangement. As her side of the conversation swirls into demurrals and red herrings, her face clouds over.

Please, let me not have stirred up a storm.

I hold that thought. Remind myself how God has salvaged so many seemingly doomed days for us. Soon Zelda and I are sliding comfortably into a long walk and another discussion about joint counseling. But I feel her resistance like a physical tautness between us and steer the conversation elsewhere.

Still later, as we exit the grocery store carrying our carton of eggs, Zelda breaks into a chorus of "In the Mood," à la Ray Stevens and the Henhouse Five. This performance requires much clucking and some wing-flapping. I join in—partly to bolster her efforts and partly in self-defense.

~~~~~

It's a troubling but recurring theme in dementia, the flip-flopping between lucidity and confusion. The sweet, bright, thoughtful person, the playful Madame Zelda, stills occupies this stooped little wisp of a body that moves, wraith-like, chin to chest, around the house. But she can drift back into the fog of her disease without warning.

Sometimes I can lead her out of the haze. She strains to dredge up the name of the restaurant where she and Dad ate last Sunday, saying, "It's the one your papa likes." I try "Perkins?" No. "Embers?" No. "Taco Bell?" No. "Long John Silver's?" No. "Culvers?" No. "Red Lobster?" No. I say, "What did you eat?" Zelda says, "Meatballs." I offer, "Olive Garden?" No. I ask, "What did Dad eat?" "Meatballs and some balls of unknown substance." I say, "Panda Buffet?" She says, "Yes!"

Sometimes she welcomes me in. Zelda and I prepare for a stroll, and a packaged toothpick falls to the floor as she pulls a facial tissue from her jacket pocket. She tucks the restaurant souvenir back in where it came from, saying, "You never know when you might run into a hippopotamus and have to do battle."

A few blocks into the walk, Zelda says she needs to stop and blow her nose and hopes the geese won't come running when they hear her honk. Then, seeing a squirrel with an acorn eyeing us with suspicion,

Zelda reassures him, "Don't fear us little one. We are squirrel admirers."

And sometimes we find a way to straddle the divide together.

9-26-05: *I make beefy, melty, crisp-grilled Reuben sandwiches for lunch and—guilt creeping over me like a slow blush—dissuade Z from cleaning up afterwards. "I should earn my keep," I fib, as my nose grows longer by the second. "Being busy helps me stay out of trouble."*

The unvarnished truth is that I have watched her lately, running cold water over a plate, making a tiny circle with her bare fingertips in the center, and then putting the still-soiled dish in the drying rack, and I worry about health issues.

So we unload the dishwasher together, instead—she plucking out utensils and cups, me stretching long arms to guide them from her contracted reach into their proper cupboards.

Practical tasks simply do not hold her interest. She is a ponderer and a philosopher, fascinated by talk of people's lives and personalities, their potential and their prospects. And so a platter headed for the dinner table ends up on the kitchen counter next to the stove and empty Boost bottles get put back in the refrigerator. She pours extra bowls of cereal in the morning for . . . she isn't sure whom. And the calcium supplement container now houses cookies as well, their crumbly yumminess snuggled up to the neatly packaged soft chews we buy because they are chocolate, and chocolate is something Zelda can still "sense" with her tongue.

~~~~~

There's a whole lotta' sleepin' goin' on around here these days, and that troubles my own slumber-deprived mind. If Dad snoozes for a few hours after lunch, he then needs a sleeping pill at bedtime. And I hate Zelda's frequent naps for what they deprive her of for hours afterward. Groggy from sleep, she might have trouble finding the bathroom that is four feet from her bedroom door. Or might have to ask repeatedly where a kitchen item belongs.

When I manage to grab a full night's rest, I feel incredible on these gorgeous fall days, which are saturated with sunlight, capped by crystal blue skies, and bulging with promise. But B's and Z's extra hours in the sack seem to generate more lethargy. I do sympathize. When a violent storm recently felled the seventy-foot pine in my backyard at home, imposing hours of heavy labor in chopping up and removing its lifeless carcass, I benefited from the physical exertion. But I had to have it forced on me.

An appointment with a neurologist should help us focus on the goal of improving Zelda's quality of life.

Wednesday, September 28. Our first visit with a specialist in vascular neurology. We leave at 8:45 for a nerve-racking, twenty-minute drive in gray, drizzly weather. Years of aggressive driving habits are carved into Dad's behavior patterns like a face on the side of Mount Rushmore—while years of living have eroded his reflexes just enough to be noticeable. And mildly terrifying.

Dr. S is genial with a rich sense of humor. He thinks Zelda is "so darned cute" and lectures her to "eat!" During her initial interview, he also notes her inability to look upward without moving her head and suggests progressive supranuclear palsy as a possible explanation.

As I help Zelda into her paper exam gown, Kleenex popcorn cascades from the inside of her wool-blend pullover—the result of unemptied pockets being sent through the Kenmore. I scramble to pluck dozens of little white puffs off the carpet before the doctor returns.

A series of assessments leads to a series of tentative diagnoses—the

105

dementia, the Parkinsonisms, and then a third condition, which has ironically skittered from my mind at the moment. He'll order an EEG and a CT scan and see Zelda again in three weeks. This plan to pursue definitive explanations boosts family morale.

To Perkins for brunch while we wait for prescriptions. Rain spits at the window just above our table, persistent and nagging, but we tune it out, relaxing into amiable chit-chat against the background hum of midday diners. Even abide the slow service with waitress banter.

Zelda orders an all-carbohydrate meal of blueberry muffin and breakfast potatoes. She polishes off the entire giant muffin and eats very few of the potatoes. But when Dad leaves to pay the tab, she cleans up his leftover hash browns as she inches her way out of the booth—one stolen bite for every incremental scoot.

~~~~~

Ignorance. It can be a lazy failure to inform yourself or a happy state of not yet knowing the truth. Sometimes it pays to be lazy. I rush to my home computer to clack out "progressive supranuclear palsy" on the keyboard. "Help," I whimper, as I bob to the surface of a sea of gloomy facts—details of a gradual, debilitating slouch toward brain deterioration, involuntary forward lunges, and feeding tubes.

Jack and I talk. His coolheaded approach to the unchangeable calms me. And . . . *poof!* It comes to me: Nothing about our situation is any different than it was before my compulsion to investigate led us into the murky waters of a still-hypothetical opinion. Dad, Zelda, and I know we don't have forever together, that the earlier days of freedom from health anxieties have shrunk into the past along with childhood memories and the sound of long-gone voices—distant, muted echoes in our heads.

As if she senses my need for consolation, the next day at lunch Zelda extends her hand. I meet her reach, dwarfing her dainty fingers in my grasp. She prays, "God is great, God is good, let us thank Him for this food."

Her voice quavers with emotion. "I used to say grace regularly before meals, before your dad and I got married." It is a mournful reflection, teeming with insight, not the ramblings of one in the throes of mental collapse.

So I offer thanks of my own that I can be at my father's and step-mother's sides as we page through these concluding chapters together, wondering how the adventure will unravel. And as my logic-grounded husband says, all prognoses are based on averages anyway. Zelda's situation is ideal—she has loving care, daily stimulation, and a living spouse.

9-29-05: *Sitting at the lunch table with Dad and Z, it could be 1978 when we used to trade quips over a pre-meal glass of Chablis—a pot of Zelda's Minnesota minestrone burbling on the stove.*

Today, Z asks Pa if he'd like a bite of her cubed cantaloupe. "No, not right now," he says.

"If you open wide, she might be able to catapult one into your mouth with her fork," I offer.

"She'd probably put my eye out," chuckles Papa, setting off a crescendo of giggles in Zelda that leaves her shoulders heaving.

It's one of those "all-is-right-with-the-world" moments. And life goes on.

Chapter Ten

Groundhog Days

Joan makes the drive from Madison for weekend visits often these days. This is both a relief and a threat. She introduces a supportive presence to Dad and Zelda's weekends. But she also introduces with regularity the idea that it's about time to get these two settled into assisted living in Wisconsin, where she can keep an eye on things. "Conveniently packaging everything up," as Dad puts it. Once dangled, this idea roils the already troubled waters of my dream life.

Dad tells me he wants to put into writing their desire to stay in Minnesota where hearth, home, and friends have been for the past thirty-two years. Zelda clenches her jaw and shrinks into herself at the mention of a move. And my own innards contract as I recall my experiences working in nursing homes—even the best of which can't offer what home care provides. Tension thickens the air like cornstarch in gravy, and it's hard to breathe normally until the topic is once again set aside.

This post-visit Tuesday, Chloé sneaks into my canvas tote, sinks her teeth into the plump, juicy breast meat of my chicken sandwich, then wins the tug of war over the whole grain bun, which she manages to secret—along with her own little self—under the couch. Scratch one tasty bag lunch.

As I buzz about doing the daily room-rescue routine, I find Zelda's comb afloat in the dishwater and her mother's gold-rimmed dinner china randomly stacked in with the paper plates. Flash back to yesterday morning before Joan left for home when Zelda admonished that it would be very kind of me to put her clothing back in place where she can find it—this after underwear turned up in the hall linen closet. "Is this yours?" asked Joan innocently. The question was a spark in the tinderbox of Zelda's dicey emotional equilibrium, and the exchange escalated into a conflagration over who put what where and why.

This never would have happened twelve months ago. But on this day, Zelda insists that she has more underwear than sits on the shelves of the hall closet. (In her dresser drawer, perhaps?) She is equally convinced that thievery has transpired and begins to eye each of us with suspicion.

When Joan happens upon the missing items in the basket of dirty laundry, the subject gets discarded faster than a stinky gym sock. Saving face. It becomes paramount when trust in your own perceptions starts slip-sliding away like a shard of soap escaping wet fingers. Still, these flare-ups can't help but stoke Joan's concerns.

October 4, 2005   **3:30 p.m.**

Dear Joan,

On your last few visits you've suggested making nursing care arrangements for your mom, and I find this troubling.

I understand the logic that a preemptive placement might simplify things down the line, but I think these conversations are premature. And I know such a move would be objectionable to Dad. At any rate, this idea probably needs to originate with him.

I know you're worried about Dad's and my stamina, and about the challenge of getting your mom to accept help with personal care, but things are still manageable at this point. Should that change, I'm sure we can jointly come up with a creative solution.

Love,

Suz

October 4, 2005   4:16 p.m.

Dear Suz,

I appreciate your reassurances. I spoke to Mom last evening, and she seemed much more like her old self, as if the anxieties of the morning had evaporated and she was no longer concerned about them. This was a tremendous relief.

It's obvious that moments of stress, like the imminent departure of loved ones, contribute to her dementia-like behavior. I've seen this before in others. Once the cause of the stress is gone, things become much more stable.

Strange as it may sound, the toenail clipping and hair washing turned out to be very nice ways to bond. I do plan to come often enough to tend to any personal care issues if need be. Believe me, Suz, you have brought such a wonderful order and harmony to the place. I can't thank you enough for that, and I don't want you to have to do even more than you already do.

Love to you and Jack.

Joan

And so the handwriting on the wall fades away like disappearing ink. Catch breath. Step into another day.

10-5-05: *Z is rattled, convinced that she must do something to prepare for this morning's MRI. Dad says he feels fuzzy, too, and asks me to come along to the imaging appointment. Three pages of paperwork and multiple signatures into our office visit, I am glad he asked.*

Decked out in her baby blue X-ray jammies, Z hums a lively folk tune and breaks into a jig. "I'm dancing out my nervous tension," she explains between hops. A pre-MRI bathroom stop seems like a good idea. Soon she summons me to untie the drawstring I had knotted tight, hoping to convince the formless costume to stay put.

After the procedure, she shuffles her way back down the hallway, both hands clutching her now-drooping scrub pants. This "one size" does not fit all.

The sky hangs heavy with dark, mist-spritzing clouds as we duck into a neon-splashed sports bar a few blocks from the MRI offices for lunch.

Pasty crab cakes, tasting of tuna and oatmeal, do nothing to lift the oppressive mood. I could use a bit of a skip in my own step, but I'm having trouble faking it.

Back home, I encourage Z to lift her chin and look to the horizon to keep from stooping. Page 37, "Living with Parkinson's Disease."

Minutes later, as we pass through the living room, Dad also reminds her to straighten her back. Upright she stiffens, snapping a salute to her brow. Next thing we know, she is down on her knees, pretending to bow subserviently at his feet but actually positioning herself to tickle them. On that note, I slip out the front door—crossing eight fingers in hopes that the mood will hold.

Back home, I encourage Z to lift her chin and look to the horizon to keep from stooping. Page 37, " Living with Parkinson's Disease."

~~~~

"To my beloved prairie dog, greetings." So wrote Zelda in a March 17, 1972 letter to Dad. "You are my love and the new and wonderful meaning in life," the note closed. Two days later: "Mine Sweetheart, after having known you, it doesn't seem that there could be another human being who could be so 'just right.' Daily, I marvel at the fact of our being able to plan a future together." Both letters are signed M.A.S.G.—short for Mary Audrey Squirrely Girl.

These voices from the past help balance exchanges in the present. But the seesaw often tilts, revealing wormholes in the timeless nature of earthly love.

Dad sits at the breakfast table wearing his aged orange-plaid flannel robe. "Yield," demands the triangular black-on-gold patch that Zelda mischievously stitched on the right sleeve during those blissful early days. His Squirrely Girl stands by the kitchen sink in her nubby pink robe, a pair of panty hose tied around the waist in lieu of a belt. As she wrestles with the troubling paper divider inside the box of powdered milk, she frets aloud about needing to prepare cereal for herself and some other unnamed person.

Her beloved—his deaf ear turned toward the kitchen confusion—reads the *Star Tribune* and munches on a buttered toaster waffle while I try to talk Zelda past the hazy delusion of having a guest to whom she owes breakfast.

"Don't forget to take your morning Reminyl," cautions Dad as he heads for the bedroom to dress. Zelda returns to him the stern look of one not to be bothered with the trivial when there are multiple breakfasts to be made.

As always, there is peace to be found in the steady, plodding pace of the morning dog walk. The crisp fall air wraps the pups and me in its 40-degree chill as startled geese trumpet a high-volume reveille at our approach and slide reluctantly into the cold pond water.

Back home, Dad clicks away at his computer keyboard downstairs, while upstairs the Reminyl sits untouched in the pill dispenser. I prod gently. Zelda picks up the pill, then returns it to the container. Prod, return, repeat. Those little flip-top compartments remind her that she doesn't know what blasted time it is, darn it. If only she would let me dispense her meds. But that is one step too far in her catalog of concessions.

And the replays continue as Zelda pops out of bed seconds after crawling into it, asking, "Is it time to get up?" and then needs telling again minutes later that, no, you've only just laid down. What doesn't loop into perpetual reruns are her stories from the past, told over pots of steeped Constant Comment, each one a marvel of rich detail and personal statistics.

There were the American Legion band concerts at Swan Park on warm Tuesday nights in Beaver Dam. Here, during her fifteenth summer, she and some girlfriends got possession of a pack of Old Golds and snuck behind a park bench to sample their first puffs.

That same summer, a classmate got "sent up" for car theft but later returned to school—reformed and on track. As I take notes, she balks at giving me names even for her cohorts in goofy kid antics. Is this paranoid alter ego talk or a reasonable request?

~~~

Most days Zelda and I make the oversized bed in Dad's room together. It bothers her, this hard-to-tidy expanse of two twin mattresses with its ill-fitting patchwork linens. So we pull and tug. Fuss with the corner-tucking and the pillow-stacking—only to walk right past a neglected mountain of clothing piled high on the cedar chest as we leave the room.

Occasional people-walks are routine, too—as long as the weather is "just right." On these mid-fall days, a wintry chill bullies its way in and robs the sunshine of its comfort. "It's always too hot or too cold in Minnesota," says Zelda with a shudder, and the comment then reminds her of a World War II lyric. "They're either too young or too old," she chirps. "Either too gray or they're green as grass." How that line finds its rhyme I am left to wonder as the fragment of memory unravels.

These ancient recollections spring forth with apparent ease. So, unfortunately, do the mood changes that transform sweethearts into fickle companions. Dad has been wanting to take an unused shelf unit to the auction house to carve out some elbow room in the overcrowded garage. I say offhandedly that Jack and I would be happy to transport it for him. Zelda walks in on this exchange and angrily demands to know which piece of furniture he plans to sell. Hearing, she resists. She can't process the logic behind the need to pare down, but it's more than that. Her anxiety ripples through the air like cartoon radio waves, and she turns her focus-cum-obsession to the empty cardboard boxes in the garage. If only they were cleared away—a plan never before suggested—it would open access to the cabinet she needs to organize her books.

Energized by distress, she makes three hasty trips up and down the stairs to Dad's office to debate this now monumental issue. Her agitated state is agonizing to behold, but her comments paint a full-color picture: An impending assault on her home environment is the only reality she comprehends; there is no room in a horror-stricken mind to entertain practical demands. The irony, of course, is that less clutter would help all of us function better.

Dad agrees that the boxes should go, and I convince Zelda to let me tackle the project while she rests. An hour later, I gleefully lead her through the newly revealed spaciousness. But she's still consumed with anguish over the close call with the shelving unit and can't begin to appreciate the improvement. Did someone reserve a letdown for two?

~~~

> On the fourth reminder, her head drops forward like a tulip on a broken stem. "Oh, Suz, this is so pitiful," she whimpers. "No, it's not," I lie, pity flooding my chest. "You're just tired. You haven't rested all day."

10-10-05: *Z talks of napping but instead entices Dad into a short walk, then plows through an entire serving of my shrimp eggs foo yung and rice and still has enough energy to shop for groceries. As this "quick trip" turns into an hour-long ordeal, my own endurance flags. So many aisles to trod, so many decisions to be made as the Parkinsonian slowness plagues her every movement.*

Once home, fatigue-induced confusion shrouds Zelda. Are the leftover eggs foo yung in the top drawer of the dining room buffet? Are we upstairs or downstairs? "We are already up," I say lightheartedly and repeatedly as she gathers grocery items in her arms and heads out of the kitchen with them.

On the fourth reminder, her head drops forward like a tulip on a broken stem. "Oh, Suz, this is so pitiful," she whimpers.

"No, it's not," I lie, pity flooding my chest. "You're just tired. You hav-

en't rested all day."

And, arm in arm, we find our way to the nest of bed and pillows where restorative sleep will work the magic I have promised her.

Promises. I promised Joan I could manage Zelda's personal care. So . . . how to tactfully ask another adult when they last bathed or shampooed? Take a stab. Mission half-accomplished. She agrees to a shampoo, fending off the insult with a frisky attitude and making up rhyming lines for every situation. ("If per chance I have dampness on my pants.") A wobbly duet of the Whiffenpoof Song—*We are poor little lambs, who have lost our way*—gets us through her rinse cycle.

Worried that her wet hair threatens pneumonia, she kneels in front of the bathroom heat vent, pushing her sparse, short do forward from the roots until it stands on end—dry but misdirected. So coifed, she seeks out Pa in the kitchen and asks if he'd like to have her sing for him. "If you must, I guess," he responds tepidly. Before mock umbrage has fully overtaken her face, Dad adds, "Your hair looks funny"—sending Zelda and me into uncontrollable spasms of glorious, nostril-flaring laughter.

And a day that started with a heated discussion about "what happened to October ninth" ends better than it began. Let's try and remember how we got here.

~~~

Dad has his own encounters with controlled anxiety, some of which he lets me in on—a rare glimpse into his private world. But he always has the power to lift me on the wings of elation.

10-13-05: *An emergency trip to Cub Foods for tomorrow morning's Maxwell House. I bring home a rotisserie chicken and slide it into the oven to keep it warm. Cut up apples, oranges, and bananas for a fruit bowl, steam fresh green beans, and thaw leftover au gratin potatoes.*

As Dad passes through the kitchen on the way to his office, I explain the dinner arrangements. He steps beside me at the counter, puts an arm around my shoulders, and plants a kiss on the top of my head. "Thank you for taking such good care of us," he says, and my heart breaks into the Hallelujah Chorus. I lean into his embrace. "Thank you for letting me be here—for the chance to give back just a little."

But repayment really doesn't describe it, not when my gain is so great. Not when countless opportunities for empathy are tucked into our every day—days that are at once both mundane and unpredictable. Cycling and recycling the same themes, yet studded with novelties.

10-18-05: *After a filling lunch of chili, coleslaw, and cornbread, we three linger at the table enjoying the peaceful, post-meal lethargy. Z asks Dad about his childhood pets and he recalls a much-loved dog named Skippy, says he remembers lying in bed one night when Skippy was ill with distemper, saying to himself, "If Skippy dies, I'm not going to believe in God anymore." My blood runs icy as he finishes with a bitter, knowing cock of his head. "And Skippy died."*

Cramped with sorrow, I say nothing. Why, why couldn't I think to speak the words that come to me now, to say that this tale is the saddest I have ever heard? That the real tragedy is that no one was there to guide him to turn toward God, not away from Him. That the horror of it is too painful to contemplate—a disconsolate eleven-year-old boy rejecting his most reliable source of comfort in a moment of despair.

~~~

An adaptable sense of humor and thick skin are helpful assets in any vocation, I suppose. I am a work in progress in both regards, and my current undertaking tests that progress regularly. At the monthly Parkinson's group meeting, I tense up when it's Zelda's turn to speak, wondering if she'll be able to stay on track. After a presentation on memory loss, the spouse of a group member gives her one of those Hollywood air hugs and tells her what a good sense of humor she has. Zelda responds with her best Henrietta Hen imitation—cluck, cluck, triple squawk—which further amuses the pseudo hugger, so all is well for the moment. Exhale.

At ten the next morning Zelda meets me at the door with her coat on, then gets irritated when I remind her that her haircut appointment isn't until 11:30. For a full hour, she protests that we must be running late, despite all efforts to reassure her otherwise. Thinking I am out of earshot, she announces to Dad that she had better make her own appointments from now on. I step in to retrace her part in agreeing to the arrangements. I offer to cancel. She stoically leaves the decision up to me, but her agitation is infectious. Stifled resentment over my ineptitude hardens her. Perhaps my coming over every day may be too much for me, she suggests.

Even knowing that those dark gulfs of emotion flow from her condition, not from her essence, I am relieved when, a day later, she is genuinely deferential, thanking Dad and me multiple times for having accompanied her to the neurologist's office last week. I see Zelda's appreciation as a form of apology and am thankful for her self-awareness. But Dad, uncomfortable with her ultra-humble attitude, quips, "Well, I thought about giving you the car keys and asking you to tell me how things went."

And that trip to the neurologist has me worried. Because Zelda hates her hand tremor, mild as it is, Dr. S casually prescribed the very Parkinson's medication that the Marshfield Clinic doctor warned against. I should have argued with vigor, but I shied away from that duty. Can't hold my tongue when I should, but there I sat mute—a wimpy victim of White Coat intimidation.

Wait and see. And pray a lot.

~~~

Eldest daughter Robin and her husband Larry visit. One day in, Rob comments that her mother no longer has a sense of humor. *Whoa. What?*

I love these girls, these stepsisters of mine. They are family to me in a distant one-sided way because I need them more than they need me. And I have enormous respect for each of them. I don't want Rob to head for home toting this misconception, but I struggle to communicate that as strongly as I feel it.

There was that moment in Dr. S's office when He Who Knows Best decided that Zelda's tremor was "a little worse" than the last time he saw her, and Zelda replied, "Yes, and I don't like it. That is, unless I have my tambourine with me." And what about her admirer from the Parkinson's group whose compliment I so casually dismissed?

Rob's next observation, that the dementia meds "are doing absolutely no good at all," throws me further off guard. Frantic rebuttals rise in my throat. I am not a big fan of pharmaceuticals, but I am here every day. I see the fallout when Zelda misses a dose. My stepsisters are privy only to strobe light illuminations of the big screen drama— passing glimpses of her behavior under the stress of visiting family. But they are also her biological children, and I wilt under the worry of adding tension to their visits. So my resistance gets tucked away to bubble inside, heartburn-like. Wait this one out, too?

With Rob and Larry gone, the aftershock plays itself out. Yesterday Zelda was obsessed with the line on the medication information sheets that reads, "Keep at a temperature of between forty and eighty degrees." At room temperature, in other words. She read it over and over again, repeated it to Dad and me as if it had great significance, then proceeded to turn off every light in sight.

Today she sits at the breakfast table with all her pill bottles lined up before her, studying the fine print and making vague references to some kind of mix-up with her meds. I ask Dad about it, and he waves off the question with a swoosh of his hand.

I reshelve a clean glass stashed in with the coffee and tea. Rescue an orphaned chunk of unwrapped Baker's chocolate from the cooking utensil drawer. Toss out conversational hooks to a preoccupied Zelda, who sits crouched in the darkened dining area absorbed by a medication mystery she can't put into words.

The last of the miniature mums Rob brought stands in a small vase on the kitchen peninsula, rotting from their fuzzy bronze centers outward and spewing dead petals across the countertop. I clear the shriveled remains, flip on a few light switches, scrub down the kitchen surfaces, and the room looks a little less sad.

Dad announces he is headed for the shower even though he really wants "to crawl back into bed"—and then crawls back into bed. At 11 a.m., Zelda eats an entire slab of long-leftover Red Baron pizza (or *pih-zah*, if we are feeling cute), having just finished her oatmeal with Boost chocolate drink drizzled on it at 10:10. Thus "stuffed to the gizzard," she heads to bed as well. Success on the eating front, but when I get back from walking the dogs, I have to rouse her to remind her to take the Razadyne—her newly prescribed more potent dementia treatment. Better days must be up for rotation.

10-25-05: *A good day today. Z looks chipper although, at one point, she says she feels like she is on a merry-go-round and sits to dispel the wooziness.*

For lunch, salmon patties with sautéed eggplant and peppers sounds good to me. Some warmed biscuits from an earlier baking session should bring Dad into agreement. We kibitz and nosh, banter and tease. "If you put me out, just don't put me out in a snow bank," says cold-hating Zelda.

"We won't put you out. It would be too hard to explain," Dad responds.

"Don't say that!" I cry in mock horror. And when I quietly remind him that she might later forget that this was a joke, he concedes. Sort of.

Post-lunch cleanup has me buzzing circles around Z as I clear and wash and dry and stack. "I think I'll start calling you Flash," she says. But when my energy level is low, momentum is the only thing that keeps me going.

A long afternoon walk. Z and I collect multi-colored leaves and talk about pumping some hilarity into the everyday routine, so it's off to Blockbuster Video in search of her favorite Pink Panther movie.

Once home, she naps; I walk the dogs and move on to dinner prep. In the newly scrubbed, relit kitchen, the mission of nurturing weary souls by nourishing weary bodies inspires me. I can't always rally the sunny sweetness that I admire in others, but I can always pour my affection into this joyful task. Meatballs in mushroom sauce on a bed of hot, fluffy rice served with fresh, steamed spinach with lemon butter. Wrap it up and stick a bow on it.

~~~

Dad is all guy when it comes to (not) talking about how he feels— emotionally or physically. When he calmly announced last week that he needed to be taken to the hospital, I went on high alert. A little digging revealed that he'd had stomach pains for days, and his own doctor had referred him, rather than trying to fit him in. Because the average emergency room wait in Minnesota is three hours, I suggested we pop into the urgent care clinic in my neighborhood—average wait time: fifteen minutes. The doctor there diagnosed and repositioned a bulging hernia. He also said he couldn't believe Dad was able to function, his oxygen levels were so low.

Today, on a mission to get Pa's issue sorted out, we all take off for the local hospital for a CAT scan of his lungs, some blood work, and an echocardiogram to rule out congestive heart failure.

This is a mammoth institution. Printed instructions guide us through the facility to various room numbers. The receptionist at the CT department asks Dad if he has other tests scheduled. Short on oxygen, with a head cold complicating his chronic obstructive pulmonary disease, he says no, and I have to correct him. At the blood draw in the lab, the same question. Again, he answers no, and again I have to correct him. This is a day of haunting concerns and confusing communications. A Twilight Zone of crossed signals.

Zelda and I seek out a restroom, but once situated in her private stall she has trouble finding the toilet paper. The double-roll dispenser is mounted high, enclosed in dark gray plastic. I locate it for her, but she has trouble figuring out how to make it surrender some tissue.

Back in the EKG waiting room, she tucks herself into a well-padded chair and falls asleep, looking for all the world like a tiny gnome in her pixie-cropped hair and brown leather, T-strapped shoes.

By default, I am driving on this little expedition. On the ride home, a guy pulls out in front of me, and Dad says, "Blast him!" I toot the horn a few times, but Dad is not satisfied. He calls out, "You dumb ship!"—or something that sounds like that—and introduces the unfortunate fellow to his middle finger with more vigor than he has displayed in weeks.

Rod Serling, are you there?

Chapter Eleven

I'm Loust! I'm Loust!

The year was 1951. The setting: a classic, midcentury Detroit apartment building. Diamond-patterned institutional carpeting. Yellowing hallway walls. Extensive, slightly musty corridors presenting an endless series of identical entry doors. Or at least that's how it appeared to two-year-old Joan and three-year-old Robin when they somehow escaped from their host's apartment, rounded a corner, and found themselves wandering one of those mazelike corridors hand in hand.

By the time a concerned adult set out to hunt for the two elfin adventurers, big sister Rob was desperate. "I'm loust! I'm loust!" rang out the quavering toddler voice just as their rescuer swooped in to lead them back to safety.

This was a favorite story of Zelda's from her daughters' early years. It became one of those esoteric taglines that gets preserved and applied to future situations—usually with a wink and a nod to other family members who share the inside joke. "Eat dot" was another of these, this time credited to a very young Julie who refused to sample what was on her dinner plate. "Eat that!" demanded her irritated father. "Eat dot!" mimicked the plucky little imp from her highchair as the whole family burst out in uncontainable laughter.

These two snippets of family history no longer have meaning for Zelda because they require the ability to excavate a targeted memory, context and all. Yet in a sadly literal way, both quotes fit her new reality.

Dad meets me at the door on the first Tuesday of November. Says that Zelda is acting psychotic—so disconnected she can't tell where she is or why. Alarm bells clang in my cranium. Talking myself off the ledge of full-fledged panic, I backtrack on the timeline, picturing myself standing in the neurologist's office, fists clenched, as he scrawls out a prescription for the tremor medication we'd been warned about.

This time it's me hunched over the table obsessively scouring medication data sheets. "Possible side effects," screams the bold print: CONFUSION. Ah, but it gets better. Additional risks include blurred vision, dizziness, lightheadedness, difficulty sleeping, decreased appetite, anxiety, and constipation. This is reading like a not-to-do list of all the complaints Zelda can hardly afford to compound, thank you very much.

So, forgive me for cursing the doctor who plunged her into a sea of bewilderment like she's never known before. Why? So he can justify his investment of time and the charges he submits to Medicare? So he can feel like he's at least done something even though that "something" offers negligible help and evident risk to this struggling patient?

I flush crimson with rage knowing that we will now spend days, possibly weeks, getting this poison out of her system. Meanwhile, Zelda suffers unnecessarily. "This is not home, of course," she says, looking around in bewilderment, "but it's a copy of home." I suggest that the new drug could be making her feel disoriented and try to sidetrack with a message from Dad. "Your Knight in Shining Armor has asked you to lunch."

Her response? "I'd like to punch him!"

Shocked, I ask, "Whatever for?"

"He should have known about this," she says through constricted lips.

And as feared, the detox period is neither short nor sweet.

11-7-05: *Monday evening. I've been home about an hour when Dad calls me in despair, asking me to come back to their place and try to calm Z. I arrive at 5:50 to find her sitting at the table nibbling on half a slice of cold, hard peanut butter toast and talking about how everything is out of place. "I don't want to be Alice in Wonderland," she laments. I cautiously remind her that we think the now discontinued new drug complicated things, left her feeling a bit muddled.*

But—confused, lightheaded, and anxious—she finds no comfort in my words. She hangs her head, tears dropping gently onto her folded hands, and says that she doesn't know what is happening to her. That she is a huge burden to Dad and me and that we should just put her away somewhere. My heart wrenches in my chest as, in my mind's eye, I slowly and methodically throttle Dr. S.

Then, incredibly, Z agrees to dinner at Pippins, the neighborhood diner. Here she remains distant and glum but makes a meal of the salad bar by adding garbanzos and chopped eggs to her tiny pile of veggies and steals an onion ring from Dad's plate. Then, minutes after our return to the townhouse, drops peacefully off to sleep.

I was busy committing imaginary assault when I should have been praying for help. But a miracle made its way to us anyway.

~~~

I have a friend whose father suffered from sundowner syndrome in his late eighties. Online resources define sundowning as "a psychological phenomenon associated with increased confusion and restlessness at day's end in patients with some forms of dementia." Sounds familiar. The Mayo Clinic website offers plenty of suggestions for altering this pattern—all of which sound eminently reasonable, but none of which seems remotely possible.

- Try to maintain a predictable routine and limit daytime napping. (Very amusing.)

- Plan for exposure to light during the day to encourage nighttime sleepiness. (Planning for year-round light exposure in St. Paul, Minnesota, is like planning for year-round poolside relaxation in Nome, Alaska.)

- Limit caffeine and sugar to morning hours. (Have they never heard of the ever-popular hot fudge sundae lunch, Dad's choice, or chocolate chip cookie dinner, Zelda's favorite?)

Even with no hope for accomplishing any of the above, Zelda gradually leaves Wonderland behind—along with the toxic drug that transported her there—and things improve. Slowly. But she resists letting loose of the sticky notion that she is a burden. Contends that she doesn't like having to be taken care of and doesn't want to freeload. A good response to these concerns? *Please*. If you have one, I'll take it. I press the idea that she would do the same for one of us, but it doesn't carry enough punch to quash her sense of not pulling her own weight. I could argue the case more effectively if it weren't so easy to see her point.

Yet even in this dour mood, there is a childlike sweetness to Zelda as she comes through her bedroom doorway, sleepy-eyed from the nap she's not supposed to be taking, and whispers, "Is this the morning I have the doctor's appointment?"

"This is afternoon," I explain quietly. "Three p.m. Your doctor's appointment is tomorrow at 11 a.m."

"Oh, OK," she whispers back.

Meanwhile, lingering lethargy and a fixation on the negative continue to haunt her. So she gets mired in musings about a recent gray weekend and curls into herself in withdrawal, even as we are blessed with a string of sunny, 60-degree days. "One gets tired of being tired," Dad says, summing things up for both of them. Maybe our trip to his heart specialist will yield some relief.

11-14-05: *There are icy teeth to the winter winds that lift the post office flag to a horizontal position. "Good morning," I brazenly assume, as I greet Z before our trip to the doctor. "I could be sarcastic and say, 'What's good about it?'" she replies sarcastically.*

During the preliminaries at the cardiologist's office, the nurse announces that my fully clothed father weighs 143 pounds—twenty-two pounds less than at his last weigh-in. This is not good.

"No way," I blurt out, remembering that I registered a beefy 144 pounds, stripped down to my hair scrunchie, the last time I ventured onto my scale at home. One more worry stirred into the pot.

On a day of mixed blessings, I try not to borrow tomorrow's unknown troubles. But I'm not quite ready to bank on tomorrow's unknown fortunes, either.

Hope flickers as a slim, attentive, silver-haired Dr. B reviews Dad's test results and assertively dismisses a diagnosis of congestive heart failure. He will make recommendations after more information is collected.

But at lunch my throat thickens with the ache of tension as Dad gets only halfway through his walleye sandwich platter and Z barely finishes the scant cup of restaurant clam chowder that cannot begin to measure up to her own version.

On a day of mixed blessings, I try not to borrow tomorrow's unknown troubles. But I'm not quite ready to bank on tomorrow's unknown fortunes, either. Then, as Z and I head for the restroom, I catch her making faces over the top rim of the booth divider at a still-seated Papa. As he returns a sweetly tolerant grin, I am warmed and heartened. And reminded that our future is in the Creator's caring hands. This is good.

~~~

"I'm here for ya." It's a phrase that gets tossed around a lot with varying degrees of sincerity. But "being there" in the intimate sense of knowing as much about a person's immediate situation as they know themselves can feel like keeping a secret you're not supposed to know.

My father sits reading in his oversized wingback chair, his lanky right leg folded over his left in the distinctive pose I have observed all my life—and in total disregard for the peripheral vascular disease that causes him so much discomfort. I become the self-aware helicopter daughter, sucking in both lips to corral my tongue.

And as Zelda feels her way back from drug-induced fantasy land, I mentally slap myself for continuing to blame every questionable event on the Big Bad Tremor Medication. That scapegoat has been driven into the wilderness. Now we learn anew to deal with what it left behind.

11-18-05: *Z ricochets around the corner like a pinball in an arcade game, fully dressed but eyes half open. "Thank you for stopping by," she offers earnestly. "I'll be here every day," I respond airily.*

It's almost eleven o'clock. Dad is back in bed, and Z is just getting around to breakfast, complaining of tough sausages, and needing redirection. "Don't forget to eat while your food is still warm," I remind her.

She adjusts her chair and dabs at her nose, her head bent over the table like the overburdened jack-in-the-pulpit in my front garden bed. Abruptly, she lifts her chin and points to the pantry door. "I hadn't realized there were two entrances to the bathroom, one behind here."

Together, we test this claim. Open the accordion door. Peer inside. Blessedly, she is neither embarrassed nor confused by the revelation that canned goods instead reside behind that mysterious portal at the west end of the breakfast room.

Then I make the idiotic blunder of asking Z if she has seen my glasses, plunging her into an urgent quest to locate them. After multiple promises to give up and take her morning nap, she heads back to her room, only to resume a dogged search of her top dresser drawer. I ask to confirm what she's doing, stealthily exit the room, and return seconds later with a big, fat, juicy peach of a lie: "Ah! I just found my glasses in my purse! Isn't that a relief . . . "

~~~

You realize just how much you've always counted on people when those dependable sorts become unreliable. Of course, unreliable isn't the right term because it implies a lack of conscientiousness. But sorting all that out emotionally isn't as easy as it should be.

On days when Zelda acts particularly confused, I forage for reasons. Lack of food, lack of sleep, lack of stimulation. When, on the heels of his observing that his wife may be declining, Dad casually announces that she is no longer taking her evening medications, I am bedazzled with incomprehension.

Well then, I seethe to myself, *perhaps that might be a good thing for you to look after, Dr. Williams, PhD.*

But then, I chastise myself, *perhaps he is fighting his own quiet battle against low oxygen levels, breathing difficulties, and a challenged circulatory system.*

But then, I chastise myself, perhaps he is fighting his own quiet battle against low oxygen levels, breathing difficulties, and a challenged circulatory system.

The voice in my head sighs as I list all the disabling possibilities. Dad has always been so sharp. And he is very much himself in demeanor and speech. It's hard for me to conceive of his being cognitively challenged, too.

I so need for him to be my partner. To help me captain this rickety craft that has us bobbing about like the three schlubs in the nursery rhyme tub. *Dear God, please give me back my father.* I can't bear to be losing them both.

Again, I muddle through attempts to get everyone on board with the pill-taking schedule even though mutiny threatens with every thump of an unseen swell. When Zelda stays in bed until 11 a.m., any semblance of a schedule is shattered.

There is her morning thyroid pill, which needs an empty stomach to work properly. So I dose her, then offer diversion with the last half-hour of *The Pink Panther Strikes Again*. The tableau of a disguised Peter Sellers in laughing-gas-induced hysterics, as his wax nose melts and droops during a heated tussle with his archenemy, once caused us to crumple into hysterics ourselves. Today it leaves Zelda with an indulgent smile barely tweaking her lips. Tires her enough to send her back to bed. Anticipating a tug-of-war over priorities, I am relieved when she first plows through half an egg salad sandwich, half a glass of milk, and a whole chocolate pecan monster cookie for her ultra-late breakfast.

But a visit from one of Zelda's old friends soon saps me of my sense of relief.

11-22-05: *A call from Anastasia strikes fear in my heart. She wants to drop by. My mind reels with snippets of dialogue from the last time she darkened our door: "My mother is ninety-four and she keeps saying, 'Why am I still here?'" Can the woman not recognize the billowing cloud of gloom that hangs in front of her open mouth?*

When Z echoed back this sentiment, Anastasia lunged ahead: "Yes, my mother has her struggles, too, and you have lived a full life," she droned on, as if speaking to a stiffened corpse in a satin-lined coffin.

Today, before her number nines have even crossed the threshold, she wails, "Oh, my! You're so thin, you're so frail, you're so feeble." Most people couldn't fathom uttering such insensitive drivel in the first place. But Anastasia repeats it. Twice.

I make a batch of blueberry scones because Z thinks we should offer her revered guest freshly baked goods with her tea. Remind myself that I need not monitor every verbal exchange for acceptability. Make tracks to the lower level to iron.

As I cart up pressed shirts to hang in Dad's closet, I overhear Anastasia speaking of assisted care arrangements and rhapsodizing about her mother's nursing home. When Zelda responds, "Well, of course Suz won't be here forever. This is just a stop between jobs for her," the dam that was my clenched teeth gives way to a torrent of pent-up responses, and I hurtle myself into the room.

"Where did you get the idea that I was here temporarily?" I sputter

cheerfully. "This is my career now. Where is all of this coming from?"
Anastasia, the source, explains patiently that Z had asked about her
mother, then lectures about the need to plan for the time when a move
becomes necessary. "IF it becomes necessary," I fire back, forgetting to
be cheerful this time. My turn to lecture. I emphasize that we have our
arrangements in place, family-care arrangements. Duh.

Later, as Z and I walk Anastasia to her car, Z leans on my arm,
unsteady on her feet—not usually a problem for her. Anastasia beams
up at us from the driver's seat as she waves goodbye. But it is a brave,
tortured smile, and tears brim in her eyes.

It's tough for people who don't see Zelda on a daily basis. I get that.
I especially empathize with those who may not have an active faith to
keep them grounded. Who may not feel secure in the knowledge that
there is a purpose behind life's difficulties, that there are opportunities
within them for acting on compassion and leaning on the Lord. And
my own eyes sting for Anastasia, who is saying a long goodbye to a
cherished friend in the only way she knows.

~~~

Holidays. They are anchors in the rough seas of life. Somehow, everything feels more stable, more normal, when we can pull out old tra-
ditions along with the festive centerpiece and follow long-practiced
customs that everyone around the table can appreciate.

11-24-2005: *It's just Dad, Zelda, Corine, Jack, and me for*
Thanksgiving at our house this year. I set the table with Mom's 1950s
china on a maroon, green, and gold plaid tablecloth that picks up the
color scheme of the apple pattern dishware.

Z converses like her old self. Expresses delight over the big platter
of roasted beets, carrots, rutabaga, and turnips, glistening like gems in
their coating of olive oil and sea salt, fresh from the hot oven.

Near disaster when a bird roasted at 450 degrees—as per Gourmet
magazine instructions—yields scorched turkey legs and pink white meat.
Ultimately, a simmering pan of chicken broth salvages enough poultry to

go around, and things go well—aside from Jack and Dad rattling with bronchial phlegm and Corine hobbling around on an injured ankle. Sounds more like a Chevy Chase "Thanksgiving Vacation" scenario now that I lay down the word picture. Didn't feel that way at the time.

But once the anchor is hauled up, an interruption in routine can be, well, interruptive.

11-28-05: *Today, after my four-day absence, the pups do frantic backflips anticipating a nice long walk, and Z meets me at the front door looking glum and stooped and drained.*

"The pills have all run out and need to be refilled, but your papa says it'll be OK to skip a day," she announces, all the while scowling in Dad's direction as if he were the derelict responsible for this mess.

I offer to make a pharmacy run, Dad can't hear what Z is saying to me, and we end up talking about three different situations. Finally, Dad says, "Oh, I think I know what she's referring to. She got up in a fog this morning and took all of her pills at once, and I said it wouldn't hurt for just one day."

Can I summon up a calm Mr. Spock imitation? Of course not. I have already cried out "Oh, no!" when Dad got to the part about taking a whole day's worth of medications in one miscalculated gulp. Now Z robes herself in my flash of anxiety and wears it around the rest of the morning. Apparently, I am incapable of squelching an impulse.

When the tension ebbs, I offer Z a warmed carrot bran muffin. By the time the microwave timer goes off, she is crawling into bed again. I intercept her. Steer her back to the table to sit and eat—her wisp-thin frame like a paper boat under the direction of my guiding hand.

So we wrap up the month with our own brand of The Usual. Dad secludes himself in his computer-illumined man cave. I pick up a stray sock here and there and some Kleenexes scattered about the hall and living room. Pulling out the couch to retrieve a Chloé-gnawed bunch of soggy tissue, I discover Dad's lost hearing aid and become the Heroine of the Moment.

But the moment passes quickly as Zelda announces in melodramatic tones that she came upon a raw potato in the chest freezer. It must have been put there after last Saturday's shopping trip, she speculates, her expression suggesting that she rather wonders whether Papa and I aren't slipping a bit.

My own irrational thoughts crouch in the shadows waiting to gang up on me at day's end when a full night's sleep is my sole and urgent goal. *What am I doing wrong,* I ask myself. I need to be ultra-productive during my waking hours because the disheartening effect of not accomplishing much is far worse than the fatigue of overdoing. Yet the fog of exhaustion that steals in at night brings no relief from insomnia.

And it doesn't seem to matter whether I have exercised and eaten well and taken steps to de-stress. I read myself to a state of grogginess, roll over, turn off the light, and snuggle hopefully into my pillow. But within seconds, like some caffeine-crazed cartoon character, I am bug-eyed awake, alert, and tingling with nervous tension.

> Within seconds, like some caffeine-crazed cartoon character, I am bug-eyed awake, alert, and tingling with nervous tension.

Heavenly Father, please rescue me from this tar pit of self-absorption. I feel tired and fat, and it is so easy to get stuck in the muck of self-reproach.

Not exactly prayerful language, but He always knows what I mean and what I need. And He always knows how to rescue me when I feel this loust.

Chapter 12

Yule Be Fine

Christmas. It's been my favorite holiday ever since I was old enough to take in the exhilarating mood and unique scents and hues of the season. As a youngster, the glamour of houses dressed in multicolored lights and indoor trees glittering with tinsel captivated me—sparkling accents piercing the deep, dark cold of winter nights. But I also sensed early on the reverent awe that infused candlelit services devoted to telling the story of the Christ child's miraculous birth.

Factored in, of course, was the breath-catching anticipation of waking at dawn on December 25th. Of sitting at the top of the stairs with big brother Bob, awaiting the parental go-ahead. Of racing down to pass around colorful, foil-wrapped packages from grandparents, aunts, and uncles miles away. This exercise likely planted in my eager young brain seeds of desire for treasures soon to be revealed.

But I also learned from the gift exchange ritual to take joy in offering others that same opportunity for delight. There were the red plastic dime store earrings shaped like bells that I gave my mother when I was in third grade. An even prouder moment, at age twelve, climaxed weeks of one-dollar layaway deposits on a rhinestone cuff bracelet purchased for her from a real jewelry store.

And decades later, the pleasure of a Christmas morning call from Dad and Zelda phoning from Florida to thank us for the six-gallon tin of holiday goodies we had sent. As Zelda doled out words of gratitude, I could hear Dad in the background in the throes of experiencing it. "Ooh, look at this one!" he declared with childlike glee as he discovered the foot-long pretzel sticks dipped first in caramel, then chocolate, then rolled in chopped pecans. She laughed at the sheer fun of it when, seconds later, he was back at her elbow enthusiastically waving a few red and green saran-wrapped popcorn balls in the air.

That moment changed my attitude toward seasonal baking from casual to committed. I compiled a list of people whose celebrations might be brightened by the gift of homemade goodies—sent across the miles or delivered next door—and launched a recurring mania that persists to this day.

So, while fully devoted to commemorating the Savior's birth as a blessed event so monumental that it determined the timeline of history, and while intent on spreading the glad tidings to a world busily striving to redefine that history, I remain a bit obsessed with my own method of sharing the Good News: the annual preparation of dozens of treats—from caramel corn to seasoned, roasted almonds; from Russian tea cakes to white chocolate macadamia nut cookies; from fantasy fudge to cranberry-orange pecan bark. Thus, through sugar and butter and dark chocolate chips, I immerse myself in the spirit of giving and of witnessing to Hope.

> Between this labor of love and all the extra activities surrounding my favorite holiday, I tend to run myself ragged every yuletide. Realizing this, more sane personalities might gear down a bit.

Between this labor of love and all the extra activities surrounding my favorite holiday, I tend to run myself ragged every yuletide. Realizing this, more sane personalities might gear down a bit, but—as with many a blinding obsession—it's tough for the obsessed to see the burnout coming.

As we enter month twelve of our family-care arrangement, clear, sunny skies redeem early mornings ushered in by two-degree temperatures, and Dad and Zelda are enjoying a qualified sort of cheerfulness. "I want you to know that I am very grateful for my fifth daughter," Zelda announces, producing a boulder-size lump in my throat. And Dad confidently plans a lunch out with a family friend, who stops upstairs to chat with Zelda.

"How *are* you?" Mike asks, leaning in to clasp Zelda's hand with a vigorous pumping gesture.

"Spookier than ever," answers a spunky, well-rested Zelda.

~~~

Several days into my Christmas baking frenzy, I drag myself out of bed and into the bathroom around 9 a.m. A hot, steamy shower always helps. Yet, too often I put it off as if it were a dreaded chore, opting for twenty minutes more to snuggle in the warmth of my plaid flannel Walmart comforter, and then regret that decision. It's a morning shower, for crying out loud. Millions of people take one every day without a second thought. Yet I might lie in bed until 9:40, then throw on some clothes and dash out the front door. All that throwing and dashing. Wears me out just describing it.

Still, the spirit of the season—plus the invigorating effects of shoveling snow off the townhouse deck—makes the days glide by. Until bits of flotsam drift in to slow things down.

12-5-05: *The telephone shrieks an unwelcome wake-up call at 6:45. It's Dad. Z's cold is worse, she feels rotten and can't talk, and could I come straightaway instead of waiting until ten? She already has a doctor's appointment, scheduled for 2 p.m., but so does Dad, at 9 a.m. I say I'll leave at eight, after the worst of the traffic has cleared.*

Then that hot, hairy monkey, Guilt, climbs onto my back and clings with a furious grip. I rummage for something to wear and head over at 7:15 instead. Z is back to sawing logs by the time I arrive.

I do dishes, bake oatmeal pecan muffins, tidy up. As I sit writing Christmas cards, Dad takes off for his appointment and Z staggers out to the kitchen table looking miserable and claiming she has slept "not one minute" the entire night. I entice her to eat a breakfast of scrambled egg, warm muffin, and juice so she can take her cognition pills on a stomach that is not completely empty.

By 11:45, she has made several fitful attempts at a nap and Dad is long since back from his podiatrist visit. Z leaps out of bed and grabs her purse and boots, ready for departure. Just as I convince her that she has plenty of time to rest before her two o'clock appointment, I hear an "oh, oh, oh" from Dad in the living room—followed by several ominous thunks and clunks.

I hightail it around the corner, visions of doing CPR dancing in my head, and find him on his knees on the floor by his chair, a toppled mug by his side, coffee dregs littering the oriental carpet. Explanations quickly follow. It was his left knee—or was it his hip? He isn't quite sure. But something "went out" on him, and he couldn't make it to a standing position after rising from the chair.

No apparent damage done, Dad naps until 12:50, and I now try to convince Z that the time has come for her to get up, get some food in her, and prepare to leave.

Hearing the magic phrase "doctor's appointment," she accepts the urgency. The lure of another warm muffin alongside her leftover chicken leg gets her speedily to the lunch table for enough calories to keep her little engine running through the afternoon.

Not every meal proceeds so smoothly. With my nutritional anxiety expanded to include both Dad and Zelda, I try my best to leave them with a colorful platterful of goodness at the end of each day. Whether they will consume enough of it to make it worth the effort, I can neither control nor predict. I can, however, make a resolute effort to leave that concern behind. To not wear my worry home like a mohair overcoat, only to strip it off impatiently in my own living room. That is not fair to my husband.

~~~

Another reason December was special for me growing up was because it's my birthday month. Dad and Zelda have never failed to honor that occasion and to do so creatively. It might have been Dad giving me the *Bhagavad Gita* in my philosophically confused twenties or a hardcover edition of the first Harry Potter book on my forty-ninth birthday. Or the time they treated Jack and me to dinner at the exclusive Forepaugh's restaurant in Saint Paul. Mini-lights aglow on the winter-bare trees in the courtyard of this impressively restored Victorian mansion, with its signature Beef Wellington and legends of hauntings, made for a magical—as they say—evening.

This year, the magic derives from a night spent with my hubby at the local Taco Bell, then cozied up with the cats at home, sipping choco-coffee and taking a night off from baking. At Dad and Zelda's, the occasion goes almost unnoticed.

12-8-05: *Today is my birthday. I remember how rotten Dad felt a week ago when he thought they had missed it, so when Z asks what day it is, I answer decisively. "I can tell you that easily because today is my birthday, December eighth."*

Z turns this information over in her mind, excuses herself, and pads down the stairs to confer with Papa. Next thing I know, he appears at my side conveying birthday wishes and an apology for not remembering.

I can only think: Why would they remember when their days flow along like a stream of warm maple syrup with nothing but the occasional appointment to set one apart from the other? And with so many emotional and physical distractions vying for their attention?

Still, it is a lonely feeling, realizing that the people who have always rejoiced the most over the observance of your birth are no longer able to make merry.

~~~

Balance. Keeping myself healthy while I encourage Dad and Zelda to do the same. Seems pretty basic. A simple one-apple-two-oranges juggling act. So why does it seem more like tackling rocket science?

While I do best on a Mediterranean diet, I'm constantly adjusting the goals for my daytime companions. And on some extra-hectic days, I end up staring down at a Wendy's Classic Double—no ketchup, extra pickles, Kaiser roll—wondering how my hand came to be wrapped around this thing.

Then there's the ongoing teeter-totter of daily activity. More is better than less, but I can't get inside Dad and Zelda to gauge their need for rest versus their need for movement. To sort out knee-jerk resistance from actual knee problems. To determine just how much encouragement is appropriate.

Zelda naps even more this month because she has a cold with bronchial congestion. She sleeps sitting upright in bed—an antigravity move to open up the sinuses. Peaceful in slumber, she bears the expression and pose of a seriously underweight Buddha, temporarily transported to nirvana.

But the chest cold further blurs her focus. She gets up at 10:45 to use the bathroom, and I intercept her as she is crawling back into bed. "What are we doing?" she asks. I say it's time for her to take some nourishment and her morning pill, and she follows me to the kitchen, not really comprehending why I am saying these things. She eats a poached egg and the small slice of light rye toast sponging up its oozing yolk, takes her Razadyne, and stands in front of the open refrigerator door, staring at the array of tubs and jars. Then she turns toward the colorful card propped on the kitchen counter and studies it as if it were a foreign object.

The strange item is a message from a friend for Zelda's birthday on December 14. The fact that we are co-Sagittarians was once a well-noted and meaningful sign to the ever-seeking Zelda.

But on this, the eighty-second anniversary of her birth, all interest in the zodiac is a mere flicker of a memory.

There is a package from daughter Robin. We slice open the brown corrugated box, pull out the gifts and stuffing, and admire the scented toiletries enclosed in dog-themed wrapping paper. But thirty minutes later Zelda seeks me out in the kitchen, her face contorted with worry.

"Suz, do you know where Rob's package is?" I reconstruct the components—box, contents, and tissue paper padding—and that seems to reassure.

Opening other gifts—handmade bookmarks and a novel from Julie and a shocking pink, sequin-bedazzled Old Navy sweater from Dad—Zelda glumly observes that her birthday is no longer worth celebrating. So I climb into my Pollyanna pinafore long enough to burble that every additional year brings even more reason to celebrate.

Meanwhile, Dad slips away to fetch himself a bag of tacos for lunch, forgetting that I planned to make French dip sandwiches in honor of Zelda's special day. As we sit at the table watching him munch his hard-shells and sip his Leinenkugel Red, Zelda's spirits brighten. She sings nonsense songs for our entertainment, then eats a chocolate cookie bar in place of lunch. So much for balance.

~~~

I will deny having said this if anybody tries to quote me, but when strategizing doesn't work, sometimes trickery does.

12-19-05 A.M.: *The skies are a smoky gray, but at thirtysomething, temperatures are flitting around the winter-balmy range. Fergie and I romp through a long start-of-the-day walk, but Z is her confused-by-morning self until she gets some food, her meds, and a nap after breakfast. My mouth puckers watching her plunge her spoon into a tiny bowl of Total cereal drizzled with chocolate protein drink, then wash that down with four ounces of watery orange juice. After several reminders to take her pills, she totters off to bed.*

When she pops back into the kitchen thirty minutes later, I convince her to eat one of Dad's leftover sausage links but can't talk her into an outdoor walk until she's had another "short snooze." Trusting that this second nap has wiped the memory slate clean, I take shameless advantage: fix her a cup of tomato soup and half a grilled ham and cheese sandwich. She wants to rest again after that mini-meal but instead retrieves a prescription package from the garbage can and shreds its label into tiny pieces for security reasons.

Eventually, we spend ten minutes bundling up, mummy-like, for a less-than-ten-minute walk. But at least she takes in a few filtered gulps of fresh air through her multiple layers of wool. She also manages several stanzas of "Hark the Herald Angels Sing" and a few muffled Otto and Ophelia Squirrel observations along the way.

As for the security issue, Zelda and Dad have a go-around about it every time she catches him recycling junk mail. He contends that name and address don't qualify as "sensitive" because they are easy enough to find in the telephone book. She contends that newspaper advice columns counsel otherwise. She's probably closer to being right on this one, but her credibility has suffered of late—one of many sad by-products of her intermittent paranoia. And so trustworthiness becomes a delicate subject, complicating the guidelines for when to speak up and when to shut up.

12-19-05 P.M.: *Z reaches into a pile of dirty dishes for a mug, and I reflexively call out a caution. She pulls her hand back as if from a live flame and retorts, "I'll just get out of your way."*

I try to explain in three different phrasings that I only wanted to warn her that those are dirty dishes, not clean. She insists that she does know which is which, and I bloat with remorse like a gross, rotund, mud-sucking worm, knowing that she now feels humiliated by my interference. I curl over and clutch my hair in my fists as Z steps briskly into the other room. Why didn't I just let her use the blasted grubby mug?

This time, her hurt from the misunderstanding fades quickly. Soon, I am upright once more, able to proceed through the day with composure.

Regrettably, composure has never been a mainstay of my temperament. And while it's a nice oasis on a cold Monday afternoon, a dose of it doesn't sustain a jaded caretaker through the week as hands cramp from addressing greeting cards for both of our households and frustration piles on top of fatigue. Déjà-vu on steroids.

12-23-05: *When I arrive at ten, Dad has already left to meet Tom McC for breakfast, and Z is standing in the middle of the kitchen looking bewildered. There are no pills in her pill-minder, and she insists she* *hasn't taken any, but the timer is set for the thirty-minute, pre-breakfast waiting period as if the thyroid pill were a done deal. I help her pour a bowl of generic Cocoa Puffs and have her take the Reminyl and thyroid—to heck with it all. I have to try to steer her back on course.*

I realize that everyday things are becoming overwhelming to them. I just wish someone would ask for my help rather than letting a little crack grow into a gaping chasm that sucks those everyday things into it.

Dad later confirms that he probably forgot to fill her pill thingy last night. Says they lost track of her prescription for thyroid, so he's been giving her his! I call the pharmacy and the doctor's office to straighten out this situation and notice that she needs other refills as well.

I realize that everyday things are becoming overwhelming to them. I just wish someone would ask for my help rather than letting a little crack grow into a gaping chasm that sucks those everyday things into it.

Knowing this may not happen, I offer to list all their prescriptions on a blank ledger sheet. Then hope that I can figure out who is taking what—since their doctors aren't always aware—so I can devise a workable system.

Again.

~~~

Everyday things, everyday angst. In my exhausted-to-the-point-of-tears state, discouragement creeps up from behind like a back-alley mugger, leaving me stunned and bereft of incentive. How will Zelda hold her ground if I can't build her up physically? And forget introducing any pleasure into her life—she rejects it. I get irritated with her for no longer trying to regain health or enjoy a birthday or see the less gloomy side of things. Then my eyes take in that stooped, small figure peering at an object as if intensifying her gaze will clear her muddied thinking, and I want to sob and engulf her in protective arms.

Not that she would welcome that last bit, mind you. This new Zelda feels negative emotions intensely but is disinclined to draw strength and comfort from others. I believe she sees herself as a doomed ship, slowly sailing over the lip of a horizon into black nothingness. A Flat Worlder in the most morose sense.

Dad's defense? Intellectual flippancy and cool detachment. Pragmatism to the nth degree. It's a dispiriting dynamic to be caught up in five days a week.

Everyday things, everyday joy. It's way too easy to forget that uplift still hides in all the usual places. I rethink my own lapse into gloom and refocus on the positive.

12-27-05: *Christmas at our place was all grown-ups this year, a quiet afternoon spent with those closest to us—Corine, Paul, Terri. An opportunity for Z to settle serenely into the subdued festivities, to tease her senses with the aroma of standing rib roast and bubbling Yorkshire pudding. A chance for her to verbally revisit beloved travel destinations. To connect with the other Anglophiles at the table in the familiar setting of her favorite spot in our house—the wormwood-paneled sunroom.*

As I enter B and Z's this morning, the breakfast table holds an interesting array of items: one used plastic milk jug filled with water, two magnifying glasses, several paper napkins torn into quarters, four vitamin bottles, a T-shirt on a hanger, dangling from a chair back, an old address book, bulging with miscellaneous clippings and lists, a colander, and a half empty juice glass—or is it half full? It strikes me that this assortment would make a great creative writing assignment. "Class, I want you to work all these objects into a short story plot."

At three o'clock, Barb and Tom stop by with a gift of fancy fudge, so we invite them to stay for tea and sugar cookies. The tray of sweets sitting out of reach on the buffet sends food-mad Chloé into fits of anxiety, whining and vibrating with unquenched longing. Ignored, her anguish-over-not-getting-any-goodies dance soon becomes an anguish-over-not-being-let-out-to-piddle jig, and she marches defiantly to the middle of the room to squat and sprinkle for the benefit of all.

Barb and I spring up simultaneously—she for paper towels and me to scoop Chloé out the front door. The chaos troubles Zelda as she remembers all those years of struggling to house-train the recalcitrant little mutt. But gloriously, she is able to remember . . . all those years of struggling to house-train the recalcitrant little mutt.

~~~

With the wonder of the Nativity account properly reinfused with awe, and with eighty-four dozen cookies and candies duly distributed, I collapse into a less frenetic routine and placidly gaze toward the new year with hopeful eyes.

At month's end, I research specialists for Dad's and Zelda's care, clip interesting new recipes to squeeze into the overstuffed "Christmas Treats" folder, and write out a hefty check to the Discover Card people.

As I overheard my husband quip to one grateful goodie-box recipient, "You should see my chocolate bill this month!" Yes. If we can keep our sense of humor and a refreshed sense of optimism, we'll be fine.

Chapter 13

Resolution Revolution

Optimism: "A disposition or tendency to look on the more favorable side of events or conditions and to expect the most favorable outcome," according to several online dictionaries.

Refreshed sense of optimism: "A transient state of giddy enthusiasm based on temporary detachment from reality," according to my current snarky mood.

Zelda, drained following an eleven-day combined visit from Joan and Julie, and I, grumpy and listless from indulgence in holiday leftovers, are seriously out of sync. Meanwhile, acute stomach cramps keep Dad housebound and miserable. Discovering a saved email in my "Family" folder reminds me that attitude adjustment isn't just a cutesy synonym for Happy Hour. It's a requirement for rational living.

This came from my father in December 2004—the month before I started my formal weekday visits:

Dear Suz,

Thanks for your clarifying memo about our pending arrangement. I like your ideas about how you can help, and I hope that high on your list will be to catch up on the tasks that have not been done since I had to cancel Merry Maids.

Certainly, time you can spend with Zelda will be good stimulation for her. She has diligently worked out ways to keep track of medications, so I have not had to do that. If you'll be able to subtly police them, I will be relieved.

Your presence will also give me time to myself without neglecting Z. Though it sounds selfish, I need to be alone sometimes. Don't mention it to her, but I am starting to see a therapist next week. She knows this, but is uncomfortable about it. I'm not facing anything earthshaking, but look forward to sounding off a little now and then.

I agree to your idea of 'one day at a time.' I am only concerned that you might experience some hardship as a result of your kind efforts on our behalf. We'll all concentrate on taking care of each other.

As I think about how it will be next month, I'm realizing how much tension I've built up trying to cope for both of us here and worrying about not doing it very well. Curbing my impatience is an effort, and I am hard on myself when I slip and make Z unhappy.

I should shut up now and save it for the therapist.

Love,

Dad

Stumbling upon a copy of my own 2004 Christmas letter pushes my expectations a smidge further in the right direction:

Sue Anne is still employed at City Hall but will be making an exciting career change in January when she leaves that position to help out her parents on weekdays in their home. This gives her a more meaningful way to spend her days and allows her father and stepmother to creatively meet their need for assistance while maintaining full independence at their residence of choice. She describes her new role as part cruise director, part housekeeper, part exercise coach, and part private chef and is deliriously happy at the prospect.

Delirium is also a transient state, thankfully. But reviewing that happy declaration gets my feet going forward again. This "one day" no longer overwhelms. Or at least it doesn't incapacitate.

1-3-06: *Relaxing with Z over a warming cup of post-lunch tea, I glance at the oversized erasable wall calendar and gasp. We've missed her regular appointment at the foot clinic because of the New Year holiday. The oversight registers like a blast in the face with a water pistol, and my brain is too sluggish to censor the impulse to blurt out my dismay.*

Hearing this, Z snorts and fumes. Glares at me in disgust. I feel troubled, too, especially knowing that she would never have noticed on her own, would have had no fuel for her churning anger, had I not brainlessly announced the blunder.

By Friday, January 6, all moods have mellowed. With a nod to Julie's parting directive to tend to her mom's weight loss and allow her more autonomy, we renew the vow to lure Zelda's rebelling taste buds out of the house for a good fill-up more often. Today, mega-lunch at Old Country Buffet. Chalk up one minor success. The autonomy thing is a much taller order—easy to censure from a distance, tricky to accomplish in the close-up world of the everyday where she no longer remembers to eat dinner or not put panty hose in the washing machine.

Monday, January 9, Zelda and I proceed to the University of Minnesota for a consultation with a dietician, but her chin is tucked in irate resistance to the plan. Intent on following up on Dr. A's referral, I unthinkingly left Zelda out of the appointment-making arrangements. And she has no memory of her favorite physician's having suggested this trip last . . . September? Who could blame her for forgetting? Or resenting?

But Fate smiles, or perhaps she smirks. We are left to sit in the waiting room for thirty-five minutes past our appointment time while the nutrition clinic staff remains casually unconcerned about a silly little thing called a schedule. Heads held high in righteous indignation, we proclaim our unwillingness to wait any longer and stomp out of the premises. I am stifling a furiously rumbling stomach, Zelda was never on board for the whole undertaking anyway, and Papa awaits us at the townhouse, nursing a severe case of diarrhea.

Speaking of which—and may I not often have occasion to do so—

we arrive home to a gag-inducing mess: a bathtub into which has been dropped poopy PJ bottoms, a feces-filled slipper, two tainted bathroom rugs, and two pairs of soiled underwear. As Dad sleeps the sleep of the innocent, I devote my afternoon to the unlovely cleanup chore ahead of me. Who knew that "taking care of each other" would be so grippingly meaningful. Or that I had the capacity to hold my breath for this long.

~~~~

As the month proceeds, I fear Zelda has lost all awareness of time and date. That her senses in general are muted. I arrive at 10 a.m. and she appears at the door with her coat on her arm even though the Parkinson's support group doesn't meet until two. And although I only come on weekdays, she frequently asks me on a Tuesday or a Wednesday if it is Sunday. Staring midday at a freshly set table, she wonders aloud whether lunch is lunch, or dinner.

At the Parkinson's meeting, she comments that she does better trotting than walking (others here have said they can dance when they can't walk), then murmurs to me that the facilitator talks too fast. At home, she often tells me that I slur my words. Between my father's compromised hearing and Zelda's comprehension challenges, it's a wonder we aren't chasing each other around the table every time someone asks for the saltshaker.

When these anxieties begin to cloud my thinking, I crave that "time to myself" that my father wrote of. Enter the sanity-saving afternoon dog walk.

1-13-06: *A sunlit 3:30 stroll as we hit our thirty-degree high for the* *day. The pups and I round a corner to hear the silken lilt of a tiny voice crying out, "Puppy, puppy!" The source is an adorable, curly-headed three-year-old playing outside with his preteen brother.*

I allow the more trustworthy Chloé enough leash to approach the pair, and the little guy squeals with delight as she gladly accepts his gentle pats. Next, Chloé rises up on her petite hind legs to greet big brother, and at that height little tyke is able to bend over and caress her head, pressing his face beside hers. Precious. Meaningful. A reset button for blurred vision.

~~~

I sensibly take in protein every four hours and put in thirty minutes on my home elliptical trainer most days, but I have blood sugar spasms just thinking about my father's diet. Today, following a corn-muffin breakfast and chocolate-chip-cookie lunch, he makes the post-nap announcement that he is heading out to hunt down a hot fudge sundae.

He also needs exercise even more than Zelda, but subscribes to a brawn-versus-brains dichotomy: either a person is athletic and dumb or he is sedentary and intellectual. Arguing that a valid third option exists is futile. So the point—at this point—remains moot as his overall activity level declines even further.

He may finish breakfast around ten, then settle into his reading chair, where he now falls asleep over the newspaper virtually every morning. If he does make it to his twice-a-week global history class, he comes home, eats lunch, then hits the sack—hard.

I've given up hinting that a physical therapy session might do Dad some good, but Zelda has developed a good rapport with her movement coach—when and if she is in the mood to engage.

1-18-06: *Physical therapy at the Parkinson's center today. Therapist Gwen observes that Z has a good sense of humor, to which Z responds, "I'm not sure if it's humor or lunacy." Her flowing wit is still on tap; her body, however, is rigid and resistant even as she hums a Sousa march* *and goose-steps her way around the therapy mat.*

This morning I observed Z locked into a kneeling position on the edge of her mattress, divested of the agility to catch herself if she were to teeter. Now, I ask her therapist to show us a safe way to get into and out of bed. Z's expression grows cloudy with irritation as Gwen takes her through the movements of a better approach: Seat yourself, then lie on your side, tuck your knees, and roll onto your back before extending your legs. Reverse the routine to get up again.

At home, I try to demonstrate the technique with her for Dad. "I hope you won't be tucking me in tonight," she spits in razor-sharp tones.

Her homework assignment of several stationary exercises and a daily, brisk, three-minute walk goes better. On the most frigid mornings, she churns out an impressive half-mile at the community center running track, humming and dancing her way around the bends in the course.

One cloud-darkened Friday afternoon, Gwen phones. Would Zelda like to participate in a sixty-second promotional television spot? My, what a compliment and an ego boost, think I. Oh dear, I'll look feeble and foolish, thinks Zelda.

> Our roles now overlap and grind against each other, and some meddling, malevolent troll seems to be rewriting the script as we sleep at night. It's very confusing.

"Duty calls," I quip merrily, and eventually she progresses from under-enthused to talking about what she should wear. She also keeps saying, "You should be doing this, Suz." I explain that they need a real patient for authenticity, but this reasoning slithers past her scope of understanding like a water snake evading a predator.

1-23-06: *I wrap up the day trying to explain to Z that the multiple toothbrushes in the upstairs bathroom are actually hers. I may as well be speaking Klingon. She is convinced that all four belong to Pa, who uses the electric toothbrush exclusively. This is one of those goofy minor* *glitches that may sustain itself for a week or go away tomorrow. I'm still not confident that I handle such discussions effectively, even with all this practice.*

As I prepare to leave today, Z is practicing the new approach for getting in and out of bed and stewing about her performance on the tape. I hope she doesn't talk herself out of it.

~~~

My father has changed dramatically since that grateful email passed between his computer and mine thirteen months ago. So has Zelda, of course. And their caretaker. Our roles now overlap and grind against each other, and some meddling, malevolent troll seems to be rewriting the script as we sleep at night. It's very confusing.

All oversight of the daily routine now falls to me—a worrisome situation since I'm not here 24/7. And still I crave control over things that fall outside my influence, such as Dad's and Zelda's states of mind and the gaps in their communication. That their lives may have dwindled to all past and no future is too painful to contemplate. Yet so often I neglect to "save it" for the Supreme Counselor. To lay my concerns at the feet of the only One who sees the full, unobstructed panoramic view. The only One with the power to grant peace to my uneasy soul.

So, on any given day, things may zigzag between really sucky and pretty darned good. But this is a new kind of variety in life—a random, less manageable flux that from time to time flings us, arms waving and legs churning, far off the smoothly paved track onto the mucky shoulder, where we become stuck and frustrated. And this thoroughfare differs in subtle ways from the one we were careening down last January.

1-27-06: *Today is glorious, weather-wise. Clear, sunny skies of an indescribable shade of blue. The ground blanketed in a crisp layer of still-white snow. An intense, wintery nip electrifies the air, which makes for motivated walking—a distinctly arctic pleasure.*

I arrive at the townhouse to find Z drifting about, dazed and con-

fused, trying to confirm what day it is. Dad sits, newspaper in lap, in his reading chair—tuned out, minus hearing aid, and not yet breakfasted.

I ask Z, who seems to be searching for something, whether she has eaten. No. I prepare her oatmeal while Dad, with an air of mild annoyance at my being in his way, sets about to feed himself. My brain expands with exasperation. Is he no longer willing to lift his eyes and take in her suffering—or no longer able?

If she had been guided to take her Reminyl upon rising, maybe she wouldn't still be in a fog at ten-thirty when I finally get her to settle onto a chair and eat some hot cereal.

Even then I must keep prodding while she sits with the little purple capsule in her left hand intent on continuing to eat with her right. She is probably ravenous. Who knows if she ate any dinner last night? She tightens her mouth and punches the air with a clenched fist on my third insistence that she swallow the blasted pill so it can take effect.

As I start out the door with the leashed pups, Dad finally says, "I'll make sure she takes it," thus ending the vicious cycle of her being too confused to take the medicine that helps with her confusion. Even as he asks why she is being so stubborn about it, his trusted, familiar voice carries the authority to get results.

On the "pretty darned good" side of the ledger, Dad dresses for an afternoon of running errands rather than returning to his chair for a nap, and Zelda and I complete the exercises Gwen assigned at the last PT session. For their evening meal, I offer up Italian meat loaf patties, ziti with peas, and eggplant Parmesan, and hope that the enticing aromas are enough to whet appetites and ring mental dinner bells.

But that mucky, off-track shoulder is always there, waiting to suck in its next flailing victim.

1-30-06: *7:20 a.m. I am awake but huddled under the covers trying not to think about how little sleep I got. The telephone rings. It's Z asking if this isn't the day of her foot clinic appointment. I refer her to the large, erasable wall calendar, but she is still befuddled. I ask if she has taken her thyroid pill, but she doesn't know.*

I speak to Dad, ask him to administer her thyroid pill now, so she can eat breakfast sooner and then get the memory meds into her system.

I arrive at the townhouse on this cold, gray morning and find Z sound asleep, her hubby off to meet Tom McC for breakfast, her Reminyl still sitting in the pill dispenser. Twenty-five minutes of hill-climbing with the dogs helps vent my fury, but I get testy with Z when I return and try to make sense of how their morning went awry. (What is wrong with me? How can I possibly aim my displeasure at someone I cherish whose natural mental processes are in disarray?)

As I help Z put together a lunch from leftovers, I discover Friday's meat loaf patties, untouched, in a container in the refrigerator, and again my temples pulsate with anger.

I exact my revenge (on whom? my father? the situation in general?) by purposefully pouring dog food crunchies into a bowl on the shelf in the garage. Ha ha! I will defiantly feed the invading mouse they have living in their garage this winter.

And I accuse them of being irrational.

~~~

I catch myself calling Zelda "Honey" at moments like that anxious and confused 7:20 a.m. phone call. And I become distraught watching her during physical therapy sessions when her expression goes blank and her head trembles with uncertainty, an overprotective guardian hovering at the sidelines, longing to shield her from embarrassment.

With my father it's different. I observe timidly as he drifts back and forth between his former competence and strange new quirks of behavior, and my own mood gets tethered to shifts in his. This has me hopping crazily between extremes. Nothing like setting yourself up for knee-weakening misery.

1-31-06: *Dad and Z are both asleep when I arrive at ten. Z hasn't had her breakfast or morning pills. I make her half an egg salad sandwich. She eats barely half of the half then returns to bed.*

In bits and pieces, I learn that they had a disagreement last night. Not able to advance her side of the argument, Z scooted across the commu-

nal driveway and brought a perplexed neighbor back with her, thinking she could enlist him as her ally in the battle.

Dad, of course, was not happy. And the back-and-forth continues into this morning with Z wanting to press a dead point based on faulty observations.

Having sought solace in sweets the night before, I enter into this setting with a chocolate hangover, gray skies drooping overhead, and not having managed a decent night's sleep myself. An impossibly challenging start to the day.

What is this nonsense? Must an unsatisfactory morning condemn us to a grim afternoon? Time to dig out that cruise director cap and pray for curbed impatience. For a more constructive attitude. And yes, even a bit of resurrected optimism.

Chapter 14

And Cupid Slept

"I wish I had known you when you were first learning to talk," my husband said to me a few months ago. At first, I assumed he meant he would have encouraged me to shut up more often. I do worry about running my mouth. But no, he clarified. He simply would have liked to have been there from the beginning of my formation as a person. Such a loving thought.

Oh, to be privy to what shaped a parent. That, too, is a wish worth entertaining. To have a glimpse of the true inner person who may have since withdrawn under the glare of life's demands and expectations.

My father once clipped an article titled "Penning Your Past" by Ina B. Chadwick and made some preliminary autobiographical notes. I sneak a peek into that file folder, hoping for insights.

In his written recollections, Dad refers to his mother, Dorothy, as Dot. Recounts the time he was five and a babysitter invited friends over to show how smart he was by having him read to them from a magazine. He also claims to remember no particulars about his parents' divorce and describes with veiled emotion his love for a younger brother, Paul, who died prematurely at the peak of his career as a journalist.

His mother was "not religious in any positive way," he divulges, but thought it best if her sons had some spiritual education through the local Methodist church. And his father was a Christian Science proponent until he lost a fourteen-month-old daughter to illness and turned away from all pious promises.

Gradually, Dad's inherited cynicism gelled into a secular dogma in its own right. "The fallacy of strict doctrine went against all I believed about human behavior," he noted, "and the continual exposure of clerical people and men of faith as seducers and mountebanks only made me more cautious."

For the young Milton Hugh, it was Aldous Huxley's *Brave New World* and Omar Khayyam's *The Rubaiyat* that "illuminated the possibilities of a logical and organized future." This is the vocabulary my father uses to express himself. It remains impressive even today as he sometimes labors to make his way in a society he once found ripe with opportunity.

2-1-06: *Just as I am climbing into a tub of hot, sudsy water following a condensed Tae Bo workout, the phone rings. Dad says, "Aren't you coming today?" "Yes," I say, "at my regular time of ten o'clock." "What time is it now?" he asks. "Nine," I reply.*

He goes on to say that he can't leave an extra-confused Z alone this morning while he goes to his global history class, and could I get there as soon as possible? I think longingly of my inviting bubble bath. "OK," I concede. But as I charge out the door minutes later, I find my car buried in a quarter ton of wet snow from the overnight deluge.

When I finally launch myself through the door of the townhouse at 9:48, Dad announces casually, "I decided not to go to class." Behind him, Z stands in the middle of the living room rummaging through her purse, oblivious to my arrival and the doggy-type commotion it has caused.

Chloé barks and howls. Fergie springs and leaps. I feel like a circus ring-master without a riding crop with which to orchestrate some order.

~~~

Where there are family needs, family support is always a blessing. Of course, family support requires family members—a resource I am short on. As those needs multiply at Dad and Zelda's, stepsister Joan's willingness to make the four-hour trip from Wisconsin most weekends redistributes the load nicely.

"I am sorry," I told Zelda yesterday following a tense en route exchange over whether she should skip her foot clinic appointment without notice. "And I know you will be mad at me for insisting that we go." "You're right," she had responded in steely, clipped tones.

Residual tension still hangs between us like soppy laundry on a flaccid clothesline.

Today she begins a sideways dig by observing that I am "very brisk this morning." I explain that I'm just trying to get as much done as possible in the hours I have here.

"This really isn't my house," Zelda continues vaguely. "Do you mind that Joan is coming? Will she get in your way?"

I am delighted, I assure her, that her second-oldest daughter lives close enough to visit often; I love having her here. Zelda then makes ambiguous noises about not being able to do anything. Is she suggesting that her disability hampers her or that I discourage her?

I choke back defensiveness. Offer the firm declaration that I am not here to take anything away from her. Point out the advantages of her having time freed for nourishment, rest, and exercise. Time to focus on getting better.

"What would you like to be doing that you haven't been doing?" I ask with all sincerity. "Vacuuming," she says.

We jointly conclude that a lightweight sweeper would help. Something easier to handle than the ancient, cumbersome contraption taking up space in the furnace room.

Bless her heart. She really doesn't grouse that often, though her frustration must be monstrous. I know I would fail a similar test of temperament.

~~~

With Joan's visit imminent, I bustle to reassemble the living room following a rug shampooing, clear out the refrigerator, clean the bathrooms, wash floors, tidy the clutter. I also sneak into the dryer some just-washed undies that Zelda has hung over the stair railings to save electricity, and put into the trash a rusty old bathroom scale that Dad set aside for Goodwill. But stealth mode always feels disloyal even with practical rationalizations.

To compensate, I double down on efforts to involve Zelda in doable tasks.

2-3-06: *I hand Z two bottles of protein drink and ask her to please put them in the refrigerator. She heads toward the bathroom with them. I remind her that they need to go in the refrigerator in the kitchen. She heads toward the bedroom with them. I repeat—ultra-casually through a theatrical smile—that they belong in the refrigerator in the kitchen.*

Z picks up on the lightness of my tone, shakes her head slowly, and chuckles. I chuckle, too, and the ill will of the past few days dissipates.

By the time I've cajoled Dad into a session of shouting out answers at Alex Trebek, Joan arrives, and the dogs begin to yodel and dance. Z steps out of her room and, in a small, playful voice, calls, "So-o-o-oz. Can you help me?"

I find her in the hallway with the arm of her bathrobe stretched over the width of a wooden hanger, leaving a swath of contorted pink fleece dangling awkwardly to the floor. Soon we enjoy another shared giggle as we gaily select an outfit for her evening with family.

~~~

As welcome as Joan's three-day visits are, I don't like missing a weekday at Dad and Zelda's. The hiccup of my skipped Monday throws Zelda off even more than it does me. When I arrive this Tuesday morning, she is in a tizzy thinking that we are running late for her dental appointment, which is tomorrow. And when I discover that she hasn't had her meds or her breakfast, the black helicopters in my head buzz into action.

> When I discover that she hasn't had her meds or her breakfast, the black helicopters in my head buzz into action.

Dad zips out the back door for his continuing education class the minute I call downstairs to announce my arrival. Does his fleeing represent a "leave it to Suz" mind-set like the recent bathroom mess? Or is there undetected bedlam in his own brain chemistry that jumbles the input?

In a calmer mood I wonder if the challenge just got the better of him this morning. Whether it often does. I picture him as a saddle-raw horse, sometimes twitching and bolting, sometimes enduring the conditions at hand. I also picture my suggesting pastoral counsel and his responding with a tense smile—rejecting as nonsense the very notion of divine assistance.

Meanwhile, Zelda and I quibble over the issue of eating until her plate is empty when she won't finish one egg and one slice of toast. ("That's a lot of food," she complains.)

And I do some twitching of my own as I wait to hear whether my husband will lose his job over his temporary visual impairment.

The strain of competing concerns tightens, anaconda-like, when Zelda insists she cannot keep her Wednesday physical therapy appointment. Getting a clear understanding of her reasons isn't easy. She tells Dad that it hurts to do the exercises. She tells me she has compelling bathroom urges. I cancel the appointment with swelling regret, knowing that she is cutting off outside connections one by one.

Relief comes from pleasurable time spent in the kitchen. Chicken chow mein for their lunch. A make-ahead dinner of pigs in a blanket and baked beans for their evening meal. Setting a Valentine's Day date with her best friends Tom and Barbara pulls Zelda into this happy place with me.

~~~

These days Dad shies away from certain everyday ventures, yet he can be disturbingly free of inhibitions once he is out there. Meanwhile, I twist in the winds of my own cyclonic emotions, and Zelda chimes in at just the right moment.

2-10-06: *Dad has a routine doctor's appointment this morning. At the last minute he asks me to come along and do the driving as well. "I just don't feel as confident going out into the world these days," he says wearily.*

It is more bitter than sweet, this sense of being there to step in and take up the slack for them. It's the detestable context. I can only play this role because they feel less able.

Then, as we exit the doctor's office and file back into the cavernous, tiled hallway, Dad releases a hearty blat of uncontainable flatulence. "We must be walking through a swamp," Zelda observes soberly, eyes forward, poker face intact.

~~~

For the first time in the history of their relationship, there will be no handmade Valentine card from Zelda to Dad this year. The calendar has become an abstract geometric outline for her. Special occasions fade into insignificance along with the blurring of the lines on that meaningless grid. I try to reattach some importance to Tuesday the 14th. A luncheon with friends. The presentation of a fancy-schmancy gourmet menu—corned beef, Gruyere, polenta roulade, and a mixed field greens salad topped with raspberry vinaigrette and roasted pine nuts. Individual molten chocolate lava cakes for dessert.

The stove timer is set. As Zelda sleeps off a bad start to the morning, the main dish is minutes away from coming out of the oven and the guests arrive. A round of raucous doggie hubbub wakes her, and she toddles tentatively into the living room wearing a sock on her right foot and a shoe on her left.

"Wee Willy Winkie," I exclaim with forced cheerfulness, ashamed of my embarrassment on her behalf. She seems not to be sure why we are all gathered here. But these dearest of friends smooth the conversational path through a well-appreciated luncheon, and my fears tiptoe onto the sidelines. Maybe it wasn't foolishness to chase after the Spirit of Valentine's Day Past after all.

~~~

Clearly, "normal" remains a highly subjective concept. And that's before you consider its evolution over an individual lifetime of growing, adjusting, rebelling, and sometimes regressing. I wistfully review the month and see arcs of change. Repeated patterns with embellishments. Reminds me of the Spirograph pictures we churned out in elementary school—elaborate meshed designs that grew progressively complex with each twist of the artist's wrist.

Far too many days now begin with that tiresome guessing game: Has Dad monitored Zelda's morning meal and medications, or did he decide against waking her? While walking the dogs, I grit my teeth against the urge to screech bitter protests into the icy air. *All I ask is that you pay attention to her morning routine and encourage her to eat dinner! I'll do the rest!* I tell myself there are too many unknowns afloat to justify my anger. Still, I want to spew my discontent into the endless heavens.

Zelda's physical ills surface with regularity now. I watch helplessly as she stumbles back to bed after a bathroom trip even though I've insisted that she first take her meds. I ask her to put into words how she feels. "Weak," she offers, and I wonder anew if she's put anything in her stomach since yesterday's lunch. She can't recall. Again, I want to scream. But seeing her lying on the bed—eyes clamped shut, her lower lip aquiver and her shoulders pulled into a rigid curl—I clasp my hands over my face and stifle a sob instead.

> **2-20-06:** *It is 2:45. Both Dad and Zelda have gone back to bed after lunch. We should be sitting in our Parkinson's support group meeting right now, but Z said she didn't feel up to it, and Dad said he was glad to have an excuse not to go. I'm feeling dejected enough to eat a sleeve or two of Oreos. Good thing there isn't any cold milk around.*

I'm feeling dejected enough to eat a sleeve or two of Oreos. Good thing there isn't any cold milk around.

~~~

Dad's failure to nurture and Zelda's succumbing to bodily ailments aren't my only sources of disillusionment. I let myself down, too, as I continually fall short in the Learning from Experience Department. But helpful lessons occasionally spring from the ashes of a repeated mistake.

> **2-23-06:** *Last night I prepared Z's favorite turkey meat loaf patties along with peas and mashed potatoes and gravy. Since I left both plates on the counter, ready to be zapped in the microwave, I didn't bother to tape the usual name labels and warming instructions to the plastic wrap covering them.*
>
> *This morning I find one untouched serving sitting on the top shelf in the refrigerator. I ask Z if she ate dinner last night. She can't remember. I ask Dad. He ate, he explains, and left her plate on the counter, assuming she wasn't hungry yet. When it was still there a few hours later, she told him she ignored it because it didn't have her name on it and nobody told her to eat it.*
>
> *As exasperating as this scenario is, it does push Dad to finally acknowledge that he needs to oversee Z's evening meals. And it pushes me to acknowledge that I can longer assume anything.*

I also acknowledge, regretfully, that these two no longer share their evenings. Or their daily trials. They speak different languages and lack the motivation or the ability or the energy—or perhaps some combination of the three—to work at translation. So the beat goes on, with me playing interpreter, as I deal with the practical so they can remain safely ensconced in their own private worlds.

Zelda and I continue the everyday tugs-of-war over hair-washing (never on a cold day or if we have plans to go outside, and not when she's tired or the furnace isn't blowing hard enough), and exercise (OK, but not very much/ hard/long/far). Meanwhile, I diagnose myself with walking depression, as in walking pneumonia, wherein the patient functions but at a subpar level. Which comes first, I wonder: the melancholy or this gray-tinged view of things? And what can I do to overcome it?

> Which comes first, I wonder: the melancholy or this gray-tinged view of things? And what can I do to overcome it?

2-28-06: *The air is a mild forty degrees and infused with sunshine, yet the ground remains snow-packed and hazardous underfoot. Jack drives me to the mall to log my 3,520 paces. But this is a dreary, neon-assaulted, greasy-edged place. And somehow, striding for wellness past throngs of people snarfing fudge-dipped peanut butter chip cookies and slurping shaved ice beverages in colors never seen in nature does nothing to counter the gravitational tug on my spirits.*

At day's end I tell myself that tomorrow will present a new month and fresh opportunities. Hearing myself sing that tired old refrain sets my pupils rolling toward the roof of my skull, so I kneel at my bedside and invite God into the process of convincing me.

As I close my eyes to sleep, I revisit a satisfying morning shared with Z today as she ate well and completed a full set of floor exercises. At one point she noted that the supine body stretch makes her hip feel strained "where the leg attaches to the cranium." A short pause, then: "No, not the cranium, although it certainly seems that way sometimes."

Recalling her simple, unemotional observation reminds me to take an objective step back and let things be what they are.

Out of bed. Back on my knees. A prayer of gratitude for help with my attitude.

Chapter 15

Hope Bobbles

Some slippery slopes can't be avoided, no matter how diligently you try to map out alternate routes. Thirteen-year-old, hearing-impaired Chloé lags behind when we walk these days. Awakened from slumber, she looks dazed, may even tremble and whimper. I often scoop her up to cradle her in my arms, my heart melting under the warmth of her tiny fleece-covered frame. Such a delicate little creature. I long to protect her by holding her close, to shield her from the younger, heftier Fergie's joyful jitterbugging as we three prepare for a stroll.

When Zelda hears me shuffling dishes, she staggers into the kitchen—still dazed from sleep herself. If only I could lift her above the fray. But the bewildering assault on her well-being comes from such a deeply buried inner source that I can do nothing but wrap her in concern and try to synchronize my pace with hers.

"Let me help. I can do that," Zelda insists as I stoop to unload the dishwasher. And so we fall into our assembly line routine in which she plucks out clean utensils, plates, and glasses and I relay them to their proper places.

Later, as she rests, I discover a neatly zip-locked baggie in the pantry with a stripped-bare chicken leg bone sealed inside. But that's an easy catch. Tracking down the basket of prescription bottles displaced to the living room hutch or her daily pill dispenser mislaid in the crisper drawer of the refrigerator takes a while. Perhaps the nap will clear her mind and erase a lingering indignity she's been nursing for two days.

3-7-06: *Tuesday morning. We are getting back into step following Joan's weekend visit, until Z's convoluted memory of an episode from Monday throws us off our footing.*

Does Z pick up on dips in my mood as I broadcast my vacillating states of mind like an overly enthusiastic deejay? I always have been a lousy poker player.

"Will someone transport me to wherever it is that I take my bath," she had asked, with decisive formality.

"Raise your eyes," I then suggested in response. "Can you look around and tell me where you are?"

At the time, she calmly identified this as home and found her way to the tub. But today she recalls it as a moment of extreme humiliation—with her being the "dumb and ugly" butt of a joke. No line of reasoning dispels her hurt. "Que sera, sera," she says mysteriously, and trips off to lick her wounds.

I turn myself inside out analyzing these smoldering trouble spots. Do I unknowingly plant seeds of disquiet? Does Z pick up on dips in my mood as I broadcast my vacillating states of mind like an overly enthusiastic deejay? I always have been a lousy poker player.

Dinnertime last night was confusing, she tells me later, because "there was this man here" who looked like Dad. Who was this man and how did he know so much about the village and all her friends and her history? Her report makes me furious—not with her but with Dr. S, who changed the memory drug prescription to 24 milligrams, all to be taken with breakfast rather than split into two 12-milligram doses as it has been.

The result? By evening, all beneficial effects have worn off, and she doesn't even know her own husband. Why this fiddling with something that was working? Add to my job description: "standing guard against the disruptive, unintended consequences of the specialists' good intentions."

~~~

Music hath charms to soothe both savage beast and savage breast, assuming both versions of the saying hold true. I invest a few bucks at Cheapo Records, pick out several CDs of traditional hymns, and plug them into Zelda's boom box at lunchtime the next day. As bacon sizzles in the frying pan, she surprises me by agreeing to a few leg exercises at the counter, and Dad returns in high spirits from his world religions class. We munch BLTs—minus the T for Zelda, who can't tolerate raw tomato—and they regale me with anecdotes from Joan's weekend visit. (As I understand it, she walked on water for them. Twice.) After they sample some fresh-baked chocolate-chunk butterscotch bars, Dad and I play boardless Trivial Pursuit. All seems well.

Seems. Until Zelda asks for help packing her bags to go home. Time to slide gently into reorientation mode. My arm around her shoulder, I choose my words with exquisite care and direct her gaze to familiar household landmarks. Still, she bristles. Edges away from her original query. Restates it as needing to pack things to send to daughter Rob. "That's all right with you, isn't it? If I do that?"

Dad tells me to back off, to not try to "be right on this one." And the hurt burrows deep. The angel on my right shoulder urges, "Maybe this is part of what you are supposed to be learning: humility and how to defer to others." But the devil on my left shoulder hisses, "If Joan were here five days a week, she—like we mortals—would slip up too." I think the angel is winning, but it may turn out to be a draw.

Meanwhile, I observe Zelda through her partially opened bedroom door as she bundles unrelated items together and stows them in various drawers and cupboards. She asks me where her "missing" suitcase is. I tell her, then I show her. She doesn't recognize it as hers but seems eager to have it handy. Even speaks of taking a trip to some unidentified destination.

Later, I round up the stashed items and return them to their proper places, hoping to interrupt the process. But then there is the large adult diaper laid open on top of the bedspread as if that will be her receptacle for these necessities should she decide to leave this place—a plan she has threatened to engineer.

I can't purge my brain of this bizarre image of Zelda as the little boy running away from home in a snit—only this time his pole is replaced by an AARP umbrella and his red bandana satchel by an oversized Depends.

~~~

There is often harmony following a discordant day. That rare good night's sleep helps too. For one thing, my intuition is more reliable when I'm rested. Zelda's stormy reactions give way to her kinder instincts in response. Or maybe it's just coincidence. Peace reigns for whatever reason.

As always, lunch out offers a chance to relax and chat. To break free of the drab townhouse walls. It's a nice change of everything—pace, focus, conversation topics, people-watching opportunities.

Zelda and I share a booth bench so my long-legged and sometimes restless father can access the salad, entrée, and dessert counters without obstruction. Dad leaves to refill his coffee mug, and Zelda pats my knee. Says I am "a sweet girl." Reminds me that the benefits of being at her side offset any temporary heaving of the pavement under our feet.

Fissures can always open up, of course. When I miss a day due to a twelve-inch snowfall and overtaxed plowing schedules, I am dumbstruck to learn that Dad let Chloé "go" inside because the weather was so intimidating. My skipped Monday also translates to a long weekend of sporadic meals and leaves a huge question mark hanging over the medication regimen.

3-14-06: *The tenor of this day follows Z's posture, pulled by chronic exhaustion into a stoop. She spends most of her time applying compresses to her irritated eyes and not being able to keep track of the passing hours.*

Dad and I indulge in another post-lunch trivia challenge. Question: What did the original U.S. Eagle symbol hold in its talons? Answer: Thirteen spears and an olive branch. Dad: "And we've been invading countries ever since." Me: "Do you really think that?" Dad, embitterment darkening his face: "Well, the Philippines and Korea and whatever."

A tense silence ripens as bewilderment numbs my brain, paralyzes my tongue. I once shared his views on virtually everything. But I held those views because I heard those views. I hate that being my own person feels like tragic alienation. Only here, only with him.

The mood lightens when Fergie plants herself directly under the pull-out cutting board where I stand mixing, kneading, and rolling out a batch of whole wheat caramel rolls. By the time I slide the buns into the oven to rise, she looks like an Australian shepherd—the floury remnants of my baking efforts having cascaded down to speckle her dark, furry little head, muzzle, and shoulders. It's enough to make all three of us laugh out loud. And that is enough.

~~~

To walk in the other guy's moccasins. It's a noble, if glib, aspiration— not so easy to accomplish when you can't also get inside their skin or their skull and they're not sharing any details.

The ongoing effort to understand why Dad won't step up and give Zelda the help she needs with meds and meals is exhausting. It drags on and on, plunges me into furious inner tirades, then jerks me back again into a shroud of shame for allowing my anger to germinate. Is it time-forged cynicism and God-forsakenness that shape his self-absorption? Or something physical, like the malady that now causes his left foot and ankle to plump up like an overstuffed sausage—yet another detail he chose not to share.

"Oh my gosh, Dad. How long has your leg been swollen like that?" I ask, startled.

"For about a week," he says nonchalantly. "I guess I'll have to call the doctor."

I take things into my own hands and return Zelda to the split Razadyne dosage—with noticeable if not stunning results. I also make that doctor's appointment for Dad, then take five to do my own deep-breathing exercises. Freshly oxygenated, I throw myself into cautiously optimistic meal planning.

3-22-06: *On the 20th, I patched together from the freezer's bounty shrimp in wine sauce on rice with French cut green beans. Last night, beef stew with cheddar biscuits. I also reminded both Dad and Z of the arrangement—individual portions awaiting them on the counter, plated, with a name and heating instructions on each.*

This system seems to work as well as any to improve the odds in the evening meal crapshoot. Tonight I will leave a simmering pot of ham-studded pea soup with chocolate marble cheesecake for a finisher and pray that Z doesn't skip right over the main dish to dessert.

This system seems to work as well as any to improve the odds in the evening meal crapshoot.

~~~

On gray, dismal days it's easy to feel as though prospects are gray and dismal as well. Zelda has always detested the cold, raw misery of a prolonged winter season. Today, she wanders aimlessly, occasionally inquiring, "What should I be doing?"

Dad reports that she now asks for basic orientation information more frequently when they are alone. "One day at a time," he reminds me. I nod in agreement, but we share the secret agony of wondering how many "one days" are ahead and how they will unfold.

3-27-06: *As I stomp the clinging snow off my boots in the entryway, Z approaches—forlorn, bent, and sagging. She puts her arm around my waist, allows me to return her side hug and cradle her head with my free hand. Neither of us has the words, but my whole body aches under the weight of her anguish. Is there anything I could be doing to better equip* *myself for the challenges of this day, or is this as good as it gets?*

Z pulls gently out from under my embrace. She says she will rest, but knowing that Dad has an appointment to have his swollen ankle examined, she climbs out of bed every ten minutes—what time is it now?—and worries over what jacket to wear and which shoes to put on.

It is damp outside, and Z feels the chill. She dons slightly wrinkled navy blue twill slacks, a wool turquoise turtleneck, and two cardigans—a royal blue cable-stitch under an oatmeal beige fisherman's sweater. Her stare locked onto some distant point in space, she slowly buttons the outer sweater halfway up on itself then fills the next few beige buttonholes with blue buttons. But she is warmed and she is dressed.

And she is still able to return to us from her private valleys of desolation and pump pleasure into an ordinary tuna salad day around the lunch table. Today she recites a Eugene Field poem she memorized at age eight to deliver to the women's auxiliary of the Beaver Dam Masonic Lodge.

"The gingham dog and the calico cat, side by side on the table sat. 'Twas something, something, something, and what do you think? Not one or t'other had slept a wink."

She can't remember "'Twas half-past-twelve" to fill in the missing section, but she recalls that she wore a yellow dress with white trim for her performance. She also pulls up partial lyrics to Artie Shaw's "Night Over Shanghai." Then reminds me that my paternal great-grandmother was the first woman chiropractor in Topeka, Kansas, before the turn of that other century, and was a member of the Women's Christian Temperance Union—which strikes us all as ironic for someone perched on a limb of my father's family tree.

~~~

As one grab bag of a day follows another, despair often nibbles at the edges of my awareness. But then I'm probably repeating myself. I tend to do that when I run out of adjectives and similes. Out of non-cliché ways to describe the three-role drama playing out at Dad and Zelda's.

It always throws me when I run out of words. Granted, I lack a fiction writer's skills, but I do have a fiction writer's imagination—not the gift you might assume it to be. Not when most of your "what ifs" culminate in anticipated disaster.

"What if" the guy approaching me on this secluded stretch of hiking trail is a machete-concealing homicidal maniac? "What if" that odd sound I hear coming from the workshop is my husband keeling over from a fatal heart attack in his fifties, like Grandad Williams and Uncle Paul and my brother?

Very seldom does this mental convention play out as "What if" I should find the Publishers Clearing House trio standing at my front door with their photo-op grins, two dozen red roses, and an oversized check for a cool mill?

It's as if a negative neural pathway has carved its way into my brain and my thoughts trickle down the rut of least resistance. I have to forcibly wrench my catastrophic thinking out of the trench and redirect it to higher ground.

I'm not sure how this trend got started. When I was eight or nine my maternal grandmother claimed, "The reason Susie doesn't worry about things is that her faith is so strong." While I enjoyed the special commendation, I'm pretty sure my attitude then had more to do with being well sheltered and, thus, freed to presume that good things would naturally come my way.

> It's hope, after all, that has you whistling as you dress for the day. Hope that puts the hop and skip into your walk to the bus stop.

I suspect the cerebral erosion took place between my seventeenth and thirty-seventh birthdays while I was bumbling through life in the dark. But what about now? Now that I again walk in the Light of faith, why can't I retrain my thinking? Tilt it toward the hopeful?

It's hope, after all, that has you whistling as you dress for the day. Hope that puts the hop and skip into your walk to the bus stop. Hope that strengthens you to sally forth into the unknowns of one of those grab bag days.

So, while I can't "What if" Dad and Zelda into restored youthful vigor, I can at least invest my expectations in the possible, stop trying to envision what's next for us all, and let God fill in the blanks. And I can certainly revel in the enchanting . . .

3-28-06: *I arrive at the townhouse to find Dad in bed and Z up and about—her Razadyne not taken but her thyroid pill already down the hatch. I hook up the dogs for their morning constitutional, anchor their leashes, and then let them out the front door while I tend to Z's morning memory pill.*

By the time I get back to start the walk, Chloé and Fergie are sitting patiently side by side on the top step—their leashes comically tangled around each other, a fallen tree branch, and the ever-stoic concrete St. Francis who stands sentry in Zelda's porch-side veggie patch. I smile a cheek-plumping smile. There is always delight to be found in the antics of these two.

. . . and the promising . . .

3-29-06: *A late lunch of chicken and rice soup and Triscuits. Strains of "In the Garden" flow from the trusty tape deck and Dad's eyes fill with tears. This was his favorite childhood hymn, he recalls, and it touches him in a place he thought was unreachable. I look forward to discovering more windows into this inscrutable human being I have loved for so long, and trust that they will open.*

. . . and the hilarious . . .

3-31-06: *Zelda and I review all four stanzas of Fields's dog versus cat poem, "The Duel," as well as the touching ode to childhood, "Pittypat and Tippytoe," then cheerfully tackle her prescribed exercise routine. During the wall slide, I lean in close to her face, steadying and instructing. "Did I tell you I chew tobacco?" she warns.*

I drink in the moment with a grateful heart and boldly lay plans to be close by when the next ad lib sprouts from the soil of her still-fertile sense of humor. No "What ifs" allowed.

Chapter 16

When the Shoe Doesn't Fit

As spring elbows the dingy crust of remaining snow off to the sidelines, Chloé seems perkier. She jogs along nicely on our walks and hasn't had an indoor "oops" in more than two weeks. She plunges her shaggy little snout into her food bowl to lap up kibble, but when I approach with the leash, her jaw drops, crunchy bits hit the floor, and she trots eagerly to the front door.

So the aging little pup is off my worry list for the moment, but those inevitable Other Things queue up to claim the empty slot. Things like whether Jack should consider cataract surgery this soon after his inner eye bleeding problems. And like the widening breach between Zelda's universe and reality.

4-2-06: *Sunday afternoon. Z calls me at home and asks, "Are my winter pants over there?" I fumble my way through a diplomatic answer and steel myself for tomorrow morning.*

Tomorrow morning reveals that Zelda bought new shoes over the weekend, 8 1/2 wides—a size she has never worn in her life. They will have to be exchanged.

A search for her current tennies—the ones that don't fall off her feet—becomes a scavenger hunt when one shoe turns up in the front hall closet and the other under her bed, a full thirty paces away. Can't imagine how that happened. Well, maybe I can.

I offer to take everyone out to lunch because Jack is here installing their new DVD player, and we are a bit off routine. The impromptu invitation throws Zelda into an angry dither—an angry dither thickened by our insistence that she come along rather than stay home alone. I truly do know better than to argue, but there are practical considerations at play here that her narrowing perspective can't accommodate. She hardens her stance, reluctant to leave the house if she can possibly avoid it.

The three-person consensus prevails, and we settle on a pub-style restaurant where Dad can have a cold beer with his patty melt. But Zelda's unhappiness taints the atmosphere, and I droop with regret for not having planned ahead for a meal at home. Before the gray haze hovering over the female half of our party can infect adjacent diners, we scoot back to the townhouse to take naps or wrap up projects, depending on whether you're on the Home Team or the Visitors.

> Before the gray haze hovering over the female half of our party can infect adjacent diners, we scoot back to the townhouse to take naps or wrap up projects, depending on whether you're on the Home Team or the Visitors.

In the hustle to declutter and cook Dad and Zelda's dinner, I find in the freezer a ceramic coffee cup, solidly frosted over—apparently placed there to preserve a solitary spoonful of Moose Tracks ice cream, now settled like tea dregs at its base. A discouraging finale to a disheartening day.

But as I pack up my tote bag at 5 p.m., Zelda emerges from her bedroom. Teary-eyed and burning with remorse for being contrary about the lunch arrangements, she offers a hug of apology. Heartened again, my world no longer tilts cockeyed on its axis.

~~~

Atlas, his shoulders trembling under the weight of the world, must have shrugged again last night. How else to account for the difference made by seventeen little hours?

4-4-06: *Z confronts me at the front door, an intense scowl etched into her brow. She is adamant that not a single thing should be done until we rush her too-large new shoes back to Walmart. When I say I need to walk the dogs first, she insists "it won't hurt them one bit" to skip that ritual. I warily point out the obvious reasons why they can't postpone their morning tinkle trot, but she digs in her heels. Will not be budged.*

It's a standoff, as Z recalls once missing an opportunity for a refund because she waited too long, and I counter that we have a full ninety days, that I can reasonably delay another half hour.

She stiffens her determination. I have no choice but to return the volley. The dogs will potty, one place or another, and my vote is for outside rather than in.

Finally, she drops her shoulders in resignation. I have tried to be firm, fair, and friendly. I think I have succeeded. But in this environment, success can be short-lived—and irrelevant.

With the oversized new shoes tucked out of sight, the urgency surrounding them also disappears. But a bile-inducing discovery throws light on Zelda's troubled demeanor. When I left the townhouse on Friday evening, there was just enough of the dementia drug on hand to get her through Tuesday, when the new prescription would be ready. Dad assures me that everything got dosed out properly, yet on Monday morning the daily pill-minder is empty and the same few tablets still sit in their original bottle. Is he correct? Did I remember wrong?

I check my notes; I counted right. Zelda has been without her most important medication for two days. How do I approach this with a seemingly coherent father who is telling me everything is on track? What magical language do you use to convince a revered elder that he is gravely mistaken? And what do you do to resolve the problem in spite of him?

You keep on keeping on, I guess.

4-11-06: *Z is better today. Being back on the Razadyne has returned her to us. She still does that thing where she stares at the floor and inquires, "Where are we?" instead of looking around to see. And that other thing, where she asks a question like, "How did we get to this place [the townhouse]?" and then proceeds to answer herself with facts connected to that move.*

But the improvement in her mood shimmers clear and bright with the quick dissipation of a misunderstanding over why she called Joan long distance to ask where her underwear went. Thankfully, we move easily along to other topics.

~~~

We will certainly continue to face the same evolving problems. To watch with intense interest as they change shape like a drop of red food coloring in undisturbed water. But we will do it together. What more could I wish for? No matter the permutations in personality and behavior, these two are mine to cherish unreservedly. God put them here, and He put me next to them. Their predicament is not an impasse to peace but a passageway. A shadowed valley offering breaking light, just when you need it.

4-14-06: *The lonely sight of Z milling about the dark, deserted kitchen stirs my soul. And then I discover, with a painful stab to the heart, that she had laid a place at the table for me at last night's dinner. I can't begin to set out in words the sense of perfected empathy that fills me at moments like this.*

She pours a bowl of puffed cereal, but I persuade her to let me cook something for her—two cream-scrambled eggs and toast and juice. The sight of her savoring a meal floods me with gratification—until she pushes me off my chair with the claim that she "shakes worse" when I am here. Probably not accurate. Unsettling nonetheless.

Dirty dishes tended to, Z announces that she wants a bath. Ahh. One thorny subject circumvented. A wave of relief washes away the layer of crusty tension the shaking comment left in its wake as—elbows linked—

we seek out the tub together.

Still a bit unsteady and disoriented, asking what the next step might be, she allows me to help with back-scrubbing and shampooing. As we select a fresh set of clothes to step into, Z is lamblike and docile. One hundred percent her familiar sweet self. What a blessing.

~~~

2-21-72

Mary, My Love:

It's Monday night and 11:30 p.m. I've prepared the income tax, called Paul, done my laundry, hidden the dirty dishes, and straightened up the place.

I also had a very productive day at the office. I feel so confident when I've been with you that I can accomplish anything.

I love you unconditionally, and I want to be with you now. But I'll sweat it out and wait a few days more. Soon we can look at each other every day and go on talking till we get caught up on each other. We'll never quit talking, though.

You make the difference.

Your constant love,

Bill

One of the personal projects I've been neglecting is a grand scheme to collect snippets of advice from people my age or older who have raised children to adulthood. Would that not be an invaluable asset for future generations—a compendium of insights from those who have seen more and done more and learned the hard lessons? I've titled the project "Advise With Consent." Should fly off the shelves, right?

Maybe I've just had more failures to learn from than most, but I'm discovering that few of my contacts are as eager to share their dazzling insights as I am. I champ at that bit; others shy from it.

Surely my psychologist father, who watched his two children muddle through plenty of questionable life choices, has some sage conclusions to contribute. I invite Dad and Zelda to chime in on the topic,

181

hoping this will give them common ground for discussion, and praying that "never" hasn't wormed its way in to nullify Dad's courtship pledge.

Regrettably, my father has seldom shown interest in retrospection. I've had to pry from him the few, skimpy nostalgic tidbits he's shared over the years. Backward glances reside in a rusty, intentionally locked compartment in his mental record-keeping system. And in an accidentally misplaced file in Zelda's. She's not quite sure what she knows or doesn't know about parenting.

They ain't talkin', and there will be no revealing glimpses into their opinions on the subject. At least they still look at each other every day. Sort of.

So the ploy dead-ends. Skips right over climax to dénouement. They ain't talkin', and there will be no revealing glimpses into their opinions on the subject. At least they still look at each other every day. Sort of.

~~~

Today Dad and Zelda are at her personal physician's office—a mission from which I am banned, presumably so that Zelda can cling to a bit of autonomy in at least this one relationship in her life.

In a detailed note to the doctor, I describe those current aspects of our situation that I know neither Dad, who doesn't enter the inner sanctum with his forgetful wife, nor Zelda will think to mention. Not-so-little things. Like the fact that the neurologist casually tosses around the possibility of progressive supranuclear palsy and that Zelda has spent five sessions with a physical therapist.

Harder to summarize is the medication chaos. Dad has a habit of cutting Zelda's half-dose pills in two, one at a time, and then putting both pieces into the daily medication dispenser because he doesn't want the loose half tumbling around in the bottle of whole pills, making it hard to fish out. This, of course, is a recipe for screwups when it comes time to take the day's dose.

I recently got his permission to cut all the pills in half at once so he doesn't have to go to the trouble. Or risk causing trouble. But how many times has one of us looked into the little compartment for pill number three, assumed that it hadn't been taken because there was still a half-pill sitting there, then doubled up by accident? My amply padded bones tremble at the thought.

More puzzling is the huge surplus of thyroid pills. Puzzling, until I determine that Dad stopped taking his Synthroid months ago. His doctor then increased his dosage based on erroneous blood test results, thinking the former dose—which he'd quit taking—wasn't sufficient to keep his TSH level up.

Stronger prescription in hand, Dad then passed his old pills on to Zelda (they are twice her dosage), whose pharmacy records show she hasn't requested a refill since early December. Out with the tiniest paring knife to slice all of these secondhand tablets in half, but the unsettled issue of how long they have both been off their proper doses chafes. To quote the inimitable Charlie Brown: AAUGH!

The same unsuspecting doctor—who obviously doesn't ask enough questions—prescribes Dad potent sleeping pills because Dad complains that he wakes often during the night. Couldn't possibly be those unreported two-hour naps that are disturbing his nighttime sleeping patterns, eh, Doc?

And all of this is happening on my so-called watch. How much more of it goes on in elderly households that don't have an outside set of eyes on site to ferret out glitches? Beyond alarming.

With so many unknowns fading in and out against the background of our own miniature gestalt, I covet help from a trustworthy expert. Good luck finding one. What we really need is a healthcare professional who deals exclusively with dementia to coordinate Zelda's treatment, and possibly even to put the specialists in communication with each other. A professional able to personalize the plan for each of the erstwhile lovebirds who inhabit this nest.

As for Zelda's psychological state, I keep rereading the literature. I know not to dispute a delusional observation; backing off gradually becomes second nature. It's the gray areas that present the greatest challenge. The in-between periods when she is somewhat in touch but still not able to properly connect the links in her chain of experience. That's when having someone confirm her limitations would be helpful.

> Perhaps I seek the unattainable. It certainly wouldn't be the first time. But I am capable of tuning in to teachable moments.

Perhaps I seek the unattainable. It certainly wouldn't be the first time. But I am capable of tuning in to teachable moments.

Both the enjoyable . . .

4-19-06: *At lunch today, Z sits in her regular chair but asks if someone else will be claiming it from her, as if she thinks she doesn't belong there. I indulge in a composure-gathering pause then coolly inquire as to who might be poised to take it from her. She flashes a little smirk of acknowledgment that she's said something off the wall. "The King," says she. "Or the Queen," say I, with a nod of my head indicating her to be that personage. "Or the court jester," she corrects, self-effacing to a fault.*

. . . and the moving.

4-24-06: *Before I leave for the day, Z wants me to show her how to work the CD player Barb McC gave her and asks for diagrammed instructions. As I try in vain to guide her through the four-step process, she wags her head dejectedly and her voice cracks. "Oh, Suz. I am really losing it."*

I encircle her shoulder with my arm. She accepts the half-hug. I tell her that I don't think she is doing poorly, that she is holding her own—which is true. Whatever it means.

I remind her that I love her very much, and she says she loves me back. We will just have to love each other past the rough spots, I pledge, and she agrees that's a fine way to proceed.

Love. It ranks smack dab in the middle of Abraham Maslow's hierarchy of needs pyramid—a theory of personality from Psych 101 that made enough sense to stick in my mind. The idea is that once the basic physical and psychological requirements are met—the needs for food and drink, and for the security of a safe environment—a sense of belonging and feeling loved becomes essential to one's well-being. Having established caring relationships, the levels layer up neatly as you climb onto the rung labeled "esteem" and from there stretch upward to attain "self-actualization," or the realization of your potential.

So rational and predictable and tidy. But no textbook discussions about stumbling back down those pretty little multicolored steps can prepare you for having the diagram collapse under your feet.

Esteem flees along with independence, and it's nigh on impossible to actualize The Self when you can't always recognize it from one day to another (Zelda) or program it the way you always have (Dad). At this confusing juncture, a flash of mindfulness from either of them provides a leg up.

4-28-06: *As the day ends, I note that trash carried downstairs by Z is likely to end up almost anywhere—in Dad's office recycling bin, in the tote basket by the back door, in the big red bucket of sidewalk salt in the garage. Even occasionally in the garbage can.*

Z catches me retrieving a rubbish bag misplaced in the kitchen pantry and closes her eyes in disgust. I sense that her disgust radiates to me as well, as the one who recovers these errant bundles.

"Let's pray," I suggest in self-defense, closing my hands around hers. She nods in solemn agreement. I bow my head, assembling my thoughts, but she preempts me by speaking her own.

"Lord, forgive me my sins, and help me to do better."

Short. Sweet. And universally applicable.

Her earnest plea reminds me once again that God is the knowable constant here. He makes the difference, grants us just what we need just when we need it. And He doesn't care where we are on Maslow's stupid chart.

Chapter 17

Man Proposes,
God Disposes

A packed-to-the-gills '62 Chevy Impala station wagon. That's how Dad and Zelda transported her worldly possessions from Michigan to Minnesota shortly after they vowed "I do" on June 20, 1972. On board were Zelda's well-used manual typewriter and a family treasure—Phoebe, the Terrier Terrifico.

Back then, Zelda liked to joke that the car, the Smith Corona, and the dog were the three main reasons Dad proposed to her. Also back then, finances were wobbly for the newlyweds. The groom's one-man management consultancy was just starting to achieve lift while his bride's teaching résumé got swallowed up in the Twin Cities' flooded education market.

Eventually Dad's private practice took flight while Zelda persevered with creative fill-in jobs and resource conservation. They invested wisely, saved regularly, and prepared well for their future needs. Financial responsibility. It's an objective many in their generation took seriously in spite of post-war commercial campaigns to ensnare them in long-term "have-it-today, pay-for-it tomorrow" schemes.

Three decades down the road, their superb planning lightens the burden of concern shouldered by those of us who care about them.

Awareness of this fills me with gratitude, knowing that some less advantaged souls must weigh a trip to the barber against an outing to McDonald's.

5-1-06: With me as chauffeur, we drive to Great Clips so Dad can get a haircut. When I suggest that Z could get a trim, too, as long as we're going, she responds, "Did I look so bad that you had to take me in to be worked on?" (Note to self: Do not attempt to answer such questions.)

I then lure them next door to the exercise equipment store—a desperate contrivance to help steer Dad toward improved blood flow to his brain and heart and legs. But he feels so sapped from this very deficiency that he flinches at the suggestion of a stationary bike, eyes me as if I may have lost my marbles for even bringing it up.

I console myself by making friends with Boo Boo—the placid gray tabby who reigns over the showroom floor from his personal fur-embedded armchair—then run to close the gap between myself and Dad as he arduously makes his way to the exit, slowed by uncooperative lower limbs.

~~~

As Ms. Roseannadanna was fond of saying, "It's always something." My husband's brother has been forced out of his workplace by a union strike, and the cantankerous disposal at Dad and Zelda's has apparently convinced the kitchen faucet to join it in a strike of their own.

The upside is that brother-in-law Paul is free to take on the nasty plumbing challenge. He mostly keeps his nose to the job at hand, but the presence of another vigorous human being enlivens what have become lackluster days of sameness and inactivity at the townhouse. With a smidgeon of luck, his congenial presence may also stimulate its residents.

5-3-06: I arrive at B and Z's at ten to find the folks heating up hot dog buns for breakfast. After some back-and-forth—is the bun in the frying pan Papa's, or is the already toasted one in the microwave his?—I convince Z to add a meatball for protein. Dad opts for a slathering of peanut butter.

Paul is coming, I remind them, ignoring the perplexed expressions that stare back at me. And the announcement a few hours later that lunch is ready stirs up another cycle of confusion.

I invite our guest to join us for grilled ham and cheese sandwiches, then try to round up both parents at the same time. Z finally completes her bathroom mission and adjusts her bearings only to have Dad turn around in mid-stride toward the table and rush off to the loo himself, calling over his shoulder, "Go ahead without me."

By this time, Z has wandered into the living room and Chloé is barking to go out. As I explain the delay to Paul, I notice Dad traipsing back and forth between the bedroom and bathroom with varying degrees of urgency and—I quickly realize—varying degrees of undress.

By round trip number four, his flapping shirttail confirms that Dad is now down to only his oxford cloth button-down. This is a scene straight from the mind of Mel Brooks. I swallow a nervous titter and focus on what Paul is saying. Maybe he'll assume my wide-eyed expression is merely polite interest, not a stupefied reaction to the bizarre events playing out ten feet behind him.

With the household pared down to three again, my father continues to behave oddly. I interrupt a round of after-lunch trivia to run an errand one Friday and find him asleep at the table when I return. Nodding and bobbing, he insists he's fine. Wants to get on with the game. But a few questions later, his head droops and his words slur as he tries to answer questions he has barely heard.

I suggest a nap before he topples off the chair and onto the floor. "Getting down there wouldn't be so hard, but getting you up might be!" He agrees with a chuckle as he teeters off to bed, and I occupy myself with kitchen therapy: Lentil Soup for the Psyche?

At home, the tension of wondering what might be happening right in front of my eyes propels me out of bed at 3:30 a.m. I sit at the dining room table, spilling onto paper a litany of fermenting concerns about Dad. The cascade gushes, like raging torrents from a dynamite-blasted dam: fading interest in outside activities, abnormal sleeping patterns, failure to take medications consistently, bowel irregularities, poor eating habits, lack of exercise, poor mobility, dulled mental functioning, changes in personality.

Unloading brings some relief and eases me past my own wakefulness. But before I can decide which doctor to consult, new thorns sprout to entangle us. Blessedly unaware, Zelda burrows deeper into her own tiny self-contained thicket.

5-8-06: *More morning chaos. Dad apparently spilled a giant mug of coffee and then threw a few paper towels down, leaving puddles everywhere beyond the boundaries of those absorbent quilted islands. Every time I move anything on the countertop, I find another pool of sable brown liquid. So we add yet another description under the heading "status quo" here at unit 2412.*

Under the old definition, I find a pan lid in the refrigerator, a meatball in the lentil soup, and the empty meatball container in the freezer with the lid neatly in place. Oh, and—big surprise—Z is again missing her evening meds.

Today she is not only confused about where she is but also morbidly depressed about her confusion. I strain to sound matter-of-fact. Explain to her that she doesn't need to get a ride to her house because she is at her house. That I haven't taken her "There's No Place Like Home" needlepoint, because the wall it hangs on is her wall. When I turn around from my pillow-fluffing to see her weeping quietly, arms dangling at her sides, my heart wants to rupture within my chest.

Dad once again appears oblivious. Shakes his head as if I were relating an unpleasant report from the nightly news as I tell him of her predicament. Now I am confused and depressed.

~~~

Rewind to June 22, 1997. Dozens of people come together to celebrate the twenty-fifth wedding anniversary that Zelda is so grateful to have reached. In honor of the occasion, I compose a mock newspaper to present to party guests. It concludes:

> So it is that Bill and Mary (Zelda) Williams look ahead to a rich future surrounded by cherished friends and loving family, warmed by memories of their second-chance years together, and ignited always by their yearning for new adventures in living and learning.

I assume the desire for loved ones to sail smoothly through their final days sharp-witted and in reasonably good health is universal. You occasionally hear about the centenarian who walks four miles each morning, lives independently, reads voraciously, and still has a fulltime job. These paragons of successful aging express an enduring zest for life. When overwhelming physical ills snuff out that igniting spark and the cold reality of cognitive decline replaces warming memories, what then?

If Dad were more able-bodied, we could co-manage this household. As things are, I can hardly bear to watch him walk twenty feet; his face grows ashen with the effort. But he won't give voice to his torment.

If Zelda's focus were more within her control, we might be able to establish a comforting routine that would offer security and help her stay acclimated. But she can't give voice to her needs.

I have to speak for them.

5-16-06: *Making morning rounds at the townhouse, I find a pair of shoes under the end table, Z's culottes spread over the back of the couch, Dad's cardigan hanging from the seat of the cane-backed chair, and Z's robe draping the coffee table. It's as if the furniture got frisky last night and decided to play "dress up" while everyone was sleeping.*

After lunch, I approach Dad as he dozes in the living room, kneel beside his chair, and rest my hand on his arm. When his eyes flutter open, I lock onto them with mine and say, "I am very worried about you." He smiles groggily and mumbles a few words of dismissal. At least I've sown the seed. Now, the wait to see if it will take root.

It's as if the furniture got frisky last night and decided to play "dress up" while everyone was sleeping.

Tension building inside me like a slowly inflating water balloon, busy-work keeps me from bursting while I bide my time. Replace light bulbs, administer Zelda's eye drops, direct her breathing exercises, and try to keep priorities in order—for all of us.

When Chloé has one of her mild seizures at my feet at the lunch table, I scoop her up and cuddle her until the spasms pass. Knowing Zelda's tenderheartedness, I describe the pup's situation to her. Try to pull her into the comforting effort. She responds with a cursory "Awww"—but quickly launches into the complaint that her waistband feels tight when she lays down. I reluctantly settle the becalmed pup into her doggie blanket and set off to investigate The Big Problem—a case of droopy drawers having been hitched up in order to stay put during a nap.

A few hours later, after she has eaten lunch and then forgotten that she has eaten lunch, and Dad has returned from the dentist to beeline it to bed and collapse into unconsciousness, Zelda settles her gaze on the painting of a British country house that hangs across from her bed. "Suz," she says in warm and caring tones, "I hope you and Jack get to go to England someday." Her compassion revived, I clutch at the wish that she would reach out to her beloved Bill, who insists on suffering in silence.

Until the silence is broken by insistent necessity.

5-17-06: *I arrive today to find Pa breakfasting on the two complementary cookies he got at his dental appointment yesterday. Unattended household paperwork piles up on his desk and dresser, and his taut features reveal how rotten he feels—rotten enough to ask me to call for a* *doctor's appointment.*

As usual, the office can't fit him in for a week. But when the scheduling clerk asks the reason for our visit, I at least get to unload all of those items from my wee hours worry list. Bet she's sorry she asked.

~~~

My beleaguered guardian angels must tire of hearing me kvetch. And on good days, I can handle the dim lighting, the sluggish pace, the uninspiring decor. On good days, I will slap a coat of peach paint on the dingy beige living room wall and find joy in the small services I am able to provide. These, however, are not particularly good days.

My mood is all the more bleak because we've been stalled under a stubborn dark cloud for more than two weeks, with no spots of light discourse breaking through the grayness. No longer do either of my charges leave the house for pleasurable pursuits. Dad is virtually chairbound. And even with continual prodding, Zelda is so distracted that it takes fifteen minutes to get a few pills down her. She also has decided that she has run out of money and, therefore, cannot purchase a new pair of slacks that fit her.

5-18-06: *I walk the dogs, then walk them again—for my benefit, not theirs—and pray, pray, pray for serenity. For the guidance to make use of my gifts to improve our plight. To even know what those gifts might be.*

I sneak out to Walmart and buy Zelda a pair of size two pearly gray pull-on pants. She steps into them and immediately pronounces them too small. I assess the situation and discover she has rolled the waistband in the back, causing it to feel tight. With a simple but impressive flick of the wrist, I, Ms. Wizard, resolve the dilemma. Z is awed. Perhaps I have discovered one of my gifts.

Chapter 18

Medical Muddles and Other Delights

Life is full of potholes, and it's easy to feel like you're hopelessly stuck in one—sucked in by circumstance, powerless to extricate yourself. I can almost hear my father advising that there's no profit in accepting the role of victim. That the only way to move forward is to put one foot in front of the other.

I haul my blender over to the townhouse and whir up two strawberry-banana protein powder smoothies, which both recipients consume with unexpected enthusiasm. No sooner do I punch the air overhead in self-congratulation than Dad announces that he can't wait until next week; he needs to see Dr. E today. He's having trouble breathing, and his inhaler offers no relief.

That's the thing about potholes. While you're bent over, shoveling gravel into the one you just clambered out of, another ankle-spraining rut may be opening up right behind you.

5-19-06: *We arrive at the doctor's office around 11:30. The nurse moves quickly to measure Dad's blood pressure, temperature, and weight, as Z and I traipse close on her heels. I read the number on the scale and my own breath fails me. Up thirty pounds from his visit last month? How can this possibly be?*

Excessive fluid buildup, the doctor explains, as he exposes his patient's grotesquely distended stomach. ("I thought my waistband was getting a little tight," declares my father, the maestro of understatement.) To further illustrate, Dr. E presses gently on Dad's calf, leaving fingertip-shaped impressions, as if the flesh has turned to memory foam.

And the blindsiding revelations keep coming. Though he had never hinted that he felt too weak to shower, today Dad tells the doctor he stopped bathing a few weeks ago. This neglect has caused angry red patches of fungal infection to blossom in crevices and body folds.

I indulge in thirty seconds of self-flagellation: He's barely been functioning; I should have known there was something appallingly wrong. I should have pressed harder for him to make an appointment weeks ago. Then I tune back in.

The bottom line, announces Dr. E: immediate hospitalization.

That is, of course, "immediate" in Medical Time, which isn't even a distant cousin of any other system known to mankind. I skip down to the coffee shop to fetch cellophane-wrapped sandwiches made with synthetic cheese, walk Zelda up and down the sage-green hallways, make numerous appeals to the receptionist for an updated ETD, and take note of the bizarre and changing assortment of individuals flowing through the clinic's afternoon scheduling cycle—all the while feeling like part of a time-lapse sequence in a depressing black-and-white movie.

Meanwhile, my quite ill father is left sitting in a wheelchair, trying to get interested in a mutilated, three-month-old copy of *Newsweek*. Twitching with impatience, I finally rouse the receptionist, who rouses a nurse, who leads us to an empty exam room where he can at least lay down and rest his fluid-engorged body, for crying out loud.

Three and a half hours after his appointment ended, we escape the doctor's waiting room. Drained but intact, we hightail ourselves to the hospital—Dad towing a corroded portable oxygen tank and me pushing him along in a grossly oversized wheelchair with lumpy tires.

Getting the patient into and out of his Toyota Sienna with the tank tethered to him is the easy part, we soon learn, since the person responsible for signage for St. Festus Hospital obviously has a malicious streak. Two full revolutions around the parking lot leave us no better informed as to the location of the blasted admissions entrance than if we had just been dropped onto this planet from a Martian space vehicle.

I finally pull up to the closest of many doors marked "Entrance," get Dad settled, shuffling and wheezing, into yet another rickety wheelchair, and begin frantically flagging down passing hospital personnel. The "OB/GYN" sign glowering down at us in neon orange does not bode well for our chances of being anywhere remotely proximate to where we want to be, but I forge ahead regardless.

The staff members I encounter are no help. They seem as confused by the layout of the building they work in daily as we first-timers. In desperation, I ask someone to direct me to the courtesy phone, and the gentleman politely points out that I'm practically knocking it off the hook with my left arm, with which I am now gesticulating wildly. "Thank you," I say coolly, trying to convey both a shade of humility and a scrap of dignity.

"You'll have to pull your car up to the south entrance [we have entered the east entrance] and check in at Guest Services," intones the adenoidally challenged voice at the other end of my SOS call. Guest, my foot; we're feeling more like lepers on the unenlightened streets of Calcutta than honored anybodies.

"How about this?" I respond, no longer interested in any semblance of humility or dignity. "My father is in a wheelchair close to the east entry door, and he is in distress. So how about you send someone over here to take us where we need to be because there is no possible way for us to navigate this labyrinth without a GPS system."

Bingo. We have an admissions supervisor on the other end of the line, saying, "What do you mean by *distress*?" I have unwittingly tapped into the red flag vocabulary of Liability Issues, which speeds things up nicely.

"Well, he can't walk very well, and he can't breathe very well, and we have spent the past four hours sitting in his physician's waiting room hoping to be admitted to this medical paradise, so he is very uncomfortable."

Madame Supervisor agrees to send someone over immediately. Meanwhile, Dad reminds me that I have left Zelda sitting in a running vehicle with the keys in it and the doors unlocked while I practice my assertiveness skills in the dimly lit hallway of the wrong wing of the hospital. Now I abandon him, race back to the van, and try to park somewhere near the hallowed portal where one is actually supposed to enter this rat's maze of hallways and unlabeled elevator banks.

Once parked, I drag poor Zelda toward where I hope Dad still sits in his wheelchair. Midway there, she leans against the wall, drained by this demanding day, and I flip-flop the remaining block-long expanse in my not-made-for-running sandals.

As instructed, we three haltingly navigate our way back to the east entrance, where a very nice lady named Tammy waits for us, and things start to get better. I think. Until I see Dad's room.

~~~

Five West is a cramped, dilapidated section of the hospital megacomplex. This tiny room will now have two patients crowded into it—the first of whom has an armed police officer soberly standing guard over him. Forever endearing myself to the individuals who now hold my father's life in their hands, I blurt out, "Oh, Zelda, what have we gotten into here?" This statement accomplishes two things: It does wonders for Zelda's delicate state of mind and establishes me as the personification of the difficult relative so universally beloved by hospital employees.

does wonders for Zelda's delicate state of mind and establishes me as the personification of the difficult relative so universally beloved by hospital employees.

The nurses are kind and helpful, anyway—possibly cutting me some slack, perhaps aware of how trying our afternoon has been. A free parking pass smooths things further, and we leave dear Papa in what seem to be caring and competent hands.

Back at the townhouse, Zelda and I pick at leftover meatloaf and scalloped potatoes, and she is fast asleep by 7:30 p.m. Certainly, I too will sail smoothly into slumber land after the energy-sapping day we've had. But tell that to my racing thoughts and tension-contracted limbs as I lay awake on the lower level futon until 2 a.m., having read myself bleary-eyed.

Independent of my will, my mind projects graphic portraits of Dad and Zelda in their heightened states of vulnerability: Zelda, her trembling lower lip and the hand vibration that worsens under stress lending an aura of innocence as she focuses intently on the task before her—unwrapping her deli sandwich or trying to remember where she put her Kleenex; Dad, pale and bloated and struggling for air. Too weak to transfer himself from the wheelchair to the hospital bed, yet still bantering with the hospital staff. My throat clenches at the powerful images I can't dismiss.

But this grip of emotion isn't fear. It's more like a rippling wave of tenderness. A deep sense of affection and an even deeper sense of longing to be able to do more. In its wake gather twinges of regret as I think of how annoyed I've been with my father for his seeming disinterest, how critical in my private assessments of his motives, never once envisioning how indescribably miserable he must have been.

~~~

5-20-06: *Saturday, the Morning After. I awaken too early and find that Chloé has spent the entire night curled up tight at my side and Fergie has now joined us for a cuddle.*

Staring at the textured ceiling above my foldout bed, I review last night's conversation with the head nurse, who described completed tests, prospective turnarounds for results, current treatment regimens. And during my groggy mental replay of yesterday's phone calls to Barb and Tom, Joan, and Deb, a blessed relapse into sleep overtakes me like a cloud of ether.

9:40 a.m. As I lie in bed planning the day as if I actually have some control over it, the phone rings. It's Dad. He wants me to come and take him home. Says he'll tell me about it when I get there. Startled into full alertness, my lips mechanically form the right questions as my brain scrambles at the notion of trying to pull off a reversal of yesterday's onerous trip.

It's because "they aren't doing anything or telling me anything, and I haven't even talked to a doctor yet," he explains. Three deep breaths—mine, not his.

"Well, I had a long conversation with the nurse in charge last night, and she was very helpful. Why don't I see if I can get her to come in and answer your questions? Then, if you still think that you want to come home, we can discuss options." Dad agrees to this strategy.

You get a good taste of aggravation trying to meld medical protocols with the multifaceted element of the Body in the Bed—who also happens to be a human being who is probably not experiencing the ideal synthesis of high emotion and rational thought at the moment.

My next talk with the nurse is both helpful and disturbing. I describe the call from Dad. Explain that—despite current appearances—he is a bright and well-educated individual. That he needs information. She will certainly go right in and speak with him, she says, "but he was told last night that he is in charge of his own care and that if he had any questions at all, he simply had to ask."

Now I'm getting nervous. This is a man whose brain is so starved of oxygen that he hasn't showered or taken his medications for more than two weeks, and you are putting him in charge of his own care? How is he supposed to know what questions to ask when he suddenly finds himself helpless and hospitalized? How would anybody know?

I'd like to see Ms. Charge Nurse take on that challenge from a prone position in a rickety old motorized bed, surrounded by strangers and suffering from cerebral hypoxia.

Call me old-fashioned, but a momentary lapse into common sense would seem to dictate an individualized approach here. A departure from the pretty-sounding, templated formal mission statement.

The nurse agrees to have a staff doctor go in and communicate their findings. She also informs me that Dad's oxygen levels are not responding well, that they have him on a full mask system—clearly not a situation from which we should remove him.

> Call me old-fashioned, but a momentary lapse into common sense would seem to dictate an individualized approach here.

I wait a bit and call Dad back. He is fine now. Crisis averted. "Yeah, the nurse came in right after I talked to you," he says naively. Because I lit a fire under her derriere, I think indignantly, battling a desire to display my efforts on his behalf like peacock plumage.

Before heading back to the hospital to check on the displaced Lord of the Manor, Zelda and I eat a late breakfast and treat the dogs to a second morning walk. Stress tremors complicating the task, she has dabbed away more than a few tears over all this. I kick myself for not better insulating her—and tuck those tail feathers between my legs where they belong.

She genuinely cares for this complex and undemonstrative character that her Prince Charming has become. At his bedside, she offers to rub his toes. "You mean give me a toe job?" he gibes. Ignoring this puckish reply, she tells him that she loves him, and he returns the sentiment.

~~~

We speak to the admitting physician. She explains that he will need additional care after release. Perhaps even a few weeks in a nursing facility. I assure her that I help out on weekdays and that my stepsister will come as needed. Dad pipes up, nodding in my direction and speaking in still-slurred words through the muffle of his oxygen mask. "When she was six years old, I promised her that if she studied hard and got good grades, she could come and take care of me when I got old."

This sympathetic doc also labels his condition as end-stage severe emphysema with an acute flare in progress, resulting in congestive heart failure. She speaks of an average three-year life expectancy and a prognosis of home oxygen therapy—following a few more days in the hospital and those weeks in a rehabilitation center. It's a lot to take in.

Meanwhile, Dad is being given high doses of prednisone to treat the flare and insulin to treat the high blood sugars caused by the prednisone—both of which stir concern. My mother's brother took his own life while under the influence of prescribed steroids. And pumping synthetic insulin into an already sick body can't be good for a stressed endocrine system. So much for being in charge of one's own care.

On the way home from today's visit, Zelda and I stop at Panda Gardens to refuel, courtesy of their ample buffet heaped with pearly grains of perfectly cooked rice and mounds of bright, glistening, steamed and buttered green beans. It's a spot of respite, a relief, and a thrill to once again share in a simple pleasure that got shuttled off our itinerary weeks ago.

5-20-06: *As her chicken stir-fry cools on the table, Z makes one protracted trip to the restroom to potty, another to wash the stickiness off her fingers. I present her with a dampened paper towel, hoping to save her another trip, but she insists on one more proper wash-up, promising—with unintentional irony—to be "back in a flash."*

At dinner, we talk about her daughters and how they got their respective names, middle names, and nicknames. It's a topic we've covered many times, but her enjoyment of it charms me and absorbs her. Transports her back to earlier, happier times spent with her beloved Aunt Hannah and other family members who have passed on.

I tell her I look forward to meeting them someday, try to remind her how all of this works, with the sacrifice of Christ securing His promise of perfect joy and perfect peace for eternity. And pray that my inadequate words bring her tranquility.

Chapter 19

The Sucker Punch

Bunking out at Dad and Zelda's reminds me of the pros and cons of having a non-spouse housemate. It's reassuring knowing there is another amiable presence close by. That you are not alone, even if you're not interacting at the moment. Then there are those trying times when your roomie does something weird and disruptive. You don't dare jeopardize the state of peaceful coexistence, so you gulp, smile, and hope this is a one-off.

Sunday morning. After another nocturnal wrestling match—me versus every negative scenario imaginable—a blanket of calm mercifully settles over my body at 1:45 a.m. Four hours later, Zelda thumps down the stairs, abruptly thwacking on the hundred-watt ceiling light and wrenching me from the depths of a coma-like sleep.

I eventually shake the shakes and get rolling. Attend to the essentials of dog walks and medications and breakfast before setting off for the cold, antiseptic-swabbed hallways of the hospital. At least we have a mission. At least Zelda is leaving the house. At least Dad is getting some help.

These are the retorts I use to shout down my fainthearted self when it screams "disaster" at the thought of my ultra-independent father sentenced to extended care.

Monday and Tuesday proceed without much drama, aside from the fact that we are all tired and disoriented and uncertain. Pretty much situation normal with a partial change of scenery. Having a superbly capable stand-in geared up to take over my role for a few days is a godsend.

5-23-06: *I call Joan with an update on Dad's likely recovery schedule, and she offers to stay with Zelda for an extra-long weekend. Before gratitude takes root, my frazzled brain clutches with disappointment: Gee, now I won't get to entertain everyone at my place on Memorial Day. Fatigue plus anxiety equals tortured logic.*

~~~

If I assumed that getting the hospital's staff physicians on the same page would be easier than coordinating communications between random family doctors, I was mistaken.

5-24-06: *Dad is hallucinating from the prednisone. He describes horrific dreams of being dragged to the electric chair, kicking and screaming. I step right into this nightmare with him when the resident, Dr. G, arrives with his snotty little intern attached at the hip to describe a radically different prognosis than we were given on day one. It is a grim death-is-right-around-the-corner rewrite of the flowery original, and I am furious with the authors of this new storyline.*

"What is your expectation?" asks the oily little sidekick, like some evil Igor, usurping his master's voice in this exchange. "Well," I begin naively, "I understand there is a three-year average life expectancy with this sort of situation . . ."

Igor shifts his hump to the other shoulder with a snort. "That is highly unrealistic," he oozes, through a barely contained smirk of disgust at my idiocy. "Without something drastic like a lung

Here, I take him by his grubby lapel and pull him out of Z's range of hearing.

"My stepmother has dementia and is already very upset," I manage, through clamped incisors.

transplant, it would be more like days, and at his age that kind of treatment wouldn't make sense," he chunters on.

Here, I take him by his grubby lapel and pull him out of Z's range of hearing. "My stepmother has dementia and is already very upset," I manage, through clamped incisors. "At least have the courtesy to exercise a modicum of tact and run things by me before you expose her to harsh realities she may not be prepared to handle. Got it?

"And besides, I didn't conjure up an opinion out of thin air. My 'expectations' were based on what the admitting physician told me mere days ago, you slimy little twerp."

That's how I remember it, anyway. I probably said some of that inside my own head later during multiple replays of the incident. And his lapel probably wasn't grubby. But I am so flabbergasted by his callous attitude—doesn't the old codger in question warrant consideration?—that I take immediate steps to fire him from the case. That old codger happens to be my father. And this unfeeling, arrogant neophyte is no longer allowed to be anywhere near him.

Remarkably, Zelda appears composed. Gives no hint as to how much she has absorbed or how it has affected her. But I am rattled and frightened, as if the Fun House floors are shifting under my feet, and I can't claim a hold on the equally unreliable surrounding walls.

It doesn't help that Dad's RN thinks that turkey bacon might be a good substitute for real bacon on his low-sodium diet, as if the salt-curing process weren't the same, and flashes bewildered doe eyes at me when I refer to steroid psychosis, which she has never heard of. And someone please explain to me, where is the sanity in telling a drug-befuddled man that he is dying but denying him the lousy cup of coffee he yearns for?

"If I could only wrap my hand around a hot mug," Dad says over his saltless, sugarless, cardiac-diet breakfast, "then I would feel more grounded." Under current circumstances, the pun passes unacknowledged.

Meanwhile, the parking attendant we've been handing money to for the past five days forces me to back up, even though there is a line of cars behind me, leave Zelda in the car, and go back inside the hospital to get my ticket stamped before he'll give me the visitor's rate. Seems like most of the bodies bouncing in and out of our personal space today have been taken over by pod people.

Seems like most of the bodies bouncing in and out of our personal space today have been taken over by pod people.

~~~

5-25-06: *Dad keeps referring to Atlanta as if he has fled there or has immediate plans to. Yet even in this delusional state, he steps back to evaluate his own drug-induced paranoia. How different it was to study the subject in clear-cut clinical terms all those years ago in college, he says, and how odd it is to be "on the other side of it" now.*

I can't commiserate with the nurse about his terrifying visions. She is completely ignorant of such a concept, has no knowledge—educational or practical—of confusion in patients thus medicated. Drip, drip, drip, as my trust erodes into pebbles of doubt. Anybody who reads the sports page or watches Entertainment Tonight has heard of "roid rage." But this trained medical professional is clueless.

I duck out from under the nimbus of uneasiness forming overhead and escape back to the townhouse. Immerse myself in tending to Zelda's needs. Within an hour, the sound of the jangling phone pierces the peaceful atmosphere. It's another RN informing me that my father is "perfectly coherent" but refuses to keep his oxygen mask on. What in the world I am supposed to do about this from twelve miles away, I have no idea. I can only conclude that the caller is scrambling to cover an assortment of uniformed rear ends.

The last time I saw my father he was talking about preparing to be transported via cargo plane to Wichita, Kansas, with Herb and Bud—his old Navy chums. He is bright and articulate, and he can still put a sentence together rather nicely. But that doesn't necessarily translate to his being "perfectly coherent." This babe gets a pink slip, too.

Kind and patient Dr. G apparently agrees with Dad's hysterical mess of a daughter because he assigns a full-time aide to monitor the oxygen delivery.

And Dad amazes. Even under the influence of neuron-altering chemicals, he reasons that it may be a good idea for him to talk to a therapist. And that a change of rooms might break his negative associations with 558/Bed Two. The Geographical Cure. It's worth a try.

My husband amazes, too. He takes care of things at home and extends a stabilizing hand in my direction. Guides me back to the solid turf of today's reality from my meanderings into the land of Catastrophia. But even as we hone our coping skills, there are polarizing forces at work.

5-26-06: *Jack is able to join us for a hospital visit this morning. While I've been around-the-clock at Z's, he has spent the last six days focusing on his mother—doctor's appointments, errands, taking her out to eat.*

At noon today, she calls him on his cell phone, interrupting his conversation with Dad. Wants him to take her to the cemetery. Where can a girl rent a decompression chamber around here?

~~~

Joan has settled in with Zelda, who won't accept a dinner invitation from Barb and Tom, and now balks at visiting the hospital. I think she senses how near the end may be and hates to confront that possibility. We've all wondered what the future held. Now that we have solid facts, we're wishing we knew less.

Papa, however, talks of nothing but going home. Doesn't sound at all as if he's given up or given in. He still peppers his statements with confusing allusions, but a cheering visit from a former colleague spurs the spot-on recollection that their friendship spans forty years.

Infected with his good spirits, Jack and I depart in peace.

5-27-06: *Saturday afternoon, 1:50. Dad rebounds from a scary-deep sleep, once again laments the inane proscription against coffee, and talks* up a storm—some here-and-now references, some plucked from one of his bizarre dream sequences.

I read to him from Bill M's email, reminiscences of their grad school antics. Funny stories I had never heard. Like the time Dad horrified a department secretary by complaining of a morning-long headache, then asked the waiter for a glass of water during their usual coffee shop lunch. The water arrives. Dad groans pathetically, covers his brow with his hand, and bends forward over the table. Plop. Suddenly an eyeball falls into his glass, sending the startled secretary screaming for help. Dad had palmed the prosthetic orb—apparently available from the psych department supply cabinet—and dropped it into the waiting glass at exactly the right moment in his improvised one-man skit.

"And then there were the sayings we'd make up, designed to sound like old maxims and delivered in serious tones," continues Bill's note. "Phrases like 'The deeper the well, the wetter the water' that left people scratching their heads trying to figure out their profound hidden meanings."

Nurse's aide Sue stops in at 3:30, and Dad tells her he dreamt that she took him home last night. "I hope we had fun!" she says with a laugh.

This is the same exceptional individual who had him sitting up in a chair yesterday evening listening to music through headphones. Bless her. And please, somebody find a way to clone her.

I exhale a fume cloud of bottled tensions. Relief fills my lungs, oxygenates my mood, and removes the lead from my shoes. And yet another infusion of hope lies ahead.

Jack and I swing by the townhouse to see Zelda, and I have a long, encouraging conversation with Joan about my desire to take Zelda into our household to care for her there. Concern over Zelda's future has gnawed at my conscience like an unfulfilled promise since the moment we heard that Dad would not be with us much longer. And for that entire time, I've dreaded Joan's automatic rejection of my offer.

But she surprises me. Displays a generous, open mind. Seems

entirely simpatico with my intentions and motives and abilities. Her unflustered reaction is like aloe to my blistering, uneasy thoughts.

~~~

Nothing changes the pace of a placid Sunday morning like getting an urgent call from the hospital as you saunter through the front door after church. It's Dr. G. Dad is nonresponsive and has very high levels of carbon dioxide in his blood.

Just yesterday afternoon, he was chuckling over his old friend's email and querying the Certified Nursing Assistant: "Now tell me about the fellow who founded St. Festus Hospital." Today, we are smacked full-on with the question of how to ease his suffering without prolonging his passing.

Jack and I meet Zelda and Joan at the hospital room door. We release a collective chorus of gasps at the sight of a full-face breathing apparatus pumping air into Dad's lungs. His body is immobile, his cheeks fluttering from the violence of the pressure. The unnatural image brings tears to every eye and evokes flinching surges of revulsion. My throat goes rock hard in painful disbelief. Joan clutches Zelda to her and shoulders the wall for support.

And then, astoundingly, Dad begins to stir. Eyes firmly closed, he wrests himself from the tangle of sheets and winces against the impact of forced air. "Stay calm," Joan urges him, as—halting breath by halting breath—he begins to revive. Zelda adds, with the twinkle of a mischievous smile, "Try staying 'clam.'"

He turns my insides to goo, saying, "Oh, Sweetie, I'm so sorry to cause all this trouble" as he labors for breath.

Everyone but Dad stiffens with apprehension as the doctor removes the BiPAP machine and his patient miraculously returns to full consciousness. He addresses us girls as if we had just walked in. Waves at Jack. Tells me I look nice today. Turns my insides to goo, saying, "Oh, Sweetie, I'm so sorry to cause all this trouble" as he labors for breath.

The nursing assistant fetches him a cold bottle of chocolate protein drink. "Boy, that's good," he smacks in appreciation. Jack puts it well: "It's as if a switch has been flipped."

Chapter 20

Slipping Through Open Doors

There is a small electronic gizmo clamped to Dad's left earlobe feeding monitored data into one of the whirring machines stationed at his bedside. Its tiny red regulator light beckons me to his good ear to speak words of comfort.

Following the frightening, late-morning fight to trick his failing lungs back into service, he nods off intermittently but allows us to fuss over him between naps. I ask if he is cold. Yes. We arrange the skimpy blanket, swaddling him for maximum coverage. And as Zelda massages his toes, he opens his eyes in gratitude and recognition.

I fold myself at the waist, aim my breath at ear level. "You know how much I love you," I whisper, then repeat the promise I've made to Zelda. "We'll get through this together."

He mumbles into his plastic face mask, "I'm not sure what 'through this' means, but . . . " The trailing words are sucked into the oxygen machine's echoing tanks.

Later, off the breathing apparatus, Dad recounts his most recent sleep hallucination as if speaking to a distant listener. "I had a bad one," he says to the mute television set suspended on the farthest wall. "One of those definitive dreams—bad in the sense that I couldn't kill myself."

"To escape the dream?" I ask.

"Well, you know, just because of the helplessness and the hopelessness," he says.

I squeeze through the crack in this opened door spurred by a cosmic sense of urgency, assure him that all is not hopeless, that there is victory over death. "I've talked to . . . " I begin, then hesitate.

"To the Big Fellow," Dad offers through a weak, lopsided grin.

The importance of the moment robs me of words, so I remind him of the lines from his favorite hymn, "In the Garden," insist that there is a reason the stanzas are comforting, that there is peace to be found in the message. "He walks with me and He talks with me, and He tells me I am His own." Dad nods in solemn compliance.

> "I've talked to . . . " I begin, then hesitate. "To the Big Fellow," Dad offers through a weak, lopsided grin.

Nursing assistant Sharon is an angel in white polyester. She has been in the room during this exchange. As Dad sleeps, I explain in strangulated utterances that I want only to ruffle his spirit. To witness to him of the faith of his childhood while he is receptive. To give him that comfort. Sharon says softly, "I think you did."

~~~

As this unsurpassable gift of a day rolls tentatively along on uncertain wheels, Dad describes an ache "up by the headband" of his inhalation mask. I ask him if he plans on playing the old glass eyeball trick on us, and he marvels over Bill M's remembering all those stories.

"Can you delve into your own memory banks for more?" I ask. He agrees to think about that for a while.

As Papa says goodbye to Joan and Zelda, he asks about his grandson. "I'd like to see Rich and tell him my tale," he smiles. He has not uttered one word of physical complaint through all of this. I tell him that he should once in a while, that it might be good for him. "Maybe you're right," he chuckles, as fatigued lids curtain his eyes once again.

Watching him rest, I bury my face in my powerless, splayed hands, not knowing where else to deposit my grief. Slowly, gently, Dad reaches out to stroke my cheek and caress my head. His lingering touch moves me beyond expression—a simple gesture, spilling over with all the tenderness I have ever hoped to experience with him.

As we talk late into the afternoon, I ask probing questions about his internship days. Dad tells me this exercise helps him feel like he's getting better. He used to write parodies about his professors, exposing their treatment of graduate students, he recalls, and we discuss the career choice booklet he wrote while still in school.

When the mood turns melancholy, I remind him of the lyrics to another of his favorite songs: "Amazing Grace, how sweet the sound, that saved a wretch like me."

"I never much liked that 'wretch' part," he protests, wrinkling his nose in distaste.

Six hours into our visit, I force myself to leave—praying I'll have tomorrow to see him and touch him and engage his fine mind.

5-29-06 A.M.: *After lying awake most of the night, my stomach knotted with fear, waiting for another bad news message from the hospital, I call Dad at 8:30. He is sitting up, taking breakfast.*

"It's Suz," I announce, and he replies, "Well, here we are again." "How are you?" I ask. "Fine, fine."

I remind him that his grandchildren and Jack and I are coming to see him this morning. "Wonderful! I'll see you in an hour."

By the time we arrive, he is less alert, nodding off every few minutes. He also displays a nasty lesion on his right forearm where an orderly grabbed hold of him to move him and peeled his delicate flesh away from the gelatinous tissue beneath it. They have applied some kind of

> His lingering touch moves me beyond expression—a simple gesture, spilling over with all the tenderness I have ever hoped to experience with him.

see-through miracle dressing to speed the healing process, but the ban-
dage's little plastic window fills with blood and scum like a special effects
gimmick in a CSI episode, magnifying the gruesome appearance of his
wound.

My mind goes vacant. As smoky anger wafts vivid images of future hospital injuries across my blank brain, Dr. G pops in to announce that Dad can be released to home hospice tomorrow.

This shocks us all, including Pa, who says with a sleep-thickened tongue that he thought he was "checking out" yesterday, that he assumed today he could simply lay down and let the "life forces" leave him. "I expected to hear a 'click,' and then everything would be quiet."

"The Big Fellow isn't quite ready for you yet," I pipe in, and I sense that Dr. G thinks I'm hanging on. I am not. I am, however, shamelessly exploiting every opportunity, thank you.

Soon the grandchildren arrive and gather around his bed. Light chatter fills the air, but these young souls are sobered by the specter of a life fading before them. Everyone here knows this is goodbye, and no one wants to let go of the moment.

Alone together again, as the late morning sun throws stripes of golden light through the mini-blinds and across the over-bleached bedding, I read the poem "High Flight" by John Gillespie Magee Jr. Dad has always been interested in aeronautics. Slipping the surly bonds of earth and touching the face of God will certainly hold new meaning for him now. (Did I say shameless?)

Sparing him my awkward a capella, I read aloud the complete lyrics of "Amazing Grace" and "In the Garden." He nods, groggily, saying, "Yes, yes." I'm not sure exactly what he's agreeing to, but I can hope.

After four hours, I have exhausted the patient with my good intentions, but my husband wants to pray. "You know how Zelda always has Jack say grace when we eat dinner at your house?" Dad nods. "Well, Jack would like to say a prayer now. Is that OK?" A double nod.

"Dear heavenly Father, who forgives all that we ask," Jack begins, then proceeds with general entreaties related to Dad's going home.

Head bowed, I take my father's warm, fragile hand in mine. He presses my palm with a firm squeeze of returned affection, and my knees go to jelly.

I kiss him again—the fourth time today—and tell him again that I love him, the fourth time today. I am compelled by the need to keep saying it, that one more time.

Almost as compelling is my desire to slap today's in-room aide, who has done nothing but sit on her luxuriously cushioned behind, whining about how Dad doesn't need a one-on-one. While she grumbles absently that he is no longer removing his oxygen tube, I look over to see the nasal cannula resting on his chin, far from where it can do him any good. And as Dad slips deeper and deeper into the V of his adjustable bed, helpless to right himself, Ms. Why-Am-I-Here slumps deeper and deeper into her chair, eyes glued to the TV. Apparently, it's not in her job description to pull herself away from *Judge Judy* long enough to tend to such things.

We have been spoiled by nursing assistants Caroline and Sharon, but this lazy, heedless attitude goes beyond disappointing. I dare not fire yet another helper, though, and tomorrow we will leave it all behind.

On our drive home from the hospital, I turn to silent prayer to exorcise my unhelpful thoughts and am astonished by the intense fervor that fills me. Everyone involved has always assumed that Zelda would go first, that there would be more time for Dad. This cataclysmic rending of our mental blueprint for the future has thrown all of us off balance.

> Everyone involved has always assumed that Zelda would go first, that there would be more time for Dad. This cataclysmic rending of our mental blueprint for the future has thrown all of us off balance.

Email becomes my means of regaining stability. Early this evening, too drained to even clack at the keyboard, I take my Golden Delicious apple and my mug of steaming tea and escape to the familiar comfort of my bedroom.

Here I doze a bit, but mostly I cry. Back to the computer to throw out a few distress signals to those friends who know best how to build up the broken-down.

5-29-06 P.M.: *I call Dad earlier than usual tonight. I need to hear his voice right now, not later. "What are you doing?" I ask. "Waiting," he says. "Waiting for what?" "To hear that 'click.' For the peace and quiet." And my heart flutters at the surrender in his voice.*

~~~

5-30-06, 8:30 A.M.: *I call Dad's room. No answer. My stomach collapses in on itself. I rush to the hospital to find him with his glasses on but slumped to one side in his bed. His right foot hangs off the edge of the mattress, and his gown has slipped, exposing his bare chest and shoulders, leaving his skin cold to the touch.*

I adjust the gown and the blanket. Reposition the goose-necked lamp. Hand him a Reader's Digest to thumb through. Think to myself, how utterly irrelevant articles on money management and weight control must seem to him right now.

I ask him what he is thinking, doing. "Waiting," he answers. "For what?" I ask. "For the end to come." "And then what?" "And then we'll see what happens."

I say, "Let's do some preparation for that. Let's get you home where you are more comfortable, and we can talk. I don't want you to just wait. I want you to tell me family stories, and I want to hear your outlook on Heaven."

His jaw set in stoic resistance to exploring what may come, he tosses me the same leftover crumb. "We'll see."

The hospice people arrive after lunch, paving the way to make the move happen by 8 p.m. But when the chaplain mentions that Dad is going home, Dad responds, "I doubt it." At this point, he probably thinks we're only making happy talk.

I burble with reassurances. Would he still like that White Castle hamburger when we finally get to blow this pop stand? And maybe a nice, hot cup of Folgers?

"That'll be too late," he says groggily, shredding my flimsy enthusiasm into itty, bitty pieces.

5-30-06, 9:00 P.M.: *Joan has returned to Madison. Between the hospice group, the Medi-Van people, and Jack's disassembling of the master bedroom furniture, we have Dad set up in his own room again—all in the course of eight hours.*

This essentially means that he is snoozing here now instead of at the hospital, but that is no small thing. And he did come around long enough to observe, "Oh, this is the old place," which gave me the chance to say, "Yeah, didn't think we could do it, huh?"

I lift Chloé up within his line of sight. This coaxes an upward curve from his parched lips as he caresses her ear with a weak hand, then nods off again.

I know our situation is more bitter than sweet, but it is still a relief to have him here. To be within shouting distance instead of thirty minutes away. To see that he gets nourishment and is covered and has access to some small comforts.

I walk the pups, tipping things a few degrees in the right direction on the normalcy scale. The girls and I pass a glass-paned door behind which sits a huge, silky-coated, licorice black dog, peering out at us with polite curiosity. Next to this beautiful creature sits a sweet-faced and equally well-behaved tuxedo-patterned cat. Such a charming color-coordinated portrait they make, framed by the door's metal trim. Smiling feels good after all the anguish.

~~~

This protracted evening takes on the feel of a twelve-act, existentialist play—complete with pathos and relieved only by a few well-placed intermissions.

Zelda is bewildered by all the activity. She suspects that she's being evicted, having taken no notice of the crew bringing Dad in on a gurney and transferring him to the rented hospital bed. Rest, reassurance, and Razadyne help. She reorients. Makes frequent trips to visit her Bill, who now shifts abruptly between extreme states—from aware and talkative to virtually comatose.

5-30-06, 10:30 P.M.: *I peek in to find Dad awake and alert with his oxygen mask out of place. I lift Fergie up for a nuzzle, replace the nose tube, fetch him some cold chocolate protein drink. As I raise the cup to his lips, he says, "This isn't the way you wanted to spend the rest of my life, is it?"*

The rims of my eyelids tingle with the threat of rising tears. "No, it isn't," I agree. "But we can make good use of this time. We can talk and share our thoughts and feelings." He shrugs, manages a faint smile. Says, "Well, I am learning how wonderful you are . . . but I knew that." The dam is breached, my eyes spill over, and my insides go squishy. "I just love you so darned much," I gush.

Embarrassed by my lapse into sappy sentimentality, Dad reverts to cool and clinical. "Someone should chronicle my illness," he says to the ceiling. I assure him that I am keeping a journal. He tips his head, satisfied.

With the spotlight focused on the gowned hostage tethered to oxygen in his makeshift medical ward, Zelda slips into the shadows and readies herself for bed. Meanwhile, I continue to lob softballs of optimism in return for my father's less hopeful swats at afterlife speculation. End-of-life perspectives likely write their own prophecies, but timely, constructive input may help shape the final forecast. Only God knows.

> What I know is this: in these last weeks of his life, I am being blessed with the kind of closeness to my father I have hungered for all of my days.

What I know is this: in these last weeks of his life, I am being blessed with the kind of closeness to my father I have hungered for all of my days. Condensed, like the contents of that dog-eared, large-print, hospital copy of *Reader's Digest*. But oh, so much more beneficial.

Chapter 21

Resting in His Promises

"When a man knows he is to be hanged . . . it concentrates his mind wonderfully." I've heard my father recite that Samuel Johnson aphorism more than once, always with a roguish grin. I think of this as I watch him now, forced to entertain concepts he has always been able to shunt out of his mind until they surged in uninvited—a tsunami of competing ideas about mortality.

There was no massive heart failure with its swift and merciful release from life. No peaceful spell of unconsciousness leading to that expected "click," leaving no time to turn things over and over in his head. The old quote would hold no humor for him today, as all the former diversions—books, crossword puzzles, computer keyboard—sit out of reach and beyond his capabilities.

5-30-06, 11:00 P.M.: *Dad watched no television his entire twelve-day stay in the hospital. I haul up the small set from downstairs and position it on his rolling tray table. Before long he has tuned in to the late night news, seeking distraction from the thoughts tumbling around in his brain like raw gems in a rock polisher. Encouraged, I tell him I'll arrange for a massage tomorrow to help with his sore back.*

"It may not be worth it," he says reflexively.

"It certainly is," I counter reflexively.

As we debate the issue, the frustrated pups sit calculating how they can possibly manage to loft themselves onto this unreasonably high foreign bed, and Z comes in for a moment of tender greetings and everyday chit-chat—a genuine back-and-forth about the weather and a favorite framed print hanging within sight in the hallway. It's good to be here together and feel a tiny bit "right" again.

Throughout this evening, during conversations interrupted by his nodding off, Dad thanks me for bringing him home, and we explore the subject of keeping someone alive. I assure him that isn't happening here, that our only goal is to make his last days as comfortable as possible, not to force his feeble body to survive any longer than it would naturally. And I drop fat tears in soft, wet patches onto the hem of his pillowcase as I tell him that, as much as I love him and will miss him terribly, I don't want him to suffer. However, I insist to my captive audience of one, he was returned to us for a reason following that brush up against eternity two days ago. A reason larger than he and I.

5-30/31-06, midnight: *I help Dad with a glass of water and note a forlorn, distant look in his eyes. I offer a penny for a peek at his thought process. "I'm thinking about goodbye," he says.*

In halting words, on loan from a source outside of myself, I speak of things we have never discussed directly. My beliefs and why I hold them, how my own spiritual quest led me to see that creation requires a Creator, and that we have a thirst within us that has only one means of being quenched.

If he could only forgive God and allow God to forgive him, I implore, it would bring us both peace. Make our goodbye so much less agonizing.

I'm convinced that the old hymns strike a chord far surpassing fond childhood associations, that they satisfy a ravenous hunger hardwired into every human being.

Working to form speech with a jaw slack from pain meds, Dad assures me that his resistance never meant that he doesn't love me very much. I know this, I tell him. But I'm convinced that the old hymns strike a chord far surpassing fond childhood associations, that they satisfy a ravenous hunger hardwired into every human being.

I have been so certain that reaching my father with the Gospel was a challenge exceeding the strength of my character, an encumbrance I am too frail to bear. But I am beginning to see things more clearly. To not be afraid. To trust in the unseen Presence who shares my mission. And the weight of the burden slips away with a sigh.

~~~

As the sleepy veil of night drapes itself over our diminishing window to the larger world, I perceive in my father's eyes a quality I have never seen there before. A fluttering awareness that he is not immune to the innate needs we've talked about.

I rush to record every last detail of this time with him. I will chronicle his illness, as he requested. But I must also log the account of a softening heart. The subtle unfurling of a spirit that has been folded away for much of a lifetime, an emerging chrysalis that I pray will flourish in the Light.

Dad pats my hand. Says we should talk more tomorrow. Throughout the evening we have covered a universe of topics. He is tired, but I sense he also needs time alone to meditate.

"Lord," I whisper, as I tiptoe downstairs to my own meditation chamber, "please walk with him and talk with him, and tell him he is Your own."

5-31-06: *Two hours into a troubled sleep, Dad rouses and calls out. Says he can't go on. That surely I can understand. That his heart and lungs are worthless.*

In his torment, he also knocks off the oxygen feed and thrashes at the alien tubes attached to various body parts. I offer the 23rd Psalm for comfort and sit with him until unconsciousness steals in to provide relief.

At 3 a.m., as I settle back into my own rumpled nest of blankets and sheets on the lower level, Z clomps down the stairs, flicks on the light, and begins loading dirty clothes into the Kenmore.

I guide her back to bed, remind her of the time, and try to look past the offended pout on her face. There is some blessing in the most recent phase of her forgetfulness in that, tomorrow, she's not likely to remember this egregious affront.

~~~

I am astounded at what this assemblage of bone and muscle and cellulite I managed to roll out of my lumpy futon can accomplish on only a few hours of fitful sleep.

Still, seeing my father suffer triggers a physical hurt inside me. His body becomes oppressively heavy as defeated motor cells wave the white flag of surrender. Alone, I can't do much for him other than stroke his forehead and plant a gentle kiss on the top rim of his ear.

Diversion lies in finishing that mistimed load of Zelda's laundry while we wait for help to arrive. Maybe the hospice worker will appreciate a mugful from the freshly brewed pot of coffee I had so hoped Dad would still want once we got him home. Having it sit untouched sets off a ripple of sadness that I cannot allow to swell.

Zelda fed, dosed, hugged, and tucked in for a morning nap, I force a small serving of Raisin Bran down my own gullet. Food holds no attraction for a stomach bound up in grief, but I know I have to give it something to convert into energy.

5-31-06, 1:00 P.M.: *The nurse arrives, reeking of tobacco—the very substance that caused Dad's COPD. She helps me change the bed, teaches me how to use the "comforting drugs" in the home-care packet. Atropine every two to four hours, a half-dropper of morphine if he seems short of breath—every hour if needed. Then there is Lorazepam for anxiety and restlessness, up to two milligrams in a two-hour period, and, if necessary, Haldol for extreme agitation.*

I should read the section in the "Saying Goodbye" booklet that refers to "days left" rather than "weeks left," the Nicotine Queen advises, and I shoot up a desperate prayer for that one last opportunity to convince my father of the unparalleled joy and peace Christ has purchased for us in Heaven.

Dad is semi-comatose today—talking in his sleep and opening his eyes for a few sips of something now and then but barely relating to those around him.

It is moving beyond description to watch Z at his bedside, speaking softly to Papa with her hand on his arm, or holding Chloé up for him to see, even though he is mostly unaware.

The nurse encourages a concerned Zelda to just keep doing what she has been doing for the past thirty-four years. It is moving beyond description to watch Z at his bedside, speaking softly to Papa with her hand on his arm, or holding Chloé up for him to see, even though he is mostly unaware.

I quietly remove the television set and replace it with the CD player. Replay again and again the disc that includes "Amazing Grace" and "In the Garden," then lean in, searching his face for hope of a few more conscious moments.

And I wait.

5-31-06, 3:00 P.M.: *My contracted stomach still unreceptive to the copious quantities of chow I generally dump into it, I ease down half a turkey sandwich for lunch, with tea—hot, soothing tea.*

Nothing, I am convinced, can prepare you to sit and wait for a loved one to slowly fade from life. Or to listen to him rale in his sleep, knowing he may never come around again for that final "goodbye," that last "I love you." This is what today feels like.

Dad slept through most of the hospice nurse's attentions earlier, the linen-changing and bathing. Even the oral hygiene care. I get him to accept a few spoonfuls of chocolate ice cream in late afternoon and catch him awake long enough to tell him I need one last thing from him before he leaves us. I need to know he is willing to accept Grace.

Z had gotten to him first with her own urgings to consider the reality of a hereafter. "I've never been philosophized to so much in my life," he says now, through a weary but tolerant smile.

"OK," I promise. "I'll back off. But it's not philosophy; it's faith. And it's very important."

Throughout the day, I trot in often to check Dad's oxygen and make sure he is covered. He shouts out in his sleep, thrusting his right arm up in a disturbing motion vaguely reminiscent of a Nazi salute. I pull calming medication from the hospice kit and clumsily administer the magical elixir, feeling unsure. Reluctant to drug away his agitation. I kiss his forehead in apology, tell him every time I enter the room that I'm still here loving him. I sense he no longer hears. I hope it matters anyway.

~~~

Zelda has been in and out of my care throughout the past two weeks, shuttled by the tumult onto the sidelines of this spanking-new playing field we're feeling our way around without the benefit of floodlights or grid lines.

We have in common hearts saddened by mutual loss, but I fear she's drifting out of my orbital path as it shifts to revolve around Dad. That we've suffered a breach in our alliance, right when we need that alliance the most.

5-31-06, 5:00 P.M.: *While Dad sleeps, Z and I reconnect via a short outing with the pups, and we both get a bit watery when she speaks of him in the past tense. Back inside later, as we make dinner plans, I get a glimpse of him wilted into the slant of his mattress, chest heaving, and my face blanches white-hot with guilt. How can I not be thinking only of him every single second?*

I pick up my copy of death's little instruction book and replay in my mind the vignette of the hospice nurse pointing me to the "Last Few Days" section. I was not shocked by her suggestion that I read it, but I didn't like hearing her say it. And I will read the booklet, because I need to know. But I don't like doing that either.

Feeling isolated and restless, I call Jack. He doesn't think he'd be of help sharing my vigil, but he will update concerned family and friends. Here at the townhouse, some of the neighbors have been touchingly generous, volunteering time, emotional support, and open-ended offers of assistance. Others are evasive. They avert their gaze and avoid all contact, choosing not to face the unpleasantness. I wish I had that option.

But do I really want to escape? I've been so busy tutoring my father in subjects he has written off as electives that I may be overlooking an opportunity to school myself.

In a neon flash of self-awareness, I finally get it—the takeaway lesson being thrust under my own nose. I've been longing for one more warm exchange with this inherently generous man I have adored through all of my years—in spite of his cheeky irreverence and walled-off emotions.

Now, disarmed by weariness, I can lay out a rather beefy list of traits he bequeathed to his only daughter and smile at the impact of genetic predetermination. There is my tendency to be impatient—with long lines, bad grammar, irresponsible people. And maybe a slight inclination to be flippant and cynical, often simultaneously.

Analytical? Oh, my. Try *over*-analytical, always trying to noodle out people's conscious or subconscious motivations but without the benefit of a PhD in the art of. And then there's that big-words habit I consistently lapse into, incognizant of my own verbosity.

As a tribute to Dad's legacy, might I try to be a smidge more forgiving of this flawed human being I call Me? To work on becoming the person I was meant to be while not despising the person I am? To embrace my highly imperfect self as if I were a lovable bullfrog—warts and all?

I truly hope so. Self-contempt requires so much energy.

~~~

During his eighty-five-plus years, my father has doled out bushels of good counsel to me and to others. If I were to say, "I can't [fill in the blank]," he'd remind me to be more careful of my words. "You can," he would correct. "You simply haven't yet learned how." Destiny-changing guidance meant to divert me from the snare of self-defeatism and steer me instead down the path of self-determination. Today I suppose they'd call it empowerment.

> Certain situations crush even the most helpful advice into atoms of unusable dust.

But certain situations crush even the most helpful advice into atoms of unusable dust.

5-31-06, 10:00 P.M.: *My cortisol levels soar, leaving my mouth parched, my muscles rigid. It's as if every intake of breath pulls molecules of disquiet into my body from the miasma of tension that surrounds us.*

Lifting leaden legs up what has become a Mount Everest of a stairway, I drop helplessly to my knees and cry out, "I can't do this any longer." Shame pulls me back to my feet, impels me through tonight's bed check—first Zelda, then Dad—and back down the stairs, clutching a microwaved bag of Gourmet Kettle Korn for my fashionably late one-course dinner.

As I finally flop onto the daybed—joined by my two loyal but bath-deprived furry sleeping companions—I think of that old quip about God not asking of you anything that you can't handle.

Such rot. Of course I can't handle this. If I could cope effectively on my own with life's trials and tribulations, I wouldn't need an active relationship with Him. Just as I took my childhood concerns to Dad, whose knowledge and influence exceeded my own, I now take my shattered, grown-up heart to my heavenly Father in my hour of greatest need.

And in this foliage-choked garden of anguish and weakness, He faithfully meets me. Reminds me that His timing has a purpose. That

Dad may need to be flat on his back, semiconscious and immobilized, before he allows God to touch him at soul level and take authorship of his future.

Rest comes in the form of assurance received. I cannot explain it, but it is as real as a candle in the dark throwing off just enough glow to light the way ahead.

Chapter 22

Oops, Goes the Apple Cart

June first. I awaken wondering how many infant souls are beginning their lives today. Extreme circumstances lead the mind in peculiar directions and open the body to unique sensations.

6-1-06: *A stirring premonition slithers over me from toes to scalp the moment my eyes open at 4:50 a.m.: Dad is gone. I lie in peaceful reverie for a while—at ease with the fact, yet not relishing the idea of confirming it. Confident that he was swathed in tranquil slumber as his spirit slipped from his body, I have no guilt over not being at his side. No guilt. Such a peculiar feeling.*

> I have no guilt over not being at his side. No guilt. Such a peculiar feeling.

I mount the stairs with lightened limbs, see no motion, hear no breathing, find no pulse. Instinctively, my hand seeks out his cheek. But there is no comfort in that, for this is no longer him.

I gently close the door to his room and call the hospice number, relieved to have them take over from here. Then I sit in my lower-level lair, stroking the pups, listening for Z to stir.

At last, her door sweeps open, and I am up the stairs in four bounding leaps. My arm encircling her back, I reluctantly report, "I'm afraid that Papa left us during the night."

She comprehends immediately. "You mean he is gone?"
"Yes."

Her head and shoulders drop, then droop—a two-stage reaction. I
draw comfort from comforting her. I would never have imagined myself
able to do the things that this morning requires, but she needs me, and
my faith strengthens me.

Zelda does well until 9:30 a.m., when the funeral parlor folks drive
off with their impersonal bundle. She has lost the love of her life,
she sobs. She tries to rest but can't tolerate being alone. I say, "Let's
pray," and she kneels right there at her bedside. Thanks God for good
friends. Asks to be worthy of them.

By 10 a.m., both the McCs are on site. While Jack installs twin beds
in the master bedroom in preparation for out-of-town relatives, Barb
suggests digging out the weeds from between the deck slats. Part of
sprucing up for visitors, she claims, but it's mainly occupational therapy.

Soon, strains of "She'll Be Coming 'Round the Mountain" and
"Row, Row, Row Your Boat" drift through the sliding screen door,
Barb's soft voice joined by Zelda's as the two fall into the comfortably
playful pattern they have repeated so many times over the last thir-
ty-plus years. Through easy familiarity, dear friends Barbara and Tom
provide a soft place for the new widow to nestle while Jack and I sort
out the minutiae involved in "making arrangements."

~~~

"One day at a time" fits some situations more aptly than others. My
own serenity quickly crumbles as I plow through the rutted terrain
of riotous emotions that losing my father has roughed up, seriously
doubting my ability to endure the next twenty-four hours. Even under
placid conditions, my thoughts hop about like a herd of rabbits in
mating mode. And these are far from placid conditions.

6-2-06: *Having just completed what was both the best two weeks of*
my life and the worst two weeks of my life, I live on green tea, wake

at 5 a.m. obsessed with what might have hit my email in-box since I last checked, and nervously attack any task that promises to absorb my attention.

With Joan looking after her mom, Jack and I deep-clean our place, ready the guest room for Z's six-month trial run stay there, and hire our pastor's daughters to weed the front flower beds. Can't hurt to upgrade the curb appeal before we four meet here to discuss the logistics of Z's move.

~~~

There's a scene in an old Laurel and Hardy movie in which one of the two, probably Hardy, has the Persian carpet he's standing on pulled right out from under him. Lands—*kerplop!*—smack on his keister. Hilarious if you're into slapstick.

Now picture yourself, feet planted on a rug of mutual understanding, as smiling friends and relations stand in front of you. Clutching the rug by its hem, they tug with all the oomph they can muster, hurling your pride into the stratosphere in a whirl of hurt and confusion.

Call me Oliver. Ask me if I'm laughing.

6-5-06: *I am a limp rag. Moving Z to a Madison nursing home is apparently a done deal, in spite of assurances that her staying with Jack and me was seriously being considered. Z casually mentions the plan during a phone conversation, adding, "I hope to still get to see you from time to time."*

I cry. Tell her I love her and I'll miss her. I am trying not to be selfish, but my world has imploded. Dad and Zelda have been my life's focus for the past seventeen months, and suddenly it's over—blam!—as if both had been killed in a devastating car crash. Everything is now a blur.

~~~

Listen, my children, and you shall hear of well-meaning people wreaking havoc and fear. In a private discussion from which I was excluded, an acquaintance, Ms. X, offers the opinion that Zelda needs to escape me—permanently.

"Sweetie, she's afraid of you," this dear misguided soul informs me later when pressed for explanations. What Zelda might have said that was open to this interpretation, I can't begin to imagine.

Then, an overly helpful male friend—who can't possibly know how meticulously my father has planned ahead—takes it for granted that legal and financial arrangements are not properly in place and issues a warning to that effect behind my back. Several of my stepsisters, swept up in it all, are understandably alarmed by the outsiders' observations and choose not to risk confronting me directly.

Exhausted, crushed by feelings of upheaval and loss, and shut out of everyday goings-on at the townhouse, have I become such a jittery mess that I cannot perceive how unhinged I look to others? Has my behavior become so erratic that I am no longer viewed as a source of rational input?

Outraged friends closer to the situation ask another question: should loosely connected acquaintances be posing loaded questions to a bereaved dementia-sufferer and then making recommendations, knowing nothing of our daily reality? And should these outsiders then make judgments about our family dynamics and venture sloppy guesses about what has and hasn't been adequately planned for?

I just wish somebody had let me in on Zelda's "stated wishes" earlier. Might've averted a heap of hopeful assumptions and battered feelings.

But Zelda's birth daughters are in charge. The "Bios." I may have power of attorney, but I am merely a stopgap. All those daily tasks I've been doing for well over a year seem now to be viewed as favors performed by an obliging stranger, requiring thanks and special mention—lightly dusted with the hint that my services are no longer required.

Can I be so expendable that I am all-in one day, only to be summarily ousted the next? I can't seem to flick the switch to the "off" position quite that easily. Now, fingertips curled over the keyboard, my brain on fire with righteous indignation, I ask myself whether to purge my opinions or put a postage stamp on them.

6-6-06, A.M.: *It's taken me awhile to tease out the cause of this chasm between the Bios and me. I speak with Z's friend X, learn that Z has been complaining about me to others; hear secondhand about warnings regarding financial disorder, and all the pieces fall into place. Bubbling with exasperation and likely adding to my reputation as a lunatic, I pour blistering responses onto the page like hot lava:*

"A little background for those not intimately familiar with Bill and Zelda's situation: Zelda also requested to speak to her three closest female friends at the same time she asked to speak to X. This is what she does when she is overwhelmed with confusion. It is also why, one evening several months ago, she trotted across the alley and fetched an unsuspecting neighbor, dragging him into her living room as support for her side of an argument with Dad.

"And any presumptions that all legal and financial matters have not been thoughtfully attended to in advance are utterly unfounded. The will, the living trust, the trusteeship, the power of attorney, the health care initiatives—all properly in place with Zelda's best interests well looked after. No loose ends. No unanticipated eventualities. No big revelation—to anyone who cared to ask.

"Perhaps you can see how I might feel like I've taken a lofted bowling ball to the solar plexus, realizing how much more smoothly things would have gone for me and my family in our time of grief if well-intentioned outside parties had simply allowed Zelda's request to talk to a friend to remain just that, rather than turning it into a medical and legal intervention."

~~~

Oh, Papa. I could use your sage advice right now. If you were here, we could debate the Madison move logically. But you are not here, and that is the difference that makes all the difference. Besides, you would probably scold me with reminders of all of Joan's amazing qualities, including her own heightened sense of loyalty and responsibility, tell me to settle down, to let someone else be right on this one.

I can only wonder, since no one is talking to me about it, what my stepsisters must think of my enflamed emotions of late. If the situation were reversed, I might be every bit as intent on putting distance between myself and them.

But no sooner do I collect my frayed nerves into a tidy bundle than another grenade lands ticking at my feet, leaving me gasping and blithering once again.

6-6-06, P.M.: *While Joan picks up Rob from the airport, Jack and I stop by the townhouse to talk over the Fort Snelling burial arrangements with Z. I ask about her move to Madison, offer the phrase "nursing home" when she searches for a term to describe her new lodgings. "No way am I living in a nursing home," she snaps.*

I fumble out an apology. Tell her I must have misunderstood. But Jack and I are stunned by her harshness and quickly skitter to new topics.

Z's chin trembles as we seek out a clean, stoppered bottle for the small portion of Dad's ashes she wants to sprinkle by the lake in Beaver Dam. Her tears well as we talk about finding new homes for the pups, the funeral service program, the burial service date.

But we also speak of more cheering topics. And she thrusts out fish lips and flares her nostrils to mimic an eccentric character Jack describes spotting at Arby's this noon. Gathering comic momentum, she lays her vibrating hands on the tabletop. "And I can play piano right here, staccato!"

Joan returns from the airport with Rob and thanks me profusely for staying with her mom and taking the pups for their trot. I clothe my bruised dignity in nonchalance. Tell her I don't require recognition. I've been walking the dogs for a long time now and suffer withdrawal when it's missing from my day, I go on—with unnaturally precise enunciation.

Am I no longer family? Was I ever?

Before Joan and Rob got to the townhouse, Zelda told me that she plans on making frequent visits back to the Twin Cities. So the deal is definitely sealed. Meanwhile, I feel petulant and misunderstood as if, after years of devotion, I am being dismissed like hired help.

In contesting this transition, I grant it the power to diminish me. Yet, like a moth flirting with the flame that will consume it, I keep returning to the scorching source of my torment.

In contesting this transition, I grant it the power to diminish me. Yet, like a moth flirting with the flame that will consume it, I keep returning to the scorching source of my torment.

I just want my stepsisters to acknowledge my wrenching loss of everything at once. Right now I feel outnumbered. Like a true outsider. An enemy force of one. Or worse, like a troublemaker who refuses to simply pass the blasted torch and be done with it.

Chapter 23

Metamorphosis

Summer in Minnesota. It's a much-anticipated, much-appreciated season. With a large portion of the citizenry poring over seed catalogues and boating brochures as early as February, hope blossoms large that warm weather will arrive soon enough to allow for four good months of gardening and water sports.

One week into this June, however, I am hunched over a keyboard, slamming out letters and emails to anyone Dad ever knew, whittling away at my need to talk about him nonstop. And when I'm not perched on the edge of my desk chair in pursuit of new outlets for telling his story, I literally cannot sit still. This perpetual state of agitation sends me not out into the sunshine to plant petunias but underground to the elliptical trainer in an unfinished, windowless corner of my basement. Here, I feverishly pump into submission the supercharged stream of energy that pulsates through every sinew in my body.

Part of this frenzy is an attempt to exorcise demon emotions which are further unsettled by claims that I've left Zelda out of the loop regarding household affairs. It's as if the pandemonium inside my skull channels itself into a physical propulsion I cannot suppress; as if my body is sloughing off the lethargy that clogged all fonts of vitality during anxious months of wondering and waiting.

The engine within revs out of control. Something has to give soon, or I will most certainly blow a gasket or two.

6-7-06: *Are my stepsisters really being cold and standoffish, or am I simply insane with grief? Is there swelling between us some species of proprietary envy over my relationship with Z? This doesn't feel like that.*

A haze of uncertainty clouds my vision. I am frantic to discover what I am missing so I can mend these broken ties. I so want to be rational and patient. To wait for Guidance.

No sooner do I scribble this appeal than my mind flits to the accusation that I have failed to explain my actions as Zelda's legal representative. *En garde*, comes the warning from my brain. It's difficult to complete a communications loop with management when you've been ushered out the front door of headquarters. But I have seen or talked to Zelda every day, asked for her participation or input in any estate business, and diligently reported back to her on outcomes.

Heavens. Could the explanation be that uncomplicated? Has Zelda's overtaxed hippocampus simply flushed all memory of these discussions like so much excess tissue swirling down the throat of the porcelain throne? Will I have to call on my husband as a witness for the defense? And on the defensive I am—against the charge that I've been secretive and other phantom indictments.

Bound up in this shroud of ill feelings, justifying why Jack and I argued to keep Zelda with us calls for a degree of diplomacy I can't dredge up. But I can tally the facts.

There's my past experience working in nursing facilities—the best of which cannot provide the reassuring familiarity that home care offers. There's the reality that all her daughters have demanding job or family obligations that I am free of. And there is Zelda's sense of belonging, her circle of dear friends, which only weeks ago she fondly laid out as what made the Twin Cities "home."

Finally, there is my own despair over a repayment uncompleted and a mission abandoned. In our little enclave of three, I shadowed Dad's and Zelda's brave, if sometimes faltering, footsteps. There, I taught and was educated; discovered actualities and rediscovered dreams; observed, challenged, and ran offense. How can mere words give life and breath to the intense sense of commitment and interpersonal bonding that flourishes in such a climate? But there I go again—justifying.

~~~

Theoretically, consulting an attorney should help plot a course that avoids roadblocks and delays. But then, theory doesn't always hold up under testing. And interpersonal bonds survive only when they're mutually coveted.

6-8-06: *Jack and I meet with the lawyer and leave with more questions than we brought—questions that will remain unanswered until we can lay our hands on a full copy of the trust.*

I call Z to tell her we will visit tomorrow. She sounds remote. Out of the blue, she declares that going to Wisconsin just feels like the right thing to do. I tell her that if she feels it's the right thing, then that's what she should do. She responds with a razor-edged "What?" "I'm just agreeing with you," I insist. But what she hears is, "I disagree with you." Instantly, the tone grows strained as if between ex-spouses.

I steer us to happier talk about having found Chloé a new home, with no word yet on Fergie, and close by saying "I love you." She says only "Goodbye."

Five minutes later I get the news from Pet Haven: The same family will take both Chloé and Fergie. I call Z immediately and Rob answers, sounding cheerful, friendly. Yet when I ask if I can tell Z the good news about the pups, she says she will handle telling her mom.

Steaming along on brewing suspicions, I wonder how Z reported our last conversation, worry that the reason there is a stepsister on site is to insulate Zelda from me, and end up knee-deep in doubt and frustration.

I feel helpless. Outnumbered by opposing forces who have become wedges in this schism between Z and me. Have I tripped over my own tangled emotions into Bonkersville?

~~~

The quandary: If you are self-aware enough to worry that you're obsessing, does that mean you are actually quite sane? Dad used to say it's not paranoia if they're really out to get you.

The quandary: If you are self-aware enough to worry that you're obsessing, does that mean you are actually quite sane? Dad used to say it's not paranoia if they're really out to get you.

Desperate to determine what went so horribly wrong, I dig up a hundred little things I may have said or done that seemed natural to me because I'd become Zelda's eyes and ears and schedule-keeper, but which could be misconstrued as overreaching by her daughters.

I draw a deep breath or three, shimmy out of the burdensome armor I'd strapped on, and dial Zelda's number. I want to enlist her help in selecting photos for the memorial picture board. Her daughter answers. Sorry, she says, her mom can't take my call. Clank, the metal breastplate snaps back into place.

So I am either delusional from a pathological sense of loss and this is merely a grand set of coincidences, or there is indeed a protective wall being constructed. How terribly sad if this mourning period should be marred by the family allegiance that cements the Bios, forever conjoined by their shared history, against the Pseudo who barged in halfway through the narrative. Or worse, if the amoebic myth that Zelda has reason to fear me has sprouted legs and now walks about as formidable fact.

If my true priority is peace and closure for Zelda, it's time to climb off this bed of pins and needles and poke around underneath it to see if anything actually lurks there.

June 9, 2006

Dear Stepsisters,

I feel like a leper. Like an outsider you sisters are circling the wagons against.

I know my response may have seemed overblown to you, but learning that you never actually considered our offer to take in your mom hit me at an emotionally volatile moment.

As for the need-to-know issue, only today was I able to put together an approximation of Z's cash-flow situation (see attached)—having felt eaten alive by the mourning process and being preoccupied with Dad's funeral arrangements.

I need to dissolve this tension. I don't want to walk on eggs, nurse paranoia, or worry that innocent remarks will get repeated out of context and reacted to, without anyone talking to me about them. And I don't want to cease being a part of the family now that Dad is no longer here.

To avoid future trust issues, I propose that we transfer the power-of-attorney assignment to Joan by July first. This gives me time to take care of burial costs and clear up some outstanding expenses.

I love your mom as if she were my own and have often told her that her marrying my father was one of the greatest blessings in my life. I truly want to help smooth the way for her.

Please tell me specifically what you want and need from me. In return, having a timeline for Ma Z's move would be helpful, so I know what to expect, and when.

Thanks for your patience as we sort through the complex feelings that are churning inside all of us.

Love,

Suz

There. I've either stepped into it or out of it. I may be shopping for new shoes tomorrow.

~~~

When you are fortunate enough to be dealing with decent, caring counterparts—they are, after all, Zelda's daughters—exposing a problem generates honest efforts to resolve it.

Joan responds with a touching description of the decision-making process from her perspective. Thanks me for my devotion over the years, reveals her conviction that her mother's decline will accelerate beyond our ability to cope, and gently reminds me that her sisters need an accommodating hub where they can gather around their mother.

Joan also humbles me with a confidence: She desperately wants to avoid the mistake of waiting too long to move an aging parent close, and she plans to cut back her hours at work so she can volunteer at whichever facility her mom ends up choosing.

She closes by sketching out an itinerary for Zelda's move to Madison, where she'll stay with Joan until a suitable, long-term placement can be arranged.

I also hear back from Deb and Julie, and Rob eases access to her mother, begins to welcome our visits with a smile and a hug.

My head still hosts a circus of reverberating thoughts but, emotionally, much has been settled. Now if only I could get my stomach to accept food, my limbs to stop twitching with impatience, and my brain to hit the snooze button for more than six hours a night.

Chapter 24

Paper Trails and Puppy Dog Tales

Some words of advice to the inexperienced: Do not delude yourself that well-organized finances and legal documents guarantee the trouble-free settling of your loved one's posthumous affairs. Life in the last lane will likely not be that simple.

Things get especially knotty when lawyers have the audacity to retire and county-specific rules and regulations are designed to make sense only to the bored legislators who churn them out for their own amusement.

Then there is dealing with the leviathan Federal government, tentacled out as the Department of Veterans Affairs, the Social Security Administration, the Internal Revenue Service, and various other frighteningly byzantine administrative bodies. Not to be left out of the jolly conspiracy to bedevil survivors in their time of loss, investment firms will resist surrendering profitable accounts and cell phone contractors will insist that only the deceased party himself is authorized to cancel service.

Parents plagued by encroaching infirmities may also bury fiscal landmines to be tripped over by the fiduciary principal left behind—who may not be operating at full mental capacity herself at the moment. (The fact that Dad never filed a 2005 tax return is worrisome, but one problem at a time, if you please.)

6-10-06: *Again I awaken at 5 a.m., electrified with nervous energy. At least with the rift between the Steps and me patched, breathing comes more naturally. I am no longer a single ping-pong ball bouncing off a fortification built four deep.*

But I am still a human sparkler—frantic to be doing something every second, even as creeping mental fatigue engulfs me like a pea soup fog. Fortunately, between personal and business correspondence, bill paying and memorial arrangements, diversionary tasks abound—most of which can be tackled in this fizzy, fuzzy state.

Jack and I stop by the townhouse to walk the dogs and have a late lunch with Z. Reduced to outside observer, I swallow the effervescent urge to counsel against the over-helping that some of my stepsisters think is necessary in dealing with their mom.

Z responds to the hovering by saying she's not used to being coddled—a polite euphemism, I'm thinking. But I must banish such speculations lest they come shooting out of my mouth and demolish our recently erected bridge of reconciliation.

My better self argues that this is simply daughterly affection and protectiveness. A matter of assuming that Z's memory challenges generalize to overall capabilities. A result, perhaps, of lack of exposure to the full range of her ups and downs—these last few weeks having cast an unflattering light on all of us.

But the reasoning behind it is not for me to sort out or critique. They care about her and she feels cared about. Anyway, it's entirely between them. None of my business. And certainly out of my hands.

~~~

The original copy of Dad and Zelda's trust is nowhere to be found. Nowhere logical, anyway. Not in the daunting collection of home files or the safety deposit box or the law office to which the disappearing family attorney transferred her records before she fell off the face of

I hear myself reassuring her. Outlining the positives. Being Suzy Sunshine. And I discover that I am a fairly good actress.

the earth. The hunt for it takes us to befuddling foreign ground, and we're trekking paperwork mountains without a Sherpa.

Meanwhile, liberated from the major tensions with the Steps, I am freed to ache for Zelda and her many losses—from spouse to furry companions to longtime friends.

6-11-06: *Today Z speaks of the move, not as if she is trying to convince me of the desirability of it, but herself. Keenly aware that I must not share any more opinions, I hear myself reassuring her. Outlining the positives. Being Suzy Sunshine. And I discover that I am a fairly good actress.*

Still, the midnight moon finds me wakeful and troubled, nursing a pulsating uncertainty and resurrecting the unhelpful question of whether this move really is the right decision.

Stop. Halt. Cease and desist, she said redundantly. Let's truly "let go and let God," whose capacity for big-picture resolution makes my squeaking efforts laughable. Besides, I chastise myself, consider Joan's throbbing fears, wakeful nights, and troubled heart. Pull yourself out of this vortex of worry and trust the ongoing process, you ninny.

~~~

The pups. Those dear, wee, mischievous critters. I simply cannot take them into my own four-cat, dog-phobic mother-in-law living arrangement. So I wring every last drop out of time spent with them. Walking them and nuzzling them. Cooing over them. Watching them romp and play.

Chloé, testing the limits of her leash, loses sight of Fergie and me over the ridge of a hill, searches the horizon intently until she has us in her sights again, then charges joyfully to my side. Bless their little pink hearts. I'll have to treat them to the doggie spa before they get introduced to their new family.

Of course, even tending to canine commitments was bound to contribute its own pebble of frustration to the pile. Paws and Rest calls to say that the dogs' rabies vaccinations are out of date so they can't be groomed. After the vaccinations, it's still a two-day wait, and their placement looms near. Drat. The best-laid plans of mice and ditsy daughters. And, absurdly, in my present state of high alert, this seems like a majorly big deal.

~~~

With Dad's memorial service put off until June 23 so out-of-towners can make travel arrangements, I have time to mull things over. Hah. Who am I kidding? I've been a persistent muller since fourth grade. And if I can't find mulling time during daylight hours, my brain will simply start the process on autopilot at 3 a.m.

Today's ponderings end with a jarring bump against the answer to a nagging concern.

Q: Why have the events of the past four weeks so thoroughly unnerved me?

A: Because deeply etched in my mind hid an unchallenged scenario of how the script at Dad and Zelda's would play out.

I took it for granted that we would drift along as we had been for another year or more, and that Chloé would be the first of the household to leave us. Eventually, I assumed, Zelda would succumb to complications from her various conditions, leaving me to care for Dad and Fergie for several additional years.

The last few weeks of Dad's life forced me into a metal-screeching U-turn and an emergency reset of the old Internal Positioning System.

6-12-06: *This evening, I crawl into Jack's lap and whimper that I am forlorn; that I know things will be OK, but that I also know that things will never be the same. He is tenderly sympathetic. Reminds me that it is all right to be sad about such a multitude of losses.*

But I am vexed by an irrational sense of failure. I've been clinging to the expectation that I could somehow make things better enough at the townhouse for Dad and Zelda to keep up their semi-independent living arrangement. Deep within my cavernous subconscious, I must have known that time was short. Yet the dream persisted, a cardboard castle afloat in the gossamer skies of my own hopeful imagination.

Unfortunately, reality doesn't support such poetic fantasies, only the sentimental heart does. Yet now I want to be angry at the pragmatists?

~~~

So, I am detaching myself from my caretaker role, right? Forming calluses to insulate my paper-thin skin and backing away from the process of deciding Zelda's future, correct? Then how come I behave like a flip-flopping fish who really, really wants to plunge back into the lake?

6-14-06: *Why am I still fighting with myself? If someone would say out loud, in plain English, that all of the Steps are in agreement, maybe I could stop wondering whether sister A knows what sister B is saying and doing. As it is, I'm like a dog with a rancid bone. I want to let it go, but my stubborn nature bares its gums in resistance.*

I hear murmurings that Z is roaming about at night, and I writhe in my chair, itching to speak up. To say that this is partly situational. That not all of her nights are spent that way.

I hold back, afraid I'll appear to be pressing my case again. But my insides flinch over the casual comment that, when Z gets settled into The Nursing Home That None Dare Call a Nursing Home, the staff there will be "adjusting her medications" to take care of that problem.

I grimace and wonder if anyone notices. Fight the need to speak out as old fears stir within. To tamp them down, I revisit Z's sweet declaration. "And we can walk in the woods and sing hymns," she predicted during a convivial exchange about what lies ahead when we visit her in her new abode.

Maybe it will all be as she trusts it will be, at least in her own hopeful imagination.

~~~

To spare Zelda the pain of days spent rattling around in a semi-empty, dog-less house, Joan plans to transport their entourage back to her place in Madison the day after we transport the pups to the vet's office, where their new family will pick them up. This

> Maybe it will all be as she trusts it will be, at least in her own hopeful imagination.

seems like a good plan. It should make the rehousing of the pets less traumatic for Zelda. Should.

But, even as untrue as it is, I feel as if I am putting Chloe and Fergie into a rowboat and pushing them out to sea, their bewildered little faces staring back at me in confusion. That's what I fear their trip to the exchange point will be like tomorrow, and I need it to be over.

6-15-06, A.M.: *The day of the last dog walk. I am despondent. Can't stop crying over those two little mutts. When one of the Steps says she doesn't think the Razadyne is doing anything for her mom, I funnel all my sad frustration into vigorous refutation. Off the Razadyne, I contend, there's a disturbing decline in rational thought, memories become irretrievable, and Z's disorientation goes from mild to profound.*

Then, of course, I stew. What will happen when she gets to Madison? Z will have a physician who sees multiple nursing home patients per visit instead of her kind, personal physician, Dr. A. And the new doc will likely use a cookie-cutter approach to keep all of his charges manageable for the staff.

With difficulty, I force myself to remember where my faith leads me: to accept the things I cannot change. Peace seeps in. My worst enemy is me. I cannot seem to sidestep the rushing current of my negative thoughts.

But telephone calls to lawyers, bankers, and investment advisors must be made. So I open myself to the calm and make those calls.

Lord, please be with me through this day. Make me a tranquil child of yours, not a manic fool who borrows tomorrow's imagined troubles.

But tension returns, creeping up my spine like a cold chill in the dark of night, and I forget my pledge to do my part in this quest for tranquility. I snap at feckless store clerks. Look at everyone with the same disapproving eye. Hold onto my stress and wield it like a weapon.

6-15-06, P.M.: *Please, Lord. Show me your plan. Rub my nose in it. Remind me what you require of me. Strengthen me to be a child of grace rather than an embittered soul always on the brink.*

When we take those two little girls to the vet tomorrow, remind me that all will work out for the best. And when Z goes away, shout into my resisting ears that I can lay my hopes in your hands, trusting that she will be content and her soul watched over.

~~~

These days I can edit myself to sound more sane and stable on paper, so I compose a long note to the family who will be taking in our little furry friends. I thank them for their kindness. Describe Chloé's long-term residency with Dad and Zelda and Fergie's early-life rescue from an abandoned apartment and add a postscript listing a few eccentricities it may be helpful to know.

– When Chloe tinkles, she does a "handstand," and when she gets down to serious business, she does a charming little crab walk, continuing in a slow zigzag until she has laid down a short trail of chocolate drops.

- Fergie, for unknown reasons, is very sensitive about having her paws touched.

- When tense, these two may get into a spat, creating a horrible ruckus. No injury has ever resulted, but prevention and/or intervention may be required.

- Last, whenever either of them relieves herself, they are both accustomed to getting half a dog biscuit as a reward. I am sending along a bag of their preferred treats.

6-16-06: *The morning of the first Grand Goodbye. I sleep less than four hours yet awaken refreshed. The inner isometrics continue, but a sense of peace about the pups and the outcome of their placement overrides the internal contractions.*

Meanwhile, I have much work to do on me—on my mild resentment that Jack and I are stuck with this dirty deed while Joan and Rob get to stay behind and be the comforters and soothers, and then get to do lunch with Barb McC on top of it all. And if one more person asks me if the dogs are going into a home with children, I may just scream, "Of course they aren't. I am competent to handle this properly, dang it!"

There. Now I promise not to spew any more bile for the rest of the day.

I am despicable. A heaving, stinking, moldy mass of wretchedness. We arrive at Zelda's to pick up Chloé and Fergie, and dear Joan is so distraught about their departure that pain distorts her face. As we leave, she blows kisses to us and to the pups, saying to me, "You have the hardest job of all. Thank you so much for doing this."

~~~

We say our goodbyes to Zelda and company, and Chloé and Fergie jump eagerly into the van and onto my lap, keen for an adventure. But they soon sense trickery, their little bodies reaching a quaking crescendo as the ride drags on.

Once inside the vet's, I request a moment to say goodbye. But there are crossed wires. The staff waits for me to signal we are ready. I wait for the staff to approach and collect our quivering, fearful little bundles. Prolonging the process intensifies the dread.

Separation. Anxiety. I am practically nonfunctional by the time we climb back into the Toyota for our ride home. Obviously, this sixty-minute excursion is far from the most tragic event I have ever experienced. Still, it ranks as one of the most distressing hours I have ever endured.

Dear Jack, calm and helpful. Ready with entertaining errands to help put the upsetting experience behind us. He is very good at constructive refocusing. If only I could arrange a Vulcan mind-meld with my levelheaded husband.

6-17-06: *I fall asleep late but easily, then dream that Chloé teeters on the ledge of a cliff and I can't make my paralyzed legs operate well enough to rescue her. My eyes fly open in terror at 4:50 a.m., the La Brea Tar Pits of emotional upheaval slogging away in my gut.*

Fortunately, I do not actually upheave—not much in there to bring up these days, anyway—but my prayers will never bring me peace as long as I cling to painful events like some sort of security blanket. Maybe I am afraid to let go of my anguish long enough to think about the future.

Chapter 25

Apoplexies and Eulogies

Little things. They can really ruffle your stuff when your emotional immune system is tapped out. My unpredictable cat, JJ, attacks my mother-in-law's petite calico in our shared backyard and I explode with screeches. Feel at risk of ripping at the seams as my heart pounds violently against my rib cage. Execute adrenaline-fueled vaults across twenty feet of turf.

Scooping the offending devil-pet back inside, I dissolve into a sputtering tirade about said mother-in-law. I've asked her dozens of times to warn me when she lets the downstairs cats out, I rant. She knows I take JJ out every afternoon, I rave. (Heaven forbid I should keep any of this insanity to myself lest my husband be allowed to think I am even remotely capable of pulling myself together.)

I actually believe that I am not entirely unlovable—when I'm in a normal frame of mind. These eruptive flares seem sinister and demonic, leave me depleted, and scare me silly. I tally the stresses: Dad's death, Zelda's move, loss of the pups, Jack's unemployment and vision issues; a dear friend's husband falsely imprisoned; another friend's son in a coma—victim of a drunken driver's drag race with police. So maybe it's not the little things after all. It's the cluster bomb of big things that hit all at once, leaving a gaping entry wound. The small irritations are just salt.

When you're feeling rubbed raw, even a smidgeon of good news renders balm.

6-20-06: *A note from Pet Haven about the girls' happy adjustment to their new home brings me peace. Even working alone at the deserted townhouse, I only break down a few times—once when I half expect to see Fergie romping toward me as I enter the back door, a second time as I overturn monogrammed Christmas stockings in a box of decorations. Then one more lapse when I come upon Dad's cornflower blue wool V-neck cardigan—so warming on a frosty winter evening. Determined to keep hacking away at the endless panorama of painful reminders, I pound my forehead with the heels of my hands to force the tears to stop and give the sweater one last hug before I thrust it into the Salvation Army bag.*

But I am OK. Not desolate and hopeless. And beginning to feel more grounded.

Alas, the staff at the bank lies in wait to uproot the grounded. I can't exercise power of attorney in Zelda's behalf without her being focused enough to add my name to her bank accounts. Not their fault, of course. There are larger governing entities that hand down the rules. But what good is power of attorney, I wonder, if it doesn't cover such contingencies as the empowerer relocating or becoming semi-incapacitated? Puzzles like this explain the large consulting fees levied by our lawyer—who has not, by the way, been in touch for three days. Time to leave another message for him.

> What good is power of attorney, I wonder, if it doesn't cover such contingencies as the empowerer relocating or becoming semi-incapacitated?

~~~

There are arguments to be made for a quick hop from bereavement date to funeral. But as Dad's memorial service approaches, I am grateful we had three weeks to prepare and get the word out. And apparently his résumé warrants extra attention from the staff at the *Star Tribune*.

This gives us the bonus of an article with photo, which covers the date and time of the service and an overview of Dad's professional life. Like a helium-inflated blimp, I swell with satisfaction each time even one more person is made aware of his contributions to society. The newspaper piece pumps me ceiling high. Anguish still wants to cling, like a bur embedded in my gym sock disrupting my gait. But this added attention provides ballast, allowing me to regain my footing—wobbly though it may be.

6-22-06: *I bake banana bread for Z's temporary return, run multiple errands, and finalize preparations for tomorrow's program; I proof the service brochure and polish my four-page eulogy, praying the audience doesn't fall asleep on each other's shoulders by page three. And I do a lot of deep-breathing.*

~~~

June 23, 2006. Days like today can pass in a blur. If providence beams brightly, it will be a blur from which you can later retrieve exactly the right set of selected memories. And there should be a bounty of memories to draw from since funeral rites tend to bring out the comforting best in those attending.

Joan graciously seats Zelda between Rob and me in the front pew for the entire service, and she and husband Rich each deliver a touching tribute to Dad from the intricately carved speaker's podium at Barb and Tom's church. The blast of bagpipes squeezing out "Amazing Grace" and "Danny Boy" overfills the small sanctuary. Had I known, I would have had the piper play from the outer lobby. Still, the overall atmosphere is lovely.

Anxious as a gnat anticipating sundown, I plunge into my oration feeling as if I've swallowed a plum pit that is now lodged halfway down my esophagus. Polite smiles see me through to the end.

"I started writing this in the present tense, addressing my father when he first entered the hospital on May 19 and I found that I needed to keep him in my mind and prayers and conversation all of my waking hours. In revising it for this occasion of both sorrow and hope, I will first share my thoughts on Milton Hugh Williams Jr. and then take a glance at his life and times through his own words. I'll close with some recollections of his best friend from graduate school."

Zelda stays composed throughout the service and luncheon, even as the lava flow of people begins to confuse and tire her. I can only imagine the strain imposed on her frail body by three hours of pomp and socializing. But the distraction of so many affectionate encounters also rescues her from her own well of grief and tires her for a good night's sleep.

Having refilled empty tanks with the loving consolations of others who knew and appreciated Dad, I should be able to run on the fragrant vapors for at least a few days . . . you'd think. But as competing viewpoints careen and collide, my passions rise to trouble the waters.

6-24-06, A.M.: *I am trying to remain calm. But if I must joust with my stepsisters much longer, disadvantaged by the slippery footing of my radically changed status, I may just scream.*

Yesterday was Dad's public commemoration. Aside from my choosing to wear a perspiration-loving polyester top that rudely released noxious molecules whenever I reached out to embrace a well-wisher, it was a very nice affair that lifted my spirits and left me even prouder of my father.

When I offer to provide fill-in support, Joan freezes in place, mortified by the suggestion. No, she decides. The answer is to get Z installed in a nursing home within the week.

Yet ever since the posse's return from Wisconsin, I've been unnerved by what I'm hearing—complaints that Z needs help even to go to the bathroom, that she breaks down just opening sympathy cards, that she wanders around all night keeping people up.

When I offer to provide fill-in support, Joan freezes in place, mortified by the suggestion. No, she decides. The answer is to get Z installed in a nursing home within the week.

I cannot fathom what is going on. The woman in question has just suffered one of life's greatest losses, and her reaction is somehow distasteful?

Afflicted with dementia, Z has lost her spouse and pets, has been hauled back and forth in a confusing trip across state lines, faces the surrender of her home and most of her belongings, and must now prepare to leave dear friends behind forever. She would be a walking miracle if she didn't exhibit symptoms of regression—especially on the heels of a taxing memorial service.

That's Despicable Me droning on in my private journal. In a more reasonable frame of mind I surmise that the on-site Bios have stepped into an atypical microcosm of their mother's daily functioning, perhaps reaching dramatic conclusions based on that hazy snapshot. Having made what they believe is the best decision, they may be homing in on details that support it. We are all capable of selective observation.

But it's buh-bye to cool, analytical thinking when my mother-in-law informs me that the acoustics in the church yesterday were so bad that not one word that came out of the speakers' mouths could be heard. *Not one word.* The fact that my mother-in-law is hearing impaired does nothing to temper my reaction.

"She doesn't mean to ruin the experience for you," Jack proposes prudently.

"She doesn't mean *not* to ruin the experience for me," I spit back petulantly.

I am such a brat. I probably need a vacation, but that wouldn't necessarily sweeten a soured attitude. And I'd probably spend the time worrying about all the things that need to be done back here anyway. Might as well keep plugging along. And keep praying for divine intervention of the personality-altering kind.

6-24-06, P.M.: *Today, as Jack and I leave the townhouse after our visit, I wrap my arms around Z and she says she misses me. I tell her I miss her, too, but didn't want to be the first to say it. Then she pauses, carefully choosing her words; says she thinks she might have made the wrong decision, especially after the time she spent in Madison last week.*

I am at a loss. What can I say or do? I tell her to give Madison a try for a month and, if she doesn't like it, she can come back. But my aching heart knows that will never be sanctioned, and I shrink into the shadow of my own lie. Lord, help me figure out all of this. And please put Zelda where she needs to be, not where I need her to be.

~~~

God takes such good care of us—when we let Him. With all the frantic exertions of the past five weeks, I've lost ten pounds. Not a bad thing. But when a muffled voice in my head tells me to slow down, something moves me to actually listen.

I skip some workouts. Do fun things instead. A Sunday potluck at church, reading away a lazy afternoon, Taco Bell for supper, neighborhood baseball games at sunset, an uplifting chat with a good friend before bed.

Still completely whacked out on Monday, I make a few trips down to the elliptical trainer for mood control, fold some laundry, wash a few dishes, then sit in my recliner—blissfully remorse-free—and watch HGTV from 3 p.m. until 10 p.m. Amazing how a two-day stint of R&R can refresh a person. But then there's that nasty, post-staycation letdown.

First, the hassle of a trip to the financial planner's office to learn how to be a personal representative. And still, the trust remains buried somewhere obscure, no doubt snickering to itself like a triumphant hide-and-seeker. But at least I have managed to stay on good terms with the stepsister who remains behind with Zelda. Or so I imagine.

6-27-06: *Following Jack's doctor's appointment at one, we drive to* *the townhouse. The plan is to take Z to the bank, have me added as a signatory on her checking account, and have Dad's name removed—all this on the advice of the personal banker, not my idea. I expect to pick up only Z, but the Resident Step turns off the washing machine mid-cycle so she can accompany us. Fine. I didn't know she was interested. Once there, my stepsister leans forward, her tense limbs pretzel-wrapped around her chair, and asks the banker in terse, insistent phrases for a copy of "anything that Zelda signs today."*

Hmm. Am I trusted, or am I not? This Step's demeanor is uncharacteristically stiff, formal, and suspicion-riddled. What could possibly be happening over there when I'm not present that leaves me splattered in dark, menacing hues I don't deserve to be painted with? That, overnight, turns everything on its head?

I am shaken. Shocked back into modus protectus. I don't like crouching behind a shield of legal explanations, but my assaulted ego ushers me there. Spine stiffened to its full expanse, I assure all parties that this procedure was recommended by the banker, gives me no more authority than I currently have, and simply avoids future problems while Zelda is out of state.

Now on full alert that others suspect I'm capable of funny business, I take pains to have one of Zelda's daughters witness all transactions. Multiple signatures are needed. There are papers making Zelda owner of Dad's IRA and documents allowing me to sign paperwork on her behalf so we won't have to send a lawyer to disturb her in Madison every time her John Hancock is required. And if I am to sell the townhouse for her and settle medical claims, I need copies of her Social Security and Medicare IDs.

As we leave for the day, hoping absence will make a certain heart grow tender, I see a card to Zelda on the coffee table. Logic tells me it's from someone offering their sympathies on the occasion of my father's death.

"Zelda, you have a card here. Shall we open it?" I say, starting for the kitchen to get a letter opener.

"She knows it's there," I am sternly rebuffed.

Just butt out and go home, my mind translates. I can't say from personal experience, but I'm thinking a bad batch of psychedelic mushrooms couldn't provide any more bizarre a trip than this.

6-27-06: *Evening falls, and I feel tossed about like a rag doll in a* Toy Story *chase scene—afraid of future dealings with the Steps because I don't know the source of all this tension or how far among them it's spread. I thought a remnant of affection still held, that respect for my integrity had been restored.*

I didn't seek out the job of tackling messy legal work and locating lost documents. Or the role of micro-accounting based on mind-reading abilities I don't possess. Dad and Zelda asked this of me. I take it on to honor their wishes. And I would rather have me in charge of the Minnesota side of things than some stranger.

Lord, I'm not doing so well here. I need your arm around my shoulder and your hand over my mouth. My crass self-focus trips me up every time. Me, me, me; I, I, I; my, my, my. I sound like a prima donna prepping for her solo. Please ease me back into the chorus where I belong.

Chapter 26

Chilly Receptions and Grueling Goodbyes

I am not Agatha Christie. I cannot knit together from shrewd observations a slick solution to the Mysterious Affair at Zelda's. Real life doesn't offer enough control over the characters to steer the action where you want it to go. Currently cast as villainess, I can only hope to redeem myself via a clever surprise ending.

I hear secondhand that Zelda is more herself now that things have quieted down. I pray that her current caretaker will follow suit. But when my niece, Rachel, on my father's side announces she's coming into town for one last visit with Grandma, the ice castle walls go up with astounding speed.

Even after phoning ahead, there is no hint of a warm welcome at the townhouse. More like a frosty blast—the kind that makes you wish you could be anywhere else. Resident Step (R.S.) sits hip-to-hip with Zelda on the couch. Glares at me for the granddaughter intrusion I had no part in planning. And here, I had naively slept through the night thinking things couldn't get any worse.

6-28-06: *In one flashing thought, I am incensed by all of this. In the next, I tear myself up wondering what I might have done to bring it on. Has Z shared her second thoughts about moving with her daughter, who now assumes that I planted that doubt? Am I viewed as a competitor* *for Z's affections, my every visit a tug at her allegiance?*

If any of this is afoot, why not respect me enough to lay it on the table so we can sort it out, rather than just turn on me?

Hurt feelings leave me mind-boggled. If I have bungled something, I am frantic to make it right. But this requires someone on "their side" who's willing to communicate my blunders to me rather than fling up barricades.

If any of this is afoot, why not respect me enough to lay it on the table so we can sort it out, rather than just turn on me?

~~~

There are oceanic depths to the turmoil that swirls around the loss of beloved family members—either to death or personality-robbing decline. This current standoff is almost as nerve-racking as what we went through with Dad, and I sincerely doubt my ability to connect enough dots to make sense of it. The Sisterhood Alliance may be a product of my own skewed thinking; I don't know. But my brain insists on wrestling with the possibility that a coalition actually exists.

That haunting all-or-nothing trait of mine plagues me, too, attaching like a caboose to the train of paranoid thoughts. If I can't clutch all four of Zelda's biological daughters to my bosom in devout, sisterly love, then must I hold all four at arm's length in wary mistrust?

"God grant me the serenity to accept the things I cannot change and the courage to change the things I can." Since I have to. I guess. But how about that "knowing the difference" part? Wisdom. That's the elusive holy grail. Stepping back a few paces sometimes puts things in focus.

6-29-06: *Taking a break from visiting Z today. Mailing photo packets to friends and relatives, hemming the living room curtains, painting our small bathroom. These tasks engage and calm me. When my mind does wander, I start filling in blanks that I should, in fairness, leave empty.*

I am so thankful for my husband. His steadying presence is a blessing always, but especially in times of confusion and doubt. God, Jack, cherished friends, exercise, and journaling; these are my lifelines. My grip, however, could definitely use some work.

~~~

I am the weakest of vessels. I crack at the slightest jarring. Slosh out my soppy contents at the least provocation. Yield my peace far too easily. But the Potter knows His creation and mends and restores and sets right.

6-30-06, A.M.: *I call the townhouse to make arrangements to see Z one last time before she leaves for Wisconsin. Joan is back. She answers, and we talk for almost an hour. She now feels no need to rush the transfer of power of attorney and suggests an explanation for the ruptured détente: When Z, who has always been daunted by finances, protests that she has no idea what's going on in that department, some of her daughters may conclude that I'm deliberately withholding information. Thus, I become suspect. A trustee with untrustworthy inclinations.*

My eyeballs vibrate with simmering frustration. My knee jerks in anger. And the tennis game begins. Shame on them for their shortsighted acceptance of Z's paranoid rumblings when they so easily write off her other abilities.

But then, shame on me for making this about . . . me. For twisting my stomach into knots of resentment, especially since Z's altered reasoning is still a closed book to them. How are they to know that at the root of their mother's anxiety there is a distorted imagination feeding on scrambled input? "Because they know you," my prideful will volleys back.

Sidestepping the Armageddon raging between my ears, I emphasize to Joan yet again that I need to be told if anyone thinks I am overstepping or being insensitive. And Joan emphasizes yet again that she has nothing but appreciation for my taking on the burden of handling the legal and financial end of things. Healing begins with that reassurance.

Reassuring news about the nursing home, too. Joan visited the brightly lit facility and discovered among its residents many retired teachers, a history professor who recently lost his wife, and a retired physician. In other words, a cheerful environment housing a stimulating set of peers.

With relations normalized, eyeballs quieted, and leg joints relaxed, I feel renewed. Honored with immediate answers to prayers for reconciliation, I am reminded not to rely solely on my own resources. To be patient and button my lip. If only I could take five paces without losing command of that understanding.

~~~

When I was ten, I began to worry about my father whenever he traveled to meet with clients: car trips within the state; flights to Canada or California. The longer-distance jaunts troubled me the most. On the day he was due back from one of those, I would turn the corner of our block on my way home from school and make careful mental notes—about the movements of bicyclists, the activities of the neighbors. If I got a general sense of things being as they should be—no unnatural stillness to the air, no unfamiliar vehicles parked along the curb—well, then, obviously no calamity could have occurred during Dad's trip.

> My heart sags within my chest, heavy with dread at facing this final farewell.

As Jack and I drive the nine miles between our place and Zelda's, nothing appears out of order. The traffic flow, the bustling activity of shoppers and service station customers. The jerks running red lights because the guy in front of them got by with it. Yet adult experience tells me it means very little that the workings of the world proceed as usual without a nod to our agonizing mission. We are mere ants within an enormous formicarium, crawling past one another with no awareness of the private joys and sorrows of our fellow tunnelers. And my heart sags within my chest, heavy with dread at facing this final farewell.

This is the lady who stepped in when my own mother was no longer able to parent but never sought to displace her. The woman of taste who introduced me to novelist Anne Tyler's genius. The nutty companion with whom I rollicked through many a madcap escapade. The home economist who taught me to love Swiss chard, fresh from the garden, and how to make pot roast on the stove top.

There is a story about a man who, although his wife's Alzheimer's disease was in its final stages, visited her in a long-term care facility every day. When a friend asked, "Why do you bother? She doesn't even know who you are," this compassionate soul replied, "But I know who she is."

It's true that Zelda no longer takes delight in the rich tapestry of our decades of kinship and friendship. But I know her significance within it.

~~~

Today is a striking example of a welcome plot twist—granted in spite of my sorry self. With all visiting daughters reassured and homeward bound, Jack and I help Joan load suitcases and boxes into the rented SUV, learn more about activities offered at the nursing home, and enjoy an upbeat visit while Zelda rests.

6-30-06, Afternoon: *Z peeks out from under her bedcovers just as I am sneaking a quick look into her room to check on her. She waggles out a small wave of the hand, and I echo the gesture. Up from her nap, the jade-green ceramic teapot centered between us on the table, she talks with me about her future, says she will miss my cooking. I promise to bring her some turkey meat loaf patties and chocolate-chocolate chunk cookies.*

Finally, the time comes to say goodbye. Or not that, but so long for now. Jack and I take turns wrapping our arms first around Joan and then Z, then force reluctant feet to trudge toward our own vehicle and begin the dismal drive home. As the familiar scenery of so many daily trips slips by, I briefly erupt in tears until a peculiar sense of numb acceptance settles in.

I will miss that impish glint of the eye and the endless supply of entertaining quips. There will be a hollow space where this now frail, birdlike character once tolerated my cautious hugs, accepted my bumbling helpfulness, and returned my love from a place deep within her essential self. But it will be better for her where she is going, I think, now that my melancholy has lifted.

Letting go is the unselfish thing to do, and here I am doing it anyway. This move gives Z more independence than she would have had staying with Jack and me. Allows her to avoid feeling burdensome.

Now, if I step cautiously and hold my head just right, I may be able to keep my eye trained on those luminous pronouncements until our first nursing home visit can confirm them.

Chapter 27

Six Degrees of Separation

My birth mother's life was a genuine American tragedy. For reasons never openly discussed, her mother kicked her father out of the house when Mom was five. Out of the house and out of his family's lives, with little concern for how two fatherless children would deal with their sense of abandonment.

It was a hush-hush subject. You just didn't talk about post-traumatic stress disorder in the World War I era. But over the decades innuendos got scattered, a few spare crumbs here and there, leaving a trail to that explanation. The callously managed loss created in my mother a vacuum of withdrawn affection.

Mom blossomed as an attractive young brunette, getting attention from a gallery of soldier boys produced by her generation's worldwide conflict. Caught my father's eye, certainly. And they were happy for a time. They married, had two babies, socialized with other G.I. Bill students. Then, later, entertained friends and colleagues and built a comfortable suburban existence during the booming '50s and '60s.

But after those two babies outgrew their need for room mothers, scout leaders, and pre-prom "Coketail party" planners, Mom began to withdraw from life outside her fashionable front door. Her self-worth anchored to a role that no longer existed, old insecurities surfaced in that ironic way they have of breeding over-reliance—the oxygen-sucking kind of neediness that drives away the very others you so desperately want to wrap yourself around.

His children grown, my father remained intrigued by life's challenges and possibilities. Rather than settle into the complacency of a lucrative company career, he was eager to strike out on his own—a terrifying prospect to my now reclusive mother.

They parted. He flourished and she withered, leaving her two adult children behind to move across country and transfer dependency to her younger brother. She spent her days in sunny California indoors, her pampered pets and the flickering glare of a twenty-two-inch Magnavox for company. Here she dragged on Benson & Hedges and tipped in measured sips of watered-down scotch like a palliative oral IV, dripping just enough alcohol into her bloodstream to calm the quaking sense of apprehension, but not enough to inspire an intervention.

The inevitable stroke hit at sixty-seven, but the senior care center would not prove to be the haven of security and personal attention she had hoped for. At seventy-two, curled into a fetal position in her mechanical bed, she broke her bond with a world she felt betrayed by, having starved herself to death.

> I refuse to let my mother's legacy of fear germinate in my marrow when things get rough. My father responded to early-life trauma with fight and resolve, my mother with frailty and resignation.

Mom believed in God, but she didn't trust Him. At least not enough to be her strength in weakness. She died as much from self-induced dread as lack of food. The soul flinches at the thought.

I relate this cheery biography only to buttress a point: I refuse to let my mother's legacy of fear germinate in my marrow when things get rough. My father responded to early-life trauma with fight and resolve, my mother with frailty and resignation. We may not be able to choose our DNA, but we can choose our role models.

And, with well-placed trust, we can deflect blinding flashes of panic that threaten to shatter our concentration.

~~~

Following Zelda's departure, there are plenty of opportunities for hope and plenty of blinding flashes. During her first weeks in Wisconsin, she stays with Joan and Rich, easing the transition to nursing home living with daily visits to Aging Acres, or whatever it's called. Once she officially makes the move, Joan visits her every morning on her way to work and every evening after work. They establish a nightly ice cream ritual that helps Zelda prepare for restful sleep. I am consoled by this thoughtful approach, moved by Joan's devotion to her mother's comfort and peace of mind.

On the Minnesota end of things, I try too hard to preserve Zelda's favorite holiday. Invite Barb and Tom for an indoor picnic on July fourth. But I'm still too spring-loaded to relax with my guests, and I end the day wondering what they must think of their manic hostess and her nonstop chatter.

I write to Zelda every Monday, call her every Friday, and chew my lip whenever hints of loneliness creep into her voice. I also push myself to the ends of my physical resources, then complain when exhaustion sweeps over me by 8 p.m. like a rush of flu symptoms. Meanwhile, preparing the townhouse for sale feels like an ongoing sandpaper scrub against raw emotions that show no sign of scabbing over.

Forays to organize and disperse thirty-four years' worth of joint accumulations—trying not to look at every object we encounter as an inextricable piece of them that I can't bear to part with—will never get easy, no matter how many months we spread them across. And some of the early trips are the most abrasive.

7-7-06: *The front door to the townhouse opens on a static, over-furnished cavern, all the animation drained from it. I want to frill my fingers in the air to stir dust particles just to initiate some movement.*

Dad's been gone for five weeks. The pups for two. Z for one. Still, each of their shadows lingers. I open curtains and blinds to flood the place with sunlight. Shoo the ghosts from their hiding places. Plop down on the couch to nurse my self-pity.

"Please, Lord, make this ache go away," I wheeze, then immediately slump in shame knowing that so many others are tortured by losses much greater than mine. I wish I weren't such a wimp.

Barb shows up, and life returns to the empty tomb of a place. We recomb the files in search of the trust, measure and shop for carpeting and hardwood flooring, bag up Zelda's clothing. Sort through cabinets and drawers, clearing volumes of paper ephemera. Prepare books for the estate sale.

> Dad's been gone for five weeks. The pups for two. Z for one. Still, each of their shadows lingers.

I do fine until I've escorted Barb back to her car. On reentering the disheveled hull solo, a surge of grief knocks me sideways like a hapless surfer overcome by a rogue wave. Too tired for self-recriminations, I wonder if I'm massaging my heartache or whether this is all part of the natural process of . . . well, processing. The simple act of pondering calms me.

~~~

Unexpected gifts. By definition they rouse a special kind of gratitude. These days consolation flows in from my father's close associates. Raf calls to say he's been thinking about us. Sympathizes with our loss. Emphasizes that Dad often said how much it meant to have me coming over. What freedom it allowed him and how much he appreciated it.

And Dad's old Navy buddy Herb writes sweet words of remembrance. Recalls examples of Papa's good works. Completes a connection with a living remnant of a fading past.

His grad school chum Bill is another link in that chain. This generous man answers daily emails within hours, patiently entertains my trivial ramblings, and contributes an uplifting memory anytime I run out of things to smile about.

So many of Dad's and Zelda's friends step forward to offer support and encouragement as we sift through the relics of two lives well lived. And oh-so-well documented with souvenirs.

7-12-06: *Jack and I run ourselves limp meeting with the real estate agent, the stager, and the appliance guy; visiting the paint store, the carpet store, and the lighting department at Home Depot; seeking out quotes for grout cleaning. As an encore, we spend six hours hauling furniture to the garage in preparation for the painter, then have to clear a path for the concrete repair people. It's a big garage, but there are limits.*

I also discover that the rule "only handle things once" doesn't apply to highly personal items. Without some reconsideration, we might impulsively toss a treasure or—flip side—compulsively hold on to every crumbling bit of personal history, like the barely recognizable corsage from B & Z's wedding. Even with a second look, reason doesn't always prevail. Z's lucky penny garter for example. That may just be a keeper.

And so we plod along, gradually pushing back the border of this mass of possessions like the slow creep of warm weather gnawing at the edges of a blanket of winter ice. I am encouraged that we've cleared a swath of space until I pivot and take in the mountains of possessions still waiting to be dealt with, and my heart sinks into my shoes. I am tired. I should not stand and stare and dwell on the impossible. In the light of a new day, it will all seem possible again.

~~~

Whenever I slouch into yearning for the sweet companionship of the dogs or begin mooning over an old stiff Polaroid of Dad and Zelda celebrating the Ceremony of the Haggis in Edinburgh, I slap myself upright with the fact that Zelda can finally enjoy the relief of being settled, and the lump of sadness in my throat softens. It's a rather astounding phenomenon. Kind of like the miracle of an enlivening surge of courage just as paralyzing cowardice sets in.

Unfortunately, neither transformation can be called up at will. And as July rolls toward August, it's not fear, per se, that terrorizes me but its petty second cousin: jealousy.

7-21-06: Joan calls to report that Z is doing so well that she may move up to the assisted living level of care, tells of all the fun they are having together. Strangely, I feel both elated and deflated. Filled with delight for Z and thrilled that Joan is seeing her mother at her best—until the sour taste of envy turns me into an embittered Cinderella. Poor me, left behind with the grubby task of shoveling out, cleaning, and repairing while Joan gets to set her mother up in a fresh, uncluttered new life full of good things.

In the background I hear Z telling Joan, "What would I do without you, Dunnie?" The jagged reality that I am utterly replaceable sinks into my chest like a dagger. Lord, please forgive my self-centeredness and help me focus on the grace in all of this.

~~~

Time, she said with supreme originality, does heal. In 1998, my fifty-three-year-old brother suffered a fatal heart attack on the steps of the Duluth Convention Center while attending a Bob Dylan concert. Shortly afterward, I experienced sternum pain so severe that my doctor decided to run a stress echocardiogram, just in case. Turns out my symptoms weren't caused by any physical defect. Two weeks after Dad died, it happened again. Lying on my side in bed, the suffocating sense that my heart might stop pounced on me like a two-hundred-pound panther springing

Two weeks after Dad died, it happened again. Lying on my side in bed, the suffocating sense that my heart might stop pounced on me like a two-hundred-pound panther springing out of the blackness.

out of the blackness. The sensation occasionally visits me still, but each time with diminished intensity and accompanied by less wild-eyed terror.

From Joan I learn that Zelda has suffered panic attacks as well, and I itch to climb into the van and zoom over to Madison. If only I could look into her eyes, see the occasional twinkle that still glints there from time to time, and know firsthand that she, too, is on the mend emotionally.

On a less dramatic scale, purging the townhouse of Dad's and Zelda's belongings makes it easier to be here. I toss Dad's last pair of short-legged PJs and his worn, chocolate brown sweater jacket without pain or remorse. Only briefly lose my breath bagging up pantry ingredients that were meant to become a Saturday night dinner.

I can now chuckle over a Mason jar of navy beans oddly intermingled with loose cracked wheat and exhale with resignation as I unpack all those boxes filled with carefully labeled folders categorizing every scrap of paper in the house. "Correspondence." "Blank Greeting Cards." "Family History." "Articles on Nutrition." The files sat untouched—well-organized dust-collectors. I can only hope that the completed project brought Dad and Zelda some peace of mind.

As I un-file and winnow, the radio weatherman yakking in the background, I hear a thunderstorm warning. *I should call Dad and Zelda to tell them.* And then I catch myself. Another quivering sigh. Another minor setback.

So, yes, healing may come with time. But it is a highly individualized progression. And physical unknowns—in collusion with sentiments stashed in the attic of your brain—may determine the schedule.

8-16-06: *I can't seem to shake this nervous sense of urgency about everything on my to-do list. Multiple daily workouts keep me from exploding with the tension of not always meeting my own goals. But no matter how often I nag myself about needing to take time for some fun, I dumbly stumble on without doing it.*

I guess I still want everything surrounding the townhouse sale to be easier. Or at least to be finished. So I pour myself into physical tasks, then wonder why my spirit feels neglected. I am a crazed hamster on an annoyingly squawky exercise wheel when I want to be an orchid flowering in the desert of my own human struggles. Lyrical, maybe. But wishing accomplishes nothing.

Instead, I run in circles when I could walk a straight line. Pop off when I should take a breather. Waste energy in a thousand ways.

The scary part is how often I've moaned about this before and how helpless I feel to change it. To change me. To conquer a world filled with reasons to give up. To not be my mother's daughter.

~~~

Fortunately, the Almighty doesn't throw in the towel as readily as we do. In fact, the Light of His guidance most often breaks through the gathering clouds precisely when we feel too enfeebled to pull on our own galoshes.

Two months into the townhouse refurbishing, I am led to the obvious cure for what ails me: a trip to Madison—practical or not.

The very thought of it restores joy.

8-30-06: *I power through a brisk, forty-minute walk under a translucent layer of white stratus that turns the firmament the palest of blues. The view fills me with gratefulness—for the able body that allows this blessing and for relief from the despair that has held me captive.*

As I march along, I cluck with disgust at what appears to be a bright red candy bar wrapper, carelessly torn to pieces then scattered by the wind. When this "litter" turns out to be velvety scarlet petals from a nearby plant, I am chastened. God is speaking to me, bold and clear. Telling me not to be so ready to assume the worst. And I burst out in self-conscious laughter.

Chapter 28

Gardening Lessons

I remember getting ready for my first boy-girl party. That enticing mix of nervousness and eager anticipation. The tortured inner debate over what to wear. The Big Decision about where my parents should drop me off.

Oddly, that's what comes to mind as we prep for our first trip to Madison. I wonder whether Jack and I will feel like outsiders. I worry that none of Zelda's professional caretakers is aware of my long history with her. Do they even know a stepdaughter exists?

Will we amble in, just a pair of well-meaning out-of-state relatives stopping by, then amble out again, having had no impact—the imprint of our visit soon filled in by the ebb and flow of paid workers? Will our presence add a spark of interest to Zelda's everyday routine, or will it complicate it?

Since the impulse to proceed persists, I assume the best and trust in a good result. We arrange a midweek trip to avoid road congestion, pack enough clothing to weather both extremes of Indian summer, box up the promised chocolate chunk cookies, and hit the road.

Zipping along I-94 East, we pass the majestic, pine-dominated cliffs of the Wisconsin Dells in all their lush, early autumn verdancy and marvel aloud at the beauty of Creation. The travel-perfect sixty-nine degree temps and cotton ball-studded skies offer reassurance.

This just feels right.

Pulling up to the entry of Zelda's new residence at 2:20 p.m. brings on a tickle of that pre-trip anxiety. *Shake it off. Inhale stiffly. Forge ahead.*

Although we're behind schedule, Zelda sits patiently waiting in the front lobby. She does seem to be expecting us, yet puts together an irrelevant sentence or two. ("I have the words in my head, but I can't get them to come out right.") Eventually, we persuade her to guide us to her room—a cheery-yellow ten-by-twelve space furnished with a few favorite pieces from the Minnesota townhouse.

"Isn't this a lovely day?" "So nice to have a view of the grounds." "The food here is fine, except that breakfast gets very boring."

Jack and I sit in chairs by the window and Zelda perches on the edge of her tidy bed as we all exchange mundane observations. "Isn't this a lovely day?" "So nice to have a view of the grounds." "The food here is fine, except that breakfast gets very boring."

My eyes shift from Zelda to the doorway behind her, and the small talk fizzles to a halt. We are being invaded by a train of uninvited guests—three women and one man, a quartet of the dazed and confused. A lost mother duck, three naive ducklings following beak-to-tail behind her with no idea where they are or why.

Mama mallard utters a string of repetitive gibberish syllables ending with, "Where am I going?" Seizing this opening, I gently steer her back out the door, and all four march off robotically, like life-sized windup toys, just as they had entered.

It's a captivating image, in a poignant sort of way. Which of these residents, I wonder, is the retired professor? Doctor? Teacher? Age and decline, the great equalizers.

This startling incident leaves me mildly flustered, but Zelda responds with indifference. I find comfort in that.

9-27-06, Afternoon: *We all are on our feet following the intrusion* *of the Senior Conga Line, so Z gives an abbreviated room tour. Two toy dogs—gifts from dear friends—nestle together on a bentwood chair. Old family photos in antique frames take up most of the small, gateleg table-top and much of the wall space. These constitute her gallery of childhood memories, her link to the carefree past; the dresser-top photos of Dad and her in camping mode or cruise attire, her link to recent loss. Both seem to pull at her core.*

She lets me take her hand and says, "I want to come home with you." A spasm of anguish disturbs the floor of my stomach. Maybe she says this to everyone who stops by. Hello, heartache, anyway.

As a diversion, we leave Jack to read a magazine while Zelda and I stroll the color-coded hallways and saunter headfirst into an encounter with an unfortunate stereotype: The Aide from Central Casting. "How are y-o-o-o-o-u-u-u-u today, Zelda?" she trills in that perfunctory, high-pitched, patronizing tone that makes any reasonable person's flesh contract until their shoulders meet their ear lobes.

"It's s-o-o-o-o-o-o nice that you have visitors! Are you having a walk?" she asks idiotically.

No, we are having a colonic cleanse, I manage to think, but not say.

This insulting creature is barely out of earshot when Zelda says, "What a twit," and proceeds to mimic her schmoozey speech in its full, phony glory, like a satirist from Saturday Night Live. She has her favorite aides—kind, respectful, playfully persuasive attendants. Clearly, this is not one of them.

~~~

Zelda needs to rest, to recoup energy for the evening meal. Jack and I head to our motel, unpack, and locate the nearest Taco Bell for a quick bite ourselves. Then it's back to the nursing home for a short evening chat while the sky is still radiant with leftover daylight.

We hunt down Zelda, who's tucked into the corner of an overstuffed couch in a communal TV room, dabbing at her eyes. As I call out, "There you are!" she raises her head, locates us with her gaze, and begins to cry.

"What's wrong?" I ask, easing down beside her and looping my arm around her spare shoulders.

"I was praying that you would come, praying so hard."

"We were here earlier today," I remind her.

"I know. I just was praying so hard that you would come now."

Laughter may be contagious, but these earnest tears could spawn a compassion epidemic. My heart wrenches, threatening to dislodge from its proper place and dislocate a rib or two. To rescue us both, Jack suggests we return to Zelda's private quarters. On the way, I tell of his latest birthday gift to me: a bottle of ketchup representing the fact that he is nine months older, so for the three months following my birthday, I temporarily catch up with him in age.

> Laughter may be contagious, but these earnest tears could spawn a compassion epidemic. My heart wrenches, threatening to dislodge from its proper place and dislocate a rib or two.

"That's romantic," Zelda intones with a smirk.

Settled into this relaxed mood, she recalls our Minnesota days of walking in the woods, singing hymns—a fantasy memory possessed only by her but one that carves a smile into every face in the room. And when her souvenir woolly black sheep from New Zealand fails to "B-a-a-a" as I upend it, Zelda observes that some devilish force must have knocked the gizzard out of him.

On this jovial note, Joan arrives to help her mom prepare for bed.

9-27-06, Evening: *Dunnie arrives around 7:30 and slides easily into the conversation with quirky anecdotes about life in the Memory Management Unit. Tells of the foreign Harlequin romance novel that turned up on Z's bedside table one evening, as if a dreamy-eyed, silver-haired Goldilocks had been testing mattresses during an afternoon reading break.*

Even better is the tale of a man's T-shirt deposited on the dresser, having mysteriously appeared out of nowhere, and Joan's discovery the following day that Z is now wearing said shirt.

The perfect foundation for our exit. We say good night and troll our way back to the Hampton Inn, more tranquil than when we first swiped the key card and stepped hesitantly into the antiseptic-tinged air of our temporary quarters.

Lying awake in the darkened motel room, fixation on Zelda lures me away from Minnesota worries—Jack remains unemployed and has been referred to an aggressive heart specialist eager to open up any chest that might require a few tweaks to its cardiac connections. But here, now, thoughts about Zelda and our Wisconsin expedition fill my mind to capacity.

So I pray for her peace of mind, that she will find nourishment for her soul in this spiritually neutral institutional environment. For her physical comfort. For her ability to derive joy from the commonplace features of her new life: ready-made meals; cheap, on-site haircuts; Joan's daily visits.

I think, also, about these past four months. About the universe of Dad's and Zelda's possessions that Jack and I continue to sort and disperse. And I am uplifted knowing that—in spite of her occasional gloomy references to having nothing—her efficiency-size apartment contains all she really requires. Her existence has been properly simplified by leaving the confusing collections of clutter behind. Her mind cleared for meeting basic needs. There is no doubt abundant blessing in this.

~~~

The unexplained surge that propelled me through those first days of dealing with Dad's illness rages on. I've lost 33 pounds and can't seem to stop the mad cycle that burns up fuel faster than I take it in. ("You look anorexic," Joan had gasped, taking me in at first sight.)

Six a.m. My usual wake-up time these days. The force thrusts me out of bed and into workout clothes to purge a buildup of frenetic energy. Trotting along on the motel's treadmill, I glance away from a rerun of HGTV's *Fixer Uppers*, catch a glimpse of myself in the wall of mirrors, and gag on the shock of my own reflection. Hollowed cheeks. Sagging flesh. I've joined Zelda's "bag of bones" club, and I don't recognize the skeletal being staring back at me.

I wanted to lose weight. The right half of my brain is elated; the chore has been accomplished without conscious willpower on my part. But the left half of my brain is horrified. This is too much, too fast, for my past-its-prime frame. Totally disregarding the strength-in-weakness homily I preach to others, I envision myself impotent to stop the trend, plunge mechanically into the shower/dress/makeup regimen, and opt not to deal with it at all.

~~~

For years, others would groan in anticipated defeat whenever Zelda and I teamed up as partners in Password or Pictionary. We could read each other so well that we often blew our opponents off the scorepad within the first few rounds of play.

This recollection flutters to the surface of my mind as we make our final nursing home visit before heading home, and Zelda welcomes us with an urgent apology. She feels guilty for not writing. Declares she "couldn't even read" when she first got to Madison. Here is true powerlessness. I am ashamed to stand beside her with a full set of basic abilities yet so unsure about how to put them to use.

Her voice thick with emotion, she adds, "I just want you to know how much I appreciate what you've done for me." She is visibly troubled. Says she hasn't adequately expressed her gratitude to me, "and to your . . . " She hesitates, finally offering "brother," meaning—I am sure—Jack.

I stammer out my standard response. How could I ever repay *her* for all she's done for me? It's an amiable standoff ending with a hug, and soon Joan arrives to chauffeur us all to a Zelda-hosted goodbye lunch.

At the China Wok buffet, we gleefully funnel fried rice and oriental chicken down our gullets. When Zelda's favorite course arrives—a spot of something sweet—Joan leans her left arm casually on the back of Zelda's chair. This frees her right hand to spoon-feed her mother a soft-serve chocolate sundae—an arrangement that seems completely natural to them. Nurturing and nourishing. A twofer.

Back at the nursing home entrance, we drag out our farewells for as long as Zelda can tolerate the cool breeze kicking up from the east. As Jack and I climb reluctantly into our van, the grip of longing crushes our hearts. Looking back and seeing Zelda's frail, bent silhouette as Joan helps her through the security door tightens the vice.

Joan kisses her mother, makes her way to her car, and waves as she tootles off to work. Jack and I linger in the parking lot not wanting to leave once Zelda comes back into view. Then, gradually, one of those miraculous transformations. As she heads down the windowed hallway toward her room, we roll slowly along with her and watch in wonder as her posture corrects, her chin lifts, and she returns a greeting to a fellow resident.

Her pace quickens now into a confident stride, and I'm reminded of what I wrote to her just last week: "I think of you throughout each day, and every time I do, I smile—assured that God is watching over you, and He's smiling, too. And that your angels are taking very good care of you."

This inspiring lady will bloom where she's planted because she is loved and well cared for and a survivor at heart. If only I can take from her example, cultivate my best self from what I have to work with, and stiffen the reluctant spine when a challenge looms. Though time and destiny have made it harder for me to get inside her head, I'm pretty

> As Jack and I climb reluctantly into our van, the grip of longing crushes our hearts. Looking back and seeing Zelda's frail, bent silhouette as Joan helps her through the security door tightens the vice.

sure I can guess what she would say to me about this last wish of mine.

"Oh, Suz. You are blossoming. You just don't know it yet."

And hearing it from her, I might even be able to believe it.

Endnotes

1 Frederick Perls, *Gestalt Therapy Verbatim* (Lafayette, CA: Real People Press, 1969), p. 4.

2 Vernon Sanders Law quote published by David H. Nathan, *The McFarland Baseball Quotations Dictionary* (McFarland & Company, 2000), p. 232.

3 Rudyard Kipping, "If," in *Stories & Poems*, edited by Daniel Karlin (New York: Oxford University Press, 2015), pp. 496, 497.